WORD CRAZY

WORD CRAZY

Broadway Lyricists from Cohan to Sondheim

Thomas S. Hischak

PRAEGER

New York
Westport, Connecticut
London

Library of Congress Cataloging-in-Publication Data

Hischak, Thomas S.
   Word Crazy : Broadway lyricists from Cohan to Sondheim / Thomas S.
Hischak.
      p. cm.
   Includes bibliographical references and index.
   ISBN 0–275–93849–2 (alk. paper)
   1. American poetry—20th century—History and criticism.
2. Songs, English—United States—History and criticism.   3. Popular
music—United States—History and criticism.   4. Musicals—New York
(N.Y.)—History and criticism.   5. Lyric poetry—History and
criticism.   6. Lyricists—New York (N.Y.)   I. Title.
PS309.L8H5   1991
782.42164'0268—dc20   90–47330

British Library Cataloguing in Publication Data is available.

Library of Congress Catalog Card Number: 90–47330
ISBN: 0–275–93849–2

First published in 1991

Praeger Publishers, One Madison Avenue, New York, NY 10010
An imprint of Greenwood Publishing Group, Inc.

Printed in the United States of America

The paper used in this book complies with the
Permanent Paper Standard issued by the National
Information Standards Organization (Z39.48-1984).

10 9 8 7 6 5 4 3 2 1

For my wife Catherine

Contents

Acknowledgments

I wish to acknowledge Leonard Cohen and Lauren A. Stiles for their library assistance; Dr. Donna K. Anderson and Dr. Stephen B. Wilson for their musical assistance; and Wayne Baker, Michael Staczar, James Wolk, Brian O'Donnell, S. J., and Teresa Wilson for their help in locating musical recordings. Thanks also to Dr. Joel L. Shatzky, Cathy Hischak and the lyricists and/or their estates and publishers for their permission to reprint sections of their songs. And a special thank you to Rosalie Kabana for her invaluable help in preparing the manuscript.

Whistling the Lyrics: An Introduction

I studied all the rhymes that all the lovers sing;
Then just for you I wrote this little thing.

> Blah, blah, blah, blah, moon
> Blah, blah, blah, above;
> Blah, blah, blah, blah, croon
> Blah, blah, blah, blah, love . . .

Ira Gershwin wrote that lyric in 1931 to go with a George Gershwin melody that had been put in and pulled out of various shows since 1928. Titled "Blah, Blah, Blah," the song failed to amuse several in the circle of the Gershwins' admirers. Why? Because Ira was poking fun at the inanity of many love song lyrics and at lyric writing in general? No. They were upset because they felt that with such silly lyrics, Ira had ruined the chances of his brother George's charming melody ever becoming a hit. The words serve the music; if they don't, the result is considered nothing less than sabotage. This is a book about American theatre lyricists. It is about how they have served (and sabotaged) from the earliest days of operetta, through the arrival of jazz, musical comedy, the "book" musical, the musical "play," and up to the conceptual musicals of the last thirty years. Histories of the Broadway musical have too rarely recorded the careers, works and distinctive characteristics of the outstanding lyricists with the same degree of attention that is given composers, playwrights, performers and directors.

This is not totally unreasonable. Lyricwriting has long been the stepchild of the production team of composer-librettist-lyricist. In opera and in operetta the lyrics are of little consequence. The music is the thing; the story, the singers, the choreography, even the scenery and costumes contribute more to the success or failure of the show than lyrics could. With the advent of musical comedy the role of the lyricist improved somewhat but the words still trailed behind the others with only a passing acknowledgment. Even today, after Hammerstein, Hart, Porter, Lerner and Sondheim have left their mark, lyrics continue to be the least essential ingredient for success. The Broadway musical continues to be about music. Deems Taylor, in his book on Rodgers and Hammerstein, examines the importance and unimportance of the lyrics in the Broadway musical. Referring to the music as the "score," Taylor comes up with this formula:

Brilliant Score + Brilliant Lyrics = Success
Brilliant Score + Dull Lyrics = Success
Dull Score + Brilliant Lyrics = Failure[1]

Critic Martin Gottfried states the case even more bluntly: "no show ever failed because of poor lyrics."[2]

The question of importance does not diminish the necessity of lyricwriting. Actors must sing something. Music does not become a score without words. In the musical theatre, music has no shape until it becomes a song; and it is the lyric that creates a song. It has been said that no one leaves the theatre whistling the lyrics. Yet they do. Richard Rodgers has argued that "the words are inherently present in every performance of the tune, amateur or professional, if only in the title, for never does a song achieve any sort of public unless the words have at some point made a joint impact with the music on the individual and public ear."[3]

This joint impact is what breathes life into the art of lyricwriting. Read "Oh, What a Beautiful Mornin' " on the page and it yawns back at you; hear it sung on the stage and it soars. No wonder so many argue that lyrics should not be read, that it is a disservice to the lyricist to have his words sitting there on the page naked without benefit of the music. The most you can achieve is the pleasant experience of reading light verse. This book on American theatre lyricists will quote from some lyrics on occasion. For various practical reasons, extensive quotations are not possible. The copyright on lyrics is fiercely protected and expense keeps lyric quotations to a minimum. (Some songwriters refuse to allow their lyrics to be quoted under any circumstances. Johnny Mercer and Irving Berlin, in their lifetimes, were of this opinion.) But there are some advantages to looking at a lyric on the page. A lyric divorced from its music often reveals wonderful and startling things about the craft of lyricwriting. Internal rhymes, for example, appear boldly on the printed page. Lyric construction is revealed and character traits solidify. On the other hand, while one could never accurately judge the quality of a song by looking only at its lyric, one does notice filler, waste words and other imperfections when viewing it under this unnatural light.

Those opposed to printing lyrics point out the opposite view: some lyrics are deceptive in print. While Lorenz Hart, Alan Jay Lerner and Ira Gershwin can make for delightful reading, others such as Oscar Hammerstein or Sheldon Harnick are poorly served on the page. These latter-mentioned lyricists are not interested in writing light verse and, like "Oh, What a Beautiful Mornin'," their lyrics are only meant to breathe with music.

The publication of lyrics is a fairly recent phenomenon. The bibliography cites collections of lyrics by Lerner, Porter, Hart and others. The finest anthology of theatre lyrics not limited to one author is Lehrman Engel's *Their Words Are Music*. Engel's information about the lyricists themselves is brief and discussion of their work is limited to select songs that are examined in detail. But it is an impressive collection of songs and a valuable introduction to some of the lyricists covered here. Lyrics can also be examined in published musical theatre librettos. Again the music is not there to support the lyrics but the libretto puts the songs in context, which is almost as important.

The purpose of this book is to look at the American musical theatre's most notable lyricists and to discuss them in terms of their careers, major works, individual styles and craftsmanship. One of the difficulties when writing about various lyricists is the tendency to judge them from our contemporary point of view. Having grown up with Rodgers and Hammerstein, Lerner and Loewe and the predominance of the book musical, one is likely to have trouble with lyrics that do not attempt to reveal character or advance the story. In the days when songs were easily interpolated from one show to another, such a specific quality in a lyric would have been damaging. Indeed, it was considered bad form even to mention a character's name in a lyric because it would keep a song from traveling—either to other shows or to the Hit Parade.

(Lorenz Hart used the character Junior's name three times in the verse for "There's a Small Hotel" and the song had to become popular for its refrain only.)

The masters of this independent approach to lyricwriting—Hart, Irving Berlin and Cole Porter—should not be judged by the same criteria as the later playwright lyricists. "A Pretty Girl Is Like a Melody" and "It's De-Lovely" create mood, sustain an idea and are fully satisfying. But they tell us little about character or situation. They can fit into most any show and indeed they both have a history for traveling. Hammerstein's book musicals eventually put an end to that and today the practice of interpolation would be considered dangerous at best. Try to imagine any lyric that Stephen Sondheim wrote for *Sweeney Todd* fitting into any other show by Sondheim, or by anyone else for that matter.

The irony about the non-book lyricists is that some of them demonstrated a particular talent for creating character and telling a story when the situation demanded it. When given a strong libretto, Berlin in *Annie Get Your Gun* and Porter in *Kiss Me, Kate* came up with character/story lyrics that stand with the best. Berlin and Porter had been capable playwrights all along but no one had ever forced them to move in that direction before.

Today we expect the lyrics not only to adhere to the book but also to blend with it effortlessly. It is hard to tell where Joseph Stein's libretto leaves off and Sheldon Harnick's lyrics take over in *Fiddler on the Roof*. We barely notice the comfortable harmony between the two because we expect it in the book musical. That is why it is often disconcerting when that blending is missing, as in *Sunday in the Park with George*, in which a character sounds so vibrant in the lyrics and then so flat in the dialogue. Or the opposite situation: Neil Simon's high-powered comic lines turning into dull, lifeless lyrics in *They're Playing Our Song*.

Trying to distinguish fairly between the playwright lyricists and the Hit Parade lyricists, this book attempts to put them in some sort of perspective of each other. Although a single lyricist is examined at a time, comparisons are inevitable and noteworthy influences are pointed out. Discussion will include Americans only and, despite the great crossover between Hollywood and Broadway, theatre lyrics will be emphasized rather than those written directly for film musicals.

Finally, an overview of the history of lyricwriting reveals important patterns in the history of the development of the Broadway musical. The words do more than serve. They have been known to startle, to amuse and to immortalize. They have created some of the theatre's most memorable moments and fostered many of its lasting impressions. So powerful and yet so easily dismissed! Or, to put it as another paradox: lyricists are the unsung heroes in the creation of the musical theatre.

NOTES

1. Deems Taylor, *Some Enchanted Evenings: The Story of Rodgers and Hammerstein* (New York: Harper & Brothers, 1953), p. 118.

2. Martin Gottfried, *Broadway Musicals* (New York: Harry N. Abrams, Inc., 1980), p. 54.

3. Oscar Hammerstein II, *Lyrics* (Milwaukee: Hal Leonard Books, 1985), p. xvi.

WORD
CRAZY

1

The Man Who Owned
Broadway: George M. Cohan

George M. Cohan is America's first influential theatre lyricist. A multi-talented one-man dynamo, Cohan was much more than a lyricist, of course. He was a musical theatre composer, director, producer, librettist and actor as well. He also managed to write twenty non-musical plays for Broadway. But it is Cohan the lyricist that concerns us here, and American theatre lyricwriting must acknowledge his early contribution. Along with Stephen Foster (who did not write for Broadway), Cohan is most responsible for establishing the American song lyric as we know it. Foster was warm and sentimental; Cohan was brash and confident. Together they created an American song vernacular that distinguished itself from the European sound.

The musical theatre was nearly forty years old when Cohan's first show opened on Broadway. During those forty years the new genre had seen remarkable innovation in terms of music, libretto, performance and technology. From *The Black Crook* (1866) through the Harrigan and Hart shows to the Victor Herbert operettas, the American musical theatre appeared to be developing in every area except lyric writing. The words for *Babes in Toyland* (1903) didn't seem to be much of an improvement over those for *Evangeline* (1874). The librettos were still negligible but they were getting better. It was the lyrics that were stagnant. It was becoming clear that musical theatre was about many things but lyricwriting was not one of them.

From the earliest shows, writing the words for the songs was considered lowly but necessary hack work. Music and spectacle came first, then the story (if any). In the case of imported European operettas, the lyricist was often a translator pounding out words to fit music already composed. In other cases the words for the songs, like those for the sketches, were routinely turned in by gag men, often several working separately on different songs for the same show. The role of the lyric writer was one of little respect and modest recognition.

It was George M. Cohan who helped change that. He despised the European operetta influence on Broadway and set out to create an American-sounding musical. He tightened up the book; made the music tuneful and simple; and wrote lyrics that were confident, forceful and spoke directly to the audience. At first the audience (and the critics, in particular) found the experience crude and "unpoetic." But once they got used to it (it took three Cohan shows) they loved it and before long the Cohan sound dominated Broadway. By the 1930s operetta was displaced by the kind of musical comedy that was descended from the Cohan show. Even when the "musical play" took over and *Oklahoma!* (1943) became the model, much of the Cohan sound remained. And it still remains. Today we expect theatre lyrics to speak directly to us. We listen for the words and we become annoyed if they do not "talk." That is Cohan's legacy.

George Michael Cohan was born in Providence, Rhode Island, in 1878. The actual date is still a matter of conjecture. Cohan himself always claimed to be "a real live nephew of my Uncle Sam's, born on the Fourth of July." But in 1943 Cohan's biographer Ward Morehouse discovered a baptismal certificate that placed the birth date on July 3. A later biographer, John McCabe, presented evidence in 1973 supporting the July Fourth claim and suggesting that the earlier certificate was a clerical error. The question will probably never be fully resolved but the issue is a noteworthy one. Cohan felt that his being "born under the Stars and Stripes" was destiny at work and his whole life got its direction from that fact. Born into a show business family, Cohan was on the stage from his earliest years. Before he was twenty he had his first songs published, was writing sketches for vaudeville and managing the family act. By 1900 The Four Cohans, as they were billed, were one of the top-drawing attractions on the vaudeville circuits, demanding as much as $1,000 a week.

But Cohan's eye was on Broadway. The leap from vaudeville to legitimate musical theatre was a difficult one and few had successfully managed it. Cohan's first attempt, *The Governor's Son* (1901), ran a month but was less than an auspicious debut. *Running for Office* (1902) didn't do much better, but in one particular lyric, "If I Were Only Mister Morgan," Cohan's unique lyrical style could be seen. Even when *Little Johnny Jones* opened on Broadway in 1904 the reception was cool. But this time Cohan made improvements while on the road and then brought the show back to New York where it became a hit. *Little Johnny Jones* is the quintessential Cohan musical. Not only did he write the libretto and the score, he co-produced it (with his new partner Sam Harris) and played the title character. The plot, about an American jockey wrongly accused of throwing a race in England, was a well-crafted melodrama filled with emotional cliffhangers. (Cohan billed the show as "a musical play.") The score was vibrant and introduced two Cohan classics: "The Yankee Doodle Boy" and "Give My Regards to Broadway." The lyric work in *Little Johnny Jones* shows a great deal of ingenuity and variety. Some songs rely on sentimentality but others are rather sly and sophisticated for 1904. "Life's a Funny Proposition After All," the hero's philosophy of life, is a deft piece of work and still holds up rather well.

While most of the critics bristled at the abrasive Cohan style, audiences were warming up to it. Cohan's next musical, *Forty-five Minutes from Broadway* (1906), was an even bigger hit. Cohan repeated all the writing/directing chores and the plot again was melodramatic (Act Two of the three-act musical had no songs) but the score was glorious. In addition to the witty title song, the show introduced "So Long, Mary," "I Want to Be a Popular Millionaire" and "Mary's a Grand Old Name."

George Washington, Jr. (1906) proved to be just as popular. The plot was a ridiculous affair about a patriotic son (Cohan), his Anglophile dad (Cohan's father Jerry), and a satirical feud between two US senators. But once again it was the score that triumphed. "You're a Grand Old Flag," the show's biggest hit, was originally titled "You're a Grand Old Rag" but pressure from civic groups convinced Cohan that his slangy sense of patriotism had gone too far. Also in the score were two favorites of the time that are not so well known today: "You Can Have Broadway" and "I Was Born in Virginia."

With three hits in a row, Cohan was at the artistic peak of his career. Although he presented many more shows up until 1928 and his work was usually very popular, much of what followed *George Washington, Jr.* was second rate or repetitive of earlier shows. Cohan had found his voice but he did not have the flexibility to let it grow or develop.

There are some superior individual songs in his later musicals but they are usually surrounded by mediocre work. Ironically, about the time the originality was disappearing from Cohan's productions, the critics were finally coming around to his kind of musical theatre. Cohan's later, more derivative shows received much better reviews than his earlier, more inventive ones.

Some of the later shows are worth noting for various reasons. The popular *The Talk of the Town* (1907) had a less than impressive score but one must admire the lyric work in "When a Fellow's on the Level with a Girl That's on the Square." *The American Idea* (1908) was not successful although it introduced the popular "Harrigan." *The Man Who Owns Broadway* (1909), as the title suggests, had an autobiographical aspect to it. *The Little Millionaire* (1911) was the biggest musical hit of that season. The plot was a trite contrivance but the score had several highlights: "Oh, You Wonderful Girl," "Barnum Had the Right Idea," "Musical Moon" and, one of Cohan's better comedy lyrics, "We Do All the Dirty Work." The musical revue was becoming more popular by this time and Cohan jumped on the bandwagon with *Hello, Broadway!* (1914). The tone of the revue was mostly satiric and some delightful songs, "Down By the Erie Canal" and "That Old-Fashioned Cakewalk," came from it. There was yet another patriotic testimonial, "My Flag," and "A Barnum and Bailey Rag" was a nod to the rising new talent, Irving Berlin. *Hello, Broadway!* was successful enough that Cohan also did revues in 1916 and 1917, simply calling them *The Cohan Revue*.

In 1919 Cohan's career was hurt by the staunch stand he took against the Actors' Strike and the young Actors' Equity Association. He did contribute to other songwriters' musicals and acted as play doctor on several occasions. Not until 1922 did Cohan again have a hit musical of his own on Broadway: *Little Nellie Kelly*. This story of an Irish policeman's daughter caught the fancy of the public and it ran for 276 performances, the longest run of his career. The last musical written by Cohan was *Billie* in 1928. Even Cohan admitted it was old-fashioned, even out of date. But the score had the charming title song and the lovely "Where Were You, Where Was I?" The musical theatre had changed quite a bit by 1928 (*Show Boat* was produced in 1927) and yet Cohan was still writing variations of *Little Johnny Jones*. He couldn't change his style of writing so he retired. Although he wrote no more musicals for Broadway he did give two highly acclaimed acting performances: the father in Eugene O'Neill's comedy *Ah, Wilderness!* (1934) and as FDR in the Rodgers and Hart musical *I'd Rather Be Right* (1937).

Cohan died in 1942, the same year the film version of his life, *Yankee Doodle Dandy*, was released. With the onset of World War Two, several of Cohan's patriotic songs became popular again. In the 1960s the same songs were anathema to many. (Cohan's lyric "Johnnie, get your gun" was answered by Dalton Trumbo's anti-war novel and film *Johnny Got His Gun*.) Yet in 1968 the musical *George M!* opened on Broadway and ran for 427 performances: Cohan's biggest hit. The show was a slapdash version of his life but it did bring dozens of Cohan songs back to the musical theatre. For a while Cohan once again owned Broadway.

What was it about George M. Cohan that made such an impact on the musical theatre? Was it his bluster and Yankee pride that appealed to so many? Was it all his patriotic fervor? Or his kinship with the ethnic working-class folk? Those factors certainly helped but patriotic shows were quite common and Harrigan and Hart had already capitalized on the ethnic possibilities. The Cohan appeal can be better attributed to his directness of language. Here was a sound that spoke without artistic embellishment. Oscar Hammerstein II put it best when he stated that "Cohan's genius was to say simply what everybody else was subconsciously feeling."[1] By being so "unpoetic," Cohan's words came over the footlights loud and clear. A song in a Cohan show engaged audiences in a friendly, chatty way. Gone was the operatic romanticism or the slick penthouse repartee. Instead we were simply told "the boys are all wild about Nellie" or that Mary "is a grand old name." Because the melodies were catchy and uncomplicated, the audience left the theatre humming the songs and soon, thanks to sheet music sales, all America was singing the praises of "Harrigan" or the "Grand Old Flag." This simplicity of Cohan's was unique in a day when even the most salient "girlie" musicals had pretensions to opera. Cohan gave his productions class by ignoring opera and expressing unaffected American ideals and emotions. There were plenty of rough edges in this kind of writing but at least it was honest. And highly moral. Cohan championed all-American values when many a musical sought to captivate audiences through its mild suggestions of a wicked life.

Today it is considered unfashionable to like Cohan and his brand of theatre. The critics pounced on the 1982 Broadway revival of *Little Johnny Jones* and, despite packed previews, it closed after one performance. (The same production had been a major success at the Goodspeed Opera

House the year before.) Many would prefer to classify Cohan with the early Tin Pan Alley songwriters rather than the musical theatre. But Cohan was pure theatre. He was not sophisticated or eloquent but he was the first Broadway producer/writer to realize the importance of the words in musicals. He not only saw the value of a sharp, fast-moving libretto, but he foresaw the essence of the relationship between book and song. The fact that these librettos do not hold up well today (How many American plays before 1920 do?) doesn't diminish his contribution. Cohan's understanding of this relationship is the basis on which Otto Harbach and Oscar Hammerstein would build. They would perfect Cohan's ideas and come up with a genuine version of a musical play.

Such ideas could only work if lyricwriting improved, and Cohan's efforts in that area must not be underestimated. He wrote his lyrics in the same gruff style as his librettos. What both lack in subtlety and poetry they compensate for in sincerity and confidence. Cohan's lyrics are never decorative or pretentious. They cry "Oh, you wonderful girl" or "Nellie Kelly, I love you." Everything is described as "swell" or "grand." The lyrics often have an ambitious, youthful naiveté that makes them engaging. The rhymes are undoubtedly simple and predictable but they still give pleasure. Lyrics at this time had barely begun to explore character, yet Cohan's do develop a personality. Of course, it is always the same character: the high-spirited Yankee. Every song is Cohan talking. It is a narrow point of view but a distinctive one all the same. Cohan's patriotic lyrics are the most familiar. ("Over There," not written for any show, remains one of the most recognizable of all American songs.) But his finest lyric work can be found in his self-mocking, more frolicsome numbers. "Down by the Erie," "Ring to the Name of Rose," "Hannah's a Hummer," "Forty-five Minutes from Broadway" and others are playful and breezy. The Cohan cockiness and blarney are satirizing themselves and the result is delicious. He even makes fun of lyricwriting itself in "Musical Moon," in which he sings of the popularity of the word *moon*, "that rhymes with June and spoon and croon." Songwriters have gone too far; he sings they "even got a sunny moon." Cohan's silliness and street corner vernacular should not be interpreted as a want of conviction. He fervently believed in all the lyric clichés. His words may have been plain but his ideas were lofty. Cohan idealized America and the Yankee character and then went out and lived it in show after show and in his personal life. He always played the role of a winner. It is no wonder he captured the hearts of America.

The flaw in both Cohan's life and work was his lack of adaptability. His headstrong philosophy of life could not change but the world and the musical theatre did. He kept trying to write the same songs over and over again. Many of his later lyrics and melodies sounded painfully familiar. Looking over his life's work, one finds that for every wonderful Cohan song there are a half dozen weak imitations. World War One forced America to look at life differently. But Cohan's pre-war sentiments continued to dominate his work deep into the 1920s. By the 1930s he was respected as an actor or a song and dance man; as a songwriter he was a has-been and an embarrassment.

What George M. Cohan has left us, apart from a collection of song favorites, is an American voice for the musical theatre. That voice got wittier in the 1930s with the lyric work of Cole Porter and Lorenz Hart. Director George Abbott maintained the Cohan style and speed in dozens of productions. Hammerstein and others refined Cohan's melodrama into palatable drama. Composers such as Jerry Herman, Cy Coleman and Charles Strouse pursued Cohan's tuneful melodies, and lyricists such as Dorothy Fields, Comden and Green, Adler and Ross, Meredith Willson and Carolyn Leigh embraced the vivacious Cohan wordage. *Of Thee I Sing*, *Annie Get Your Gun*, *The Pajama Game*, *Fiorello!*, *The Music Man*, *Guys and Dolls*, *Barnum* and *Annie* all have more than their share of the Cohan spirit and directness.

So the legacy continues. Whenever the American musical gets brash, cocky and full of grit, Cohan is there. The resilient nature of Broadway comes from the Yankee Prince himself. He still refuses to change. He is still singing.

NOTE

1. John McCabe, *George M. Cohan: The Man Who Owned Broadway* (Garden City, N.Y.: Doubleday & Co., Inc., 1973), p. 51.

2

As Thousands Cheered: Irving Berlin

Irving Berlin, America's most popular and beloved songwriter, started out as a lyricist for other composers' music. Despite the fact that he never learned to read music, Berlin eventually became his own composer and wrote over three thousand songs, about half of which were published. It is no secret that Berlin almost single-handledly invented American popular music. Cohan had broken away from European operetta, but it was Berlin who made popular music more personal. He captured the spirit of the era (of several eras, in fact) and spoke for a whole nation. Cohan dazzled his audiences; Berlin seduced his.

Berlin's threefold career with Tin Pan Alley, Broadway and Hollywood is a long and astonishing one. He most loved writing individual songs but he did find time to produce seventeen film scores and twenty-one Broadway scores. His work in all three areas is similar in its simplicity, direct manner and large number of hits. Berlin had no intention of changing the musical theatre but he did just that when he redefined America's notion of popular music.

Irving Berlin was born Israel Baline in 1888 in a small village in Russian Siberia. When Berlin was four years old his family fled Russia because of a czarist pogrom and immigrated to New York, where they settled on the Lower East Side. He went to work at age eight selling newspapers, and by his teens Berlin was employed as a singing waiter at various taverns and restaurants. He eventually worked himself up to song plugger at Tony Pastor's Music Hall in Union Square, pushing the latest tunes in order to sell sheet music. George M. Cohan was Berlin's idol. Not only did he love to sing his songs, but Berlin's early lyric work showed a strong Cohan influence. While working as a singing waiter at Pelham's Cafe in Chinatown, Berlin and a pianist, Nick Nickolson, were asked by the proprietor to write an original song for the cafe because a rival tavern had had their own song published. "Marie from Sunny Italy" was the result and it was soon published. The song was hardly a hit (Berlin later said it earned him thirty-seven cents) but it gave Berlin a new career and a new name: Israel Baline was misprinted as "I. Berlin" on the sheet music.

Berlin started contributing lyrics regularly to various Tin Pan Alley composers, most frequently with Ted Snyder, and by 1908 a song of theirs was interpolated into a Broadway show. For the next twenty years a season would not go by without at least one new Berlin song or score heard on Broadway. For the *Ziegfeld Follies of 1910* Snyder and Berlin provided "Goodbye Becky Cohen" for Fanny Brice's debut. The next year Berlin's solo effort, "Alexander's Ragtime Band," was introduced in the *Friars' Frolic of 1911*. The song did not catch on right away. Not until popular songstress Emma Carus sang it in a Chicago vaudeville house did its notoriety begin. Before the year was out all America was singing it.

If any one song ever changed the direction of American music, it was "Alexander's Ragtime Band." Ragtime was hardly new and, as even Berlin noted, the song was more about ragtime than an accurate example of it. But "Alexander's Ragtime Band" made ragtime accessible to the general public and soon rags were all the rage. The popularity of this one song has no modern equivalent; it was heard not only coast to coast but in all the major cities in Europe. And all this in an age before radio. Irving Berlin instantly became America's most well known songwriter. After 1911 Berlin provided his own music and rarely collaborated with other composers. While concentrating on Tin Pan Alley hits, Berlin did continue to contribute to Broadway. For the 1911 *Ziegfeld Follies* he provided the comic "Woodman, Woodman, Save That Tree" for Bert Williams and even had a song interpolated into *The Little Millionaire* (1911), a musical by his idol George M. Cohan. Berlin's first full score for Broadway was *Watch Your Step* (1914), that season's biggest hit with Vernon and Irene Castle doing "The Syncopated Walk." Another song from that show, "Play a Simple Melody," did not get much recognition at the time but eventually became a Berlin favorite. Another notable pre–World War One show for Berlin was *Stop! Look! Listen!* (1915), which introduced "The Girl on the Magazine Cover" and "I Love a Piano."

As a member of the military getting ready to go to France in 1918, Berlin put together the service show fundraiser *Yip-Yip-Yaphank*, one of the most famous of all revues. Billed as "a military mess cooked up by the boys of Camp Upton," *Yip-Yip-Yaphank* had a cast of 350 members of the armed forces and a Berlin score that included "I Can Always Find a Little Sunshine in the Y.M.C.A.," "Mandy," "We're on Our Way to France" and "Oh, How I Hate to Get Up in the Morning," the last sung by Berlin himself. After the war Berlin became a more regular contributor to the *Ziegfeld Follies*. For the 1919 edition, which most consider the best of the series, he introduced "I Want to See a Minstrel Show," "You'd Be Surprised" and the theme song for the rest of the *Follies*, "A Pretty Girl is Like a Melody."

With producer Sam H. Harris, Berlin built the Music Box Theatre and produced four editions of the *Music Box Revues* (1921–1924). The first edition introduced the theme song for the series, "Say It with Music." These revues were not as lavish as Ziegfeld's extravaganzas; nor were they as intimate or witty as the later *Garrick Gaieties* and *The Little Shows*. But they were impeccably produced with top-quality casts and exceptional scores, all by Berlin. Among the songs to come from the four *Music Box Revues*: the dance numbers "Everybody Step" and "They Call It Dancing," the comic songs "I Want to Be a Ballet Dancer" and "Pack Up Your Sins and Go to the Devil," and the ballads "A Waltz of Long Ago," "Lady of the Evening," "What'll I Do?" and "All Alone," the last two being Tin Pan Alley hits by Berlin that he added to the shows. Until the 1940s Berlin favored revues over book musicals. An exception was *The Cocoanuts* (1925), the hilarious Marx Brothers vehicle that was very successful but yielded no popular songs. (Berlin wrote "Always" for the show but librettist George S. Kaufman disliked it and cut it before opening.)

The thirties brought two outstanding Berlin-scored revues: *Face the Music* (1932) and *As Thousands Cheer* (1933). Moss Hart wrote the satirical sketches for *Face the Music* and the brilliant score included the charming "On a Roof in Manhattan," the hypnotic "Manhattan Madness" and the Depression-era favorite "Let's Have Another Cup of Coffee." The next year's *As Thousands Cheer* was probably Berlin's best revue, with a score that contained such gems as "Lonely Heart," "Easter Parade" and three memorable songs delivered by Ethel Waters: "Heat Wave," "Harlem on My Mind" and "Supper Time." The last, a haunting ballad about racial bigotry, was unusually weighty for a musical revue but Ethel Waters' rendition of the song was so powerful that producer Harris defied tradition and kept it in the show.

Berlin spent the rest of the 1930s in Hollywood, where he wrote a trunkful of songs that remain favorites, two of them ("Cheek to Cheek" and "White Christmas") winning Academy Awards. When he returned to Broadway in 1940 the musical revue was out of fashion so Berlin moved on to book musicals. *Louisiana Purchase* (1940), a musical satire on Southern Governor Huey Long, was that season's biggest hit. The book has aged poorly but the show provided Berlin's first truly theatrical Broadway score. There's the cheery title song, the wry "What Chance Have I with Love?," the breezy "It'll Come to You" and the ballads "Fools Fall in Love," "You're Lonely and I'm Lonely" and "It's a Lovely Day Tomorrow." *Louisiana Purchase* was hardly the integrated kind of musical that the Gershwins or Rodgers and Hart had achieved but it showed that Berlin could adapt to the times and write songs for characters and story. Because the flawed book makes revivals of *Louisiana Purchase* difficult, the score, though one of his finest, is not well known.

America's entry into World War Two prompted Berlin to repeat the success of *Yip-Yip-Yaphank*. This time the fundraiser ("Produced by Uncle Sam") was called *This Is the Army* (1942). Again the cast was made up from the military and again Berlin sang "Oh, How I Hate to Get Up in the Morning." Also in the score was "This Is the Army, Mr. Jones" and two popular ballads: "I'm Getting Tired So I Can Sleep" and "I Left My Heart at the Stage Door Canteen."

When Berlin returned to Broadway in 1946 he had the greatest success of his career. *Annie Get Your Gun* had a superior libretto by Herbert and Dorothy Fields. Jerome Kern was slated to do the music but his death in 1945 caused producers Rodgers and Hammerstein to approach Berlin. At first he refused, saying he knew nothing about writing "hillbilly music."[1] But the producers persisted and, after writing a few songs to experiment with, Berlin agreed. With Ethel Merman as Annie Oakley, the show ran for 1,147 performances and Berlin's Broadway career reached its climax. *Annie Get Your Gun* is Berlin's best musical theatre score not because of the number of hits it contains but because its songs successfully combine character and plot development in the manner of *Oklahoma!* and other great book musicals. Unlike previous Berlin works, most of the songs are appropriate only for the show they appear in. (Berlin used no old trunk songs for *Annie Get Your Gun*.) The score also contains a variety of songs unique to Berlin: the rousing "I Got the Sun in the Morning" and "There's No Business Like Show Business," the tender "They Say It's Wonderful" and "I Got Lost in His Arms," the swinging "Moonshine Lullaby," the character songs "Doin' What Comes Natur'lly," "The Girl That I Marry" and "You Can't Get a Man with a Gun," and the comic numbers "I'm an Indian Too" and "Anything You Can Do (I Can Do Better)."

The success of *Annie Get Your Gun* raised expectations too high for Berlin's next Broadway musical, *Miss Liberty* (1949). The too-solemn libretto by Moss Hart and Robert Sherwood about the Statue of Liberty was not what audiences wanted and the absence of a strong star such as Merman didn't help. Berlin's score was again in the true book musical style, this time approaching operetta, but the show didn't run long enough for any of the songs to catch on. It remains a neglected and enchanting score with the lovely "Just One Way to Say I Love You," the gentle "Paris Wakes Up and Smiles" and, gaining some recognition, "Let's Take an Old-Fashioned Walk." A song cut from the show, "Mr. Monotony," did become a cult favorite years later and was finally heard on Broadway in 1989 in *Jerome Robbins' Broadway*. (Robbins was the choreographer for *Miss Liberty*.)

Insisting on a star to guarantee his next venture on Broadway, Berlin wrote *Call Me Madam* (1950) for Ethel Merman. The book by Howard Lindsay and Russel Crouse, based on the real-life Washington hostess Pearl Mesta, was light and comic and the show was a success. While many feel that its score was not as engaging as that for *Miss Liberty*, it did have its share of hits: "The Hostess with the Mostes' on the Ball," "It's a Lovely Day Today," "They Like Ike" and "You're Just in Love (I Wonder Why?)." Much of the 1950s found Berlin in Hollywood again, and twelve years would pass before he worked on another musical. When *Mr. President* arrived on Broadway in 1962 it had the largest advance yet seen for a musical: over two million dollars. But the reaction to the show once it opened was so tepid that *Mr. President* closed after only 265 performances. The libretto, by Lindsay and Crouse again, was lackluster but even more disappointing was Berlin's score. He tried to adapt to the times (the show even had a dance called "The Washington Twist") but the ballads were pale shadows of his older songs, the character and comic numbers were bloodless, and the rousing patriotic song "This Is a Great Country" was an embarrassing reminder of Berlin's past greatness.

The failure of *Mr. President* convinced Berlin to retire. He had always judged the success of his efforts solely by their popularity. When he felt he ceased to be popular, he stopped. When Berlin died in 1989 he was considered a national hero. But the career that had conquered the ragtime era, the Roaring Twenties, the Depression, the anxious forties and the booming post-war years ended in 1962 when Broadway suddenly found Berlin old-fashioned. A song from *Mr. President* argued "Let's Go Back to the Waltz." America thought otherwise.

Enough time has gone by that Irving Berlin has, in a way, been redis-covered. He was never totally forgotten (songs like "White Christmas" and "God Bless America" saw to that); but until recently he was too often still considered old-fashioned. Clichéd descriptions of his work (primitive, patriotic, sentimental, simpleminded) overwhelmed the truth. People forgot that it was Berlin who had written many of their favorite songs. They even attributed his work to others. Many assumed "Puttin' on the Ritz" was by Cole Porter, that Rodgers and Hart wrote "Blue Skies," or that "Let's Face the Music and Dance" had to be the Gershwins. "Cheek to Cheek" was much too sophisticated for homespun old Berlin; and surely someone else wrote "Harlem on My Mind" or "Shaking the Blues Away."

Today Berlin has been rediscovered as being much more versatile and sophisticated than formerly thought. His chameleon-like ability to adapt to the latest trends and styles over his fifty-four-year career still amazes. But one wonders if he had any personal vision of his own. Was he merely talented at cleverly determining the pulse of the times? Is Berlin America's most popular songwriter because he told people what they wanted to hear when they most needed to hear it? There is no doubt that Berlin had a talent for anticipating the latest craze. Ragtime had been around for decades but he saw it in a democratic vein and wrote "Alexander's Ragtime Band." He foresaw the dancing phenomenon that would sweep the country in the 1910s and provided songs to feed it: everything from "The Dance of the Grizzly Bear" to "The Syncopated Walk" to "The Monkey Doodle-Doo." Berlin wrote madcap songs for the twenties, optimism for the Depression, patriotism for the war years, and swing for the late forties. Sometimes he helped start the fashion, other times he just joined in. But he always managed to write hits in whatever style was in vogue.

Yet there is a personal side to Berlin's work that is not conscious of the popular music band wagon. Consider his influence on the ballad. The sentimental American ballad goes back to Stephen Foster, but Berlin revitalized the form in the 1910s. "When I Lost You," a very personal song Berlin wrote after the untimely death of his young wife, went beyond fads or trends. It was straightforward, simple and timeless. "Always," "What'll I Do?" and "Remember" are among his most beloved ballads and all grew from situations in Berlin's life. For very personal testimonies they were extremely popular because Berlin's private voice echoed the public's feelings. He taught America that it was all right to be sentimental.

Berlin did have a personal vision and his own set of criteria when it came to songwriting. He was immensely aware of his own limitations ("Brahms wrote music, I just write songs"[2]) and allowed no pretension to infiltrate his work. Having the equivalent of a second grade education, he knew that his approach to lyricwriting would have to be emotional rather than intellectual. He limited his vocabulary to what was comfortable for him and kept his subject matter very practical. Berlin once said a song will be a success if it is based on one of four topics: home, love, self-pity and happiness. They were simple guidelines but ones he always abided by.

Berlin's lyrics are characterized by their simplicity and honesty. They express everyday sentiments but are rarely banal. Berlin found eloquence in the vernacular; in his hand the most everyday phrases became new and poetic. His lyrics often defy analysis because they are written to be understood and appreciated on first hearing. One may criticize such writing as unchallenging and even pandering to the lowest common denominator. But one also finds in Berlin's songs a respect for the audience that is not evident in most popular music. Berlin's uncalculated emotions are never vulgar or moralizing. The audience recognizes Berlin's honesty and immediately connects with it. Cohan had a rigid philosophy and proclaimed it loudly; Berlin just tells you how he feels. Both reflected America's sentiments of the time but only Berlin's lyrics retain their potency from decade to decade.

Most Berlin songs repeat the title frequently. There was a practical reason for this: Berlin felt that listening to an often-repeated title helped the audience remember it when they went to buy sheet music. It was a practice he continued long after radio, films and television replaced the parlor piano. As practical as Berlin always was, he did harbor some lofty ambitions. It was always his dream to write an American tragic ragtime opera but he felt it was beyond his talents. He watched his contemporaries and younger colleagues, like George Gershwin and Jerome Kern, gain respect in wider musical circles and graduate to "composer" status. Berlin stuck to songwriting.

Yet these others always had the greatest respect for Berlin and admired his work. (Gershwin called him "America's Franz Schubert.") Surprisingly they did not envy his success or belittle his talents. When musicologists scorned the little man who could only plunk out tunes on the black keys, the Broadway songwriters were quick to defend Berlin. Jerome Kern, who was a much bolder experimenter than Berlin, was always the first to credit the unpretentious quality of Berlin's work. Kern's famous quotation to Alexander Woollcott ("Irving Berlin has no place in American music; he *is* American music"[3]) shows his admiration, but a better explanation of Berlin's individual talent was expressed in these words by Kern: "He doesn't attempt to stuff the public's ears with psuedo-original, ultra-modernism, but he honestly absorbs the vibrations emanating from the people, manners and life of his time, and in turn, gives these impressions back to the world—simplified—clarified—glorified."[4]

On the other hand, Berlin never participated in creating any of the landmark musicals because he was never, by his nature, very experimental. There is nothing quite as influential as *Oklahoma!* or *West Side Story* in his credits. (Berlin turned down the offer to do *Show Boat*; he thought the idea preposterous.) Even his best book musicals were only high-quality examples of models developed by others. By his own admission, Berlin wrote many "bad" or "amateurish" songs; more than anyone else, he claimed.[5] But then he had more hits than anyone else. His average for success, even considering his thousands of efforts, was quite good. But Berlin's accomplishments cannot be judged merely by the law of averages. What he left behind was a conscious, deliberate body of work that was no accident.

Berlin's primary interest was never the musical theatre. He spent less than a third of his career there and usually tackled safe projects. His interest was in songs, not scores, and it is through his individual songs that he made his important contribution to Broadway. Like Cohan, he helped move the focus from European operetta to the American song and dance show. Berlin was one of the few songwriters to move back and forth effortlessly between Tin Pan Alley and Broadway. More importantly, he demonstrated that songs could make the transition as well. There have always been musical theatre songs that caught on but never on the scale and with the frequency of Berlin's work. His legacy for the theatre was the concept of Broadway's providing America with its popular songs. It was a legacy that lasted until the mid-1950s, when popular music and theatre music started to move in different directions. By the 1960s the link would be totally broken. No longer does Broadway produce the popular songs of the day. Only an occasional song from a musical ever appears on a *Billboard* chart. Coincidentally, Berlin's career concludes with the end of popular theatre music.

Perhaps our admiration for Irving Berlin is a nostalgia for the days when the musical theatre did provide song hits. But that can only be part of the story; nostalgia is a superficial reason for such longevity. *Annie Get Your Gun* may be the only Berlin musical that future generations will frequently revive, but Berlin's more lasting gift, his vast collection of songs, will be valued as long as audiences wish to see life "simplified—clarified—glorified."

NOTES

1. Michael Freeland, *Irving Berlin* (New York: Stein and Day, 1974), p. 168.

2. Martin Gottfried, *Broadway Musicals* (New York: Harry N. Abrams, Inc., 1980), p. 235.

3. Stanley Green, *The World of Musical Comedy* (New York: A. S. Barnes & Co., Inc., 1980). p. 83.

4. Green, p. 83.

5. Freeland, p. 12.

3

Going Up: Otto Harbach

Otto Harbach is not as well known today as some of the other early songwriters for Broadway. But during the 1920s he contributed to dozens of Broadway hits; at one point in 1925 Otto Harbach had five plays running simultaneously on Broadway, something no one before or since has been able to claim. But Harbach's importance is not due to his prolific output; he belongs with the influential early songwriters because he brought lyric and libretto writing to an adult level. In a day when most book writers and lyricists were gag men or hacks, Harbach approached the craft with great seriousness and high expectation. While much of his work has paled with time, Harbach laid the groundwork for Oscar Hammerstein II and others who would develop his ideas and shape the musical theatre into what we now have.

Despite his Teutonic-sounding name, Otto Harbach was born in 1873 into a working class family of Danish descent. The family name, Christiansen, was changed to Hauerbach when his ancestors settled in Salt Lake City in the 1830s and adopted the name of their employer's farm, a common practice at the time. Otto Hauerbach worked his way through college and became an English and public speaking teacher at Whitman College in the state of Washington. By 1901 he moved to New York to take graduate courses at Columbia, but soon his money ran out and he took a series of jobs, mostly with small newspapers. (He would change his name to Harbach during World War One because of the strong anti-German sentiment that prevailed.) According to a story he later told Alan Jay Lerner, Harbach was inspired to write for the musical theatre when, riding on a streetcar one day, he saw an ad for Fay Templeton in a Weber and Fields show.[1] That streetcar ride would lead to one of the longest and most prodigious careers on Broadway. There are far too many Otto Harbach collaborations to consider them all separately but some of the highlights will be examined.

Harbach wrote the book and lyrics for nine musicals with composer Karl Hoschna. *The Three Twins* (1907) was Broadway's biggest hit that season, due partly to the song "Cuddle Up a Little Closer." *Madame Sherry* (1910) was the team's most successful musical. It had an outstanding score that included "Every Little Movement (Has a Meaning All Its Own)" and a libretto that was superior to the usual Broadway fare. But the Hoschna/Harbach collaboration ended suddenly with Hoschna's death in 1911 at the age of thirty-four; Harbach would spend the rest of his career collaborating with a variety of different composers, librettists and lyricists.

His first hit without Hoschna was *The Firefly* (1912), with music by the young Rudolf Friml. Harbach's book and lyrics provided a well-constructed plot in the European style but set in contemporary America. The characters were well drawn and the score included such song favorites as "Sympathy," "Giamina Mia" and "Love Is Like a Firefly." Harbach's next venture with Friml was *High-Jinks* (1913), the biggest hit of that season, and provided two song standards of the day: "All Aboard for Dixie" and "Something Seems Tingle-Ingling." Harbach worked with Leo Dietrichstein on the book and lyrics and proved to be as adept at musical comedy as at operetta. Harbach also worked with Louis A. Hirsch, the composer for several of the early *Ziegfeld Follies*. In 1917 they presented *Going Up*, a musical farce about an aviation race. Both the title song and a dance song, "(Ev'rybody Ought to Know How to Do the) Tickle Toe," were very popular. Harbach and Hirsch's *Mary* (1920) was equally successful and the song "Love Nest" swept the country. *Mary* had a foolish plot about a man who sells "portable houses." Besides being prophetic about the appeal of mobile homes, *Mary* served as the source for much of the satire in Sandy Wilson's 1954 spoof *The Boy Friend*. With *Wildflower* (1923), Harbach worked with beginning lyricist Oscar Hammerstein II. With various composers, Harbach and Hammerstein did *Rose-Marie* (1924), *Sunny* (1925), *The Song of the*

Flame (1925) and *The Desert Song* (1926), all of which are discussed in Chapter 5.

Harbach's participation in *No, No, Nanette* deserves special mention because the 1925 sensation is considered by many to be the archetypal 1920s musical comedy. Harbach was slated to do the lyrics alone for Vincent Youmans' music and write the book with Frank Mandel. But Harbach had found Youmans difficult to work with in the past (as did many others) and suggested Irving Caesar be brought in for lyric collaboration. The show's two biggest hits, "I Want to Be Happy" and "Tea for Two," were last minute additions by Caesar but the whole score for *No, No, Nanette* was exceptional. Songs such as "You Can Dance with Any Girl," "I've Confessed to the Breeze (I Love You)," "Too Many Rings Around Rosie" and the title song represent all that is wonderfully giddy about 1920s musical comedy. *No, No, Nanette* was a phenomenal hit, with tours across the country as well as to South America, New Zealand, the Philippines and even China. When the musical was revived on Broadway in 1971 it was a hit all over again.

Of all his many composer collaborations, Harbach's finest lyrics would be with Jerome Kern. They first worked together on *Sunny* in 1925 and the next year did *Criss Cross*, a musical farce with a globe-trotting plot starring comedian Fred Stone. The score, with lyric help by Anne Caldwell, was delightfully silly with songs like "In Araby with You," "You Will, Won't You?" and "I Love My Little Susie," which Stone sang to a camel. Harbach's best scores with Kern are *The Cat and the Fiddle* (1931) and *Roberta* (1933). Just as Hammerstein and Kern broke new ground with *Show Boat* in 1927, Harbach and Kern would take some adventurous steps with *The Cat and the Fiddle*. Harbach did book and lyrics alone this time and wrote "a musical love story" (his description) in which music and story were indispensable to each other. Set in contemporary Brussels, the plot about a would-be opera composer allowed the score to integrate with the story and characters in a way rarely done. There was a small cast, no chorus-girl numbers and no dazzling spectacles. The characters were believable and the score was memorable: "Try to Forget," "She Didn't Say 'Yes' (She Didn't Say 'No')," "The Breeze Kissed Your Hair" and "The Night Was Made for Love." *The Cat and the Fiddle* was Harbach's earnest attempt to write a timely modern operetta. *Roberta* was much more conventional. Harbach again did solo work on the book and lyrics, devising a familiar plot about a dress shop in Paris. Business for *Roberta* was moderate but when "Smoke Gets in Your

Eyes" was broadcast over the radio, the show became a hit. Also in the magnificent score were "Yesterdays," "You're Devastating" and "The Touch of Your Hand."

Roberta would mark the end of twenty-five years of hits for Otto Harbach. The Depression signaled the end of operetta and few of Harbach's many collaborations after 1933 would gain favor. When he and the great operetta composer Sigmund Romberg wrote *Forbidden Melody* in 1936, the show was hopelessly out of date and quickly closed. Harbach contributed to different productions off and on up to 1950. He died in 1963 when he was nearly ninety, a forgotten songwriter who had helped create dozens of Broadway productions.

In the long run, Harbach is important, if only because he trained and guided Oscar Hammerstein and it was Hammerstein who most influenced musical theatre from the late 1920s to the 1960s. Harbach was twenty years older than Hammerstein but he saw the potential in the young lyricist and insisted on his getting equal billing and equal percentage of royalties. Hammerstein's gratitude to Harbach was both professional and personal. In later years he stated that Harbach "was the best play analyst" and "the kindest, most tolerant and wisest man I have ever met."[2] It was Harbach who first suggested to Hammerstein the importance of strong story structure and a score that could be integrated with it. Hammerstein would carry this idea to fruition with *Show Boat*, *Oklahoma!* and other musical plays; but it was Harbach who first preached the basic principles.

Harbach was an educated, literary man, unlike most librettists and lyricists writing in the 1910s. Harbach approached the writing of musicals with the slow, careful and thorough procedure of an academic. He constantly revised, rewrote and perfected while most others rushed through their work knowing that the music and the stars were the only things that mattered. Harbach taught Hammerstein (and others) to think about a lyric or a character for a length of time before actually writing. In the days when many musical theatre writers put together three or four shows each season, such deliberation must have seemed excessive. But Harbach's efforts showed in the final product. While some of his lyrics may seem dated or over-romanticized, they are never sloppy or inconsistent.

One cannot dismiss Harbach as merely the teacher of an important pupil. Harbach's work, either with others or alone, does have its own merits and did contribute to the overall quality of Broadway. Because he collaborated with so many (on some of his shows there were as many as three lyricists), it is difficult to pinpoint the Harbach style. And, to add to the confusion, many times different lyricists worked on the same song, so it is hard to determine where Harbach leaves off and where Hammerstein or Caesar comes in.

But there are some Harbach characteristics that seem consistent throughout his career. His vocabulary, for example, consists of words that are usually educated but not stuffy, romantic but not saccharine. He avoids the common vernacular in his lyrics and eschews slang. Harbach at his best writes about straightforward emotions and develops them in a direct manner. A song simply states "Love is Like a Firefly" or "The Breeze Kissed Your Hair." His metaphors may involve the familiar moonlight, fire or red lips but they are not embellished to a ridiculous level. The image of lost love being like a dying fire with smoke that "gets in your eyes" is eloquent because it stops short of mawkishness. One of the reasons so many of Harbach's lyrics from the old operettas can still be enjoyed today is his talent for restrained emotion. *The Desert Song*, *Rose-Marie* and *The Firefly* can be successfully revived now because, in addition to the superb music, the lyrics please us with their old-fashioned sentiment but do not embarrass us.

Harbach's lyrics for the musical comedies are just as carefully written but often tend toward the cute, as was the style. *No, No, Nanette* and *Going Up* have been revived but too often as camp. But even in musical comedy Harbach's words can convey great power and warmth. Although not as well known today as some of his songs, "The Touch of Your Hand" is a good example of Harbach's simplicity, gentleness and potency.

When you shall see flowers that lie on the plain,
Lying there sighing for one drop of rain;
Then you may borrow
Some glimpse of my sorrow,
And you'll understand
How I long for the touch of your hand.

Both the operettas and the musical comedies worked because they offered such a romanticized view of reality. Harbach was consistent in this view and showed that intelligent and passionate words could raise the level of lyricwriting. The plots and the settings may have been exotic but the emotions were simple and familiar. And, most significantly, the story supported the lyrics so Harbach's love songs could take on a greater depth than those casually inserted into other shows. Like P. G. Wodehouse, Harbach cannot be grouped with the popular Tin Pan Alley songwriters. Many of his songs became hits but their original context in a story was essential to their creation.

On the other hand, Harbach's shortcomings as a lyricist cannot be ignored; his technique does not rival that of Berlin or Hammerstein. He purposely uses antiquated words or phrasing in his efforts to reach high levels of romanticism. Sometimes the strain shows. There are more 'twas's and forsooth's than one would like. Phrases like "so I chaffed them" or heaven "opened its golden portal" don't sit well in a lyric. And Harbach's rhymes are often awkward; who else would rhyme "yesterdays" with "sequester'd days"?

But it is not his technique that places Harbach among the most consequential of the early musical theatre writers. His serious approach to an art form that was considered frivolous by most was unique for his time. He was a perfectionist in a business that was often dominated by the careless and the sloppy. He respected the musical theatre, or at least the possibilities such a theatre offered. When he was in his eighties, wheelchair-ridden and nearly blind, Harbach one day complained to his son that he couldn't sleep all the night before. He said he had suddenly realized what was wrong with the lyric to "Smoke Gets in Your Eyes." Such a sense of perfection is worth noting. It allowed Harbach to make substantial demands of the musical. Those demands were met by later writers and the musical theatre kept "going up." Otto Harbach does not get the recognition he deserves but his influence still surrounds us.

NOTES

1. Alan Jay Lerner, *The Musical Theatre: A Celebration* (New York: McGraw Hill Book Co., 1986), p. 63.

2. Oscar Hammerstein II, *Lyrics* (Milwaukee: Hal Leonard Books, 1985), pp. 42-43.

4

Leave It To Plum:
P. G. Wodehouse

If Otto Harbach prepared the way for Oscar Hammerstein, it was P. G. Wodehouse who laid the groundwork for Ira Gershwin, Cole Porter and Lorenz Hart. While very different from Harbach in temperament, Wodehouse was just as influential. He brought a new sophistication to lyricwriting that was more subtle than Cohan and more graceful than Berlin. Wodehouse, who was British (he became a US citizen in 1955), introduced a W. S. Gilbert quality to the Broadway musical. Yet his shows, particularly those with Guy Bolton and Jerome Kern at the Princess Theatre, were uniquely American in style and attitude.

During his ninety-three years, Wodehouse wrote ninety-six novels, over three hundred short stories, sixteen nonmusical plays, several filmscripts and essays. Somehow he also found time to write the lyrics and/or librettos for twenty-eight musical comedies. His most consequential work for the musical theatre was done between 1917 and 1928. During that short time he did more than any other lyricist to change the sound and shape of the Broadway musical.

Pelham Grenville Wodehouse (nicknamed "Plum") was born in Guildford, England, in 1881. Educated at London's Dulwich College, he pursued the banking profession until he decided to make writing his vocation. By 1902 his first of many comic novels was published, and two years later he started contributing lyrics to London musicals. For one of them, *The*

Beauty of Bath (1906), he collaborated with the visiting Jerome Kern on one song. Wodehouse's stories and novels became more and more popular (the delightful character Psmith was introduced in 1910, Jeeves in 1915), and he also served as a columnist for the London *Globe*. His career was taking off rapidly, and by the age of twenty-four he had twenty novels to his credit. But two brief visits to the United States convinced Wodehouse that he'd like to try his luck in New York, so he moved there in 1915.

It was as drama critic for *Vanity Fair* that Wodehouse attended the opening night performance of *Very Good Eddie* (1915), the second of the Princess Theatre shows. This series of small, intimate musical comedies had begun with Jerome Kern's *Nobody Home* (1915) and had attracted some attention. The cast, scenery and orchestra were limited by the small size of the Princess Theatre. (Wodehouse jokingly called the series "Midget Musical Comedy.") The intention was to focus on book musicals that unified plot and songs and to move away from the big stars, individualized comics, large chorus lines and lavish scenery. *Nobody Home*, with a book by Guy Bolton and lyrics by Schulyer Greene, Kern and others, was a modest success. But *Very Good Eddie* was an unqualified hit and the goals of the Princess Theatre were being realized.

At the show's opening Kern introduced Bolton to Wodehouse, who said he liked everything about the new-style musical except the lyrics. Bolton, an American born in England, liked Plum immediately, and that night the most important triumvirate of the early American musical theatre was born. Ironically, the first Bolton-Wodehouse-Kern musical, *Have A Heart* (1917), was not at the Princess Theatre, but it retained all the ideals of the series. Called "an up-to-date musical comedy" by its creators, *Have A Heart* was a frivolous comedy about a second honeymoon, but the silliness was literate and adult in tone. Kern's music, Wodehouse's lyrics, and Bolton and Wodehouse's book blended together gracefully and the result forecast what was to be expected of the new team.

Oh, Boy! (1917), this time at the Princess Theatre, was a triumph. Besides being a popular success (463 performances), it was the nearest the team had yet come to pure musical comedy. Most of the songs continued the plotline and the humor grew from the characters and the situations, not from added comics. Two hits came from *Oh, Boy!*: "Till the Clouds Roll By" and "An Old Fashioned Wife." Wodehouse also provided a wonderful comic duet, "You Never Knew About Me," and an amusing parody of "Apple Blossom Time" called "Nesting Time in

Flatbush." *Leave It To Jane* (1917) did not run as long, but it was an even better show and has held up well over the years. (A 1959 revival ran for two years.) *Leave It To Jane* was one of the first shows to use that most serviceable of musical settings, the college campus, which Bolton-Wodehouse-Kern called Atwater College. Once again the plot and the songs went hand in hand. In addition to the lively title song, the score included "Just You Watch My Step," "The Sun Shines Brighter," and "Wait Till Tomorrow," as well as the seductive "The Siren's Song" and the comic "Cleopaterer."

Wodehouse contributed lyrics to some unsuccessful shows in between these hits (all in all, he did lyrics for five musicals in 1917), but the Bolton-Wodehouse-Kern team was again in top form with *Oh, Lady, Lady!* (1918). Again the score was superior, with Wodehouse's lyrics for "Greenwich Village" and "Not Yet" providing the comedy and "When the Ships Come Home" and "Before I Met You" supplying the tender moments. The best song in the score, "Bill," was dropped during rehearsals when its lyrics didn't fit the actor cast as Bill. With slightly revised lyrics, "Bill" appeared in Kern/Hammerstein's *Show Boat* in 1927.

Oh, Lady, Lady! was the last Princess Theatre musical with Kern. He did reteam with Bolton and Wodehouse for the excellent score for *Sitting Pretty* in 1924 but the famous triumvirate had come to an end. Kern moved on to "serious" musicals and, working with Harbach and Hammerstein, pursued new directions in musical theatre. Wodehouse and Bolton stayed together for a while and worked on a handful of musicals and revues with other composers, but none matched the earlier Princess Theatre shows. (The exception was *Anything Goes* in 1934, for which they wrote the original libretto.) Wodehouse's novels and stories began to dominate his time, and by World War Two he left the musical theatre completely. No one, with so few shows, has had more impact on the musical theatre than Plum.

Wodehouse must be viewed in terms of what preceded him for his impact to be fully appreciated. European operettas, English Gaiety shows (named after the Gaiety Theatre in London) and various forms of music hall entertainments were in favor. The words were unimportant. Cohan and Berlin broke through with popular songs, but the score as a whole usually didn't speak. Wodehouse gave musical theatre lyricwriting a sound; it was a sound that bridged the stuffiness of the old operettas and the brassy, confident voice of the Jazz Age. It was a tone that was uniquely American: direct, charming, wholesome and eager.

Musicals had been trying to find an American voice for some time. Cohan attempted it through bold, patriotic fervor and slam-bang feelings. Berlin introduced the ragtime element to Broadway and let the words express simple, cross-cultural emotions. Both fought against the European operetta by denying it. Wodehouse went so far as to replace it with something better. If operetta had exotic settings and lush lyrics, Wodehouse gave the musical familiar, contemporary locales and conversational wit. Operettas capitalized on passion and romance; Wodehouse substituted charm. The Princess Theatre musicals were neither hysterically funny nor emotionally heartrending. They were light, fast, logical and literate. No one could be insulted by their silly plots because the authors developed them with youthful good intentions.

When it came to the lyrics, Wodehouse was careful to put a touch of reality behind all this charm. The lovers sing to each other playfully (they'll survive "on bread and cheese and kisses," one song states) but you cannot dismiss their earnest gumption. The imagery in the lyrics is down to earth. No one dies of passion or walks on air; the raptures are on a more modest scale. "The Church Around the Corner," which Wodehouse wrote with Kern for *Sally* (1920), is a good example of this unpretentious kind of charm.

Dear little, dear little Church Around the Corner,
Where so many lives have begun,
Where folks without money see nothing that funny
In two living cheaper than one.
Our hearts to each other we've trusted:
We're busted, but what do we care?
For a moderate price
You can start dodging rice
At the Church Around the Corner,
It's just around the corner,
The corner of Madison Square.

The words are cozy, silly and touching. In operetta this kind of song would never work. But in the airy world of musical comedy it soars.

It would be Hammerstein who would perfect the homespun kind of lyric that started with Wodehouse. No wonder Wodehouse's "Bill" fit in so well with Hammerstein's lyrics for *Show Boat*. The final lines of

"Bill" are justly famous. They are that winning combination of pathos and self-mockery.

And I can't explain,
It's surely not his brain
That makes me thrill.
I love him because he's— I don't know—
Because he's just my Bill.

That simple "I don't know" is bold and knowing. Wodehouse has taken the torch song and made it conversational. The operetta writers would never recover from the shock.

As stated earlier, Wodehouse had a profound effect on Cole Porter, Lorenz Hart and Ira Gershwin. All three of them (and others) at one time or another publicly acknowledged Wodehouse as their inspiration. The reasons are sometimes obvious. All three were word crazy, and it was Wodehouse who first showed American musicals the fun that could be had with words. He gave the lyricist new power because he demonstrated that the words could be as potent as the music. Later lyricists saw Plum as their hero and their teacher.

It is in their comedy songs that the three lyricists most imitated Wodehouse. His comic lyrics reveal the seeds for all the delightfully witty songs that these three would later write. One sees in "Cleopaterer," for example, the future of lyric comedy.

She gave those poor Egyptian ginks
Something else to watch besides the sphinx

You can see Gershwin's slang, Porter's risqué humor, and Hart's wit foreshadowed in those two lines.

Wodehouse's lyric craftsmanship, like the plots of his novels, is intricate, well constructed and lighthearted. He chose his words carefully, often simplifying phrases to their minimum length and their greatest impact.

No small part of his lyric craftsmanship is his use of rhyme. Wodehouse is the first Broadway lyricist to capitalize on the power (and joy) of rhyming. Cohan's rhymes were blunt and obvious. Berlin's could be subtle and warm but rarely frolicsome. It was Wodehouse who opened up the comic and dramatic possibilities of rhyme. He used all forms of rhyme (masculine, feminine, internal and so on) and he used them expertly. The comic song "Napoleon" is a feast of delectable rhyming: "talking mean/Josephine . . . injure/ginger . . . galleries/calories . . . all foemen/a guy's abdomen." Such playful rhyming would reach a peak in the 1930s, but Wodehouse started all the fun in the 1910s.

It is interesting to consider what Wodehouse would have contributed to the musical theatre had he remained with it longer. Would he have become another Porter or Hart or, instead, an outdated songwriter overshadowed by that new generation? Wodehouse was a man of infinite talent and energy but not flexibility. Would he have succeeded in writing the kind of musical play that *Show Boat* introduced? One way or the other, P. G. Wodehouse's major contribution had been made. He taught the American musical comedy that it could be charming, literate and, perhaps most of all, American. Then he went elsewhere. Leave it to Plum.

5

No More Make-Believe:
Oscar Hammerstein II

If one considers *Show Boat* and *Oklahoma!* the two most influential Broadway musicals of the twentieth century, then Oscar Hammerstein II, who wrote not only the lyrics but also the librettos for both shows, must be ranked as the giant in the history of the musical theatre. He has been called the Master, either out of affection or derision. The title seems inappropriate for such a careful, sentimental man, but he did play a major role in shaping the musical stage as we now know it. Few men have had longer careers (from 1919 to 1960) and none has had so varied a career. Oscar Hammerstein was, at times, the most honored and applauded of all theatre craftsmen; at other times he was regarded as a has-been, the ultimate failure. It was a roller coaster career held together only by Hammerstein's constant dedication and steadfastness of purpose.

Today the man who developed the musical play is looked upon with mixed emotions. To some he represents all that was inspired and glorious about the musical theatre. To others he symbolizes all that is antiquated and tiresome about it. Just as in Hammerstein's lifetime, public opinion today seems to vary according to whom you talk to and what day of the week it is. But regardless of which emotion his name conjures up, Oscar Hammerstein is the American theatre's most influential lyricist. To the unending joy or despair of us all, he will not go away.

Oscar Hammerstein II was born in New York City in 1895 into a notable theatrical family. His grandfather and namesake was the most colorful and innovative opera impresario of his day. Oscar II's father, William Hammerstein, was the shrewd manager of the Victoria Theatre, a leading vaudeville house owned by the Hammerstein family. Uncle Arthur Hammerstein was a Broadway producer with an impressive list of hits to his credit. Despite this background, the family wanted young Oscar to become a lawyer. He entered Columbia College in 1912, where his classmates included Howard Dietz, Morrie Ryskind, Bennett Cerf, Herman Mankiewicz and Lorenz Hart. Drawn to the Varsity Shows, Hammerstein was soon performing and writing original musical comedies. Even after he graduated and started law school, he continued to contribute to the annual shows. (For one of them he wrote two songs with a new undergraduate named Richard Rodgers.)

When his Uncle Arthur employed Hammerstein as an assistant stage manager for one of his productions, the law career was soon forgotten, and by 1919 he had written a non-musical play called *The Light* that closed in New Haven. But the next year Hammerstein's first Broadway musical, *Always You*, was presented by Arthur Hammerstein and was successful enough to warrant a road company. The music was by his friend Herbert Stothart and, as would be the pattern, Hammerstein wrote both the book and lyrics. Three more musicals with Stothart followed, the most significant being *Tickle Me* (1920) because Hammerstein worked with Otto Harbach on the lyrics. Harbach became the mentor for the young Hammerstein and taught him about lyric structure and the importance of having the songs complement the whole story. It was a practice not followed by many at the time but it formed the basis of Hammerstein's approach to musical theatre. (Years later Hammerstein would act as mentor to a handful of young songwriters, Stephen Sondheim in particular.)

Wildflower (1923) was Hammerstein's first major hit. Otto Harbach again assisted on the book and lyrics and the incomparable Vincent Youmans wrote the music. The show ran for 477 performances and, while impossibly dated now, it did make efforts to integrate the songs into the story. These efforts would be more fruitful in *Rose-Marie* (1924), the highest-grossing musical of the decade and the most successful Broadway show until *Oklahoma! Rose-Marie*, with its Canadian Rockies setting, its "Indian Love Call" and "Song of the Mounties," and its lush romantic music by Rudolf Friml, may seem today like the quintessential antique operetta. But, in fact, Hammerstein and Harbach made some bold advances in musical theatre structure and even managed to put a murder in the plot, something very unusual on the musical stage. *Rose-Marie* broke records, spawned five road companies and played in London and Paris. But more importantly, it convinced Hammerstein that audiences would be able to accept a fully integrated musical play someday.

Hammerstein and Harbach's next show, *Sunny* (1925), with music by Jerome Kern, was a throwback to an earlier style, with the plot and songs moving in individual directions. But Hammerstein did find in Jerome Kern a composer with a similar outlook, and they began a long personal friendship and professional collaboration. *The Desert Song* (1926) was Hammerstein's first of five shows with composer Sigmund Romberg. Together (with the ever-diligent Otto Harbach) they fashioned for *The Desert Song* an exotic story set in romantic North Africa that capitalized on the Rudolf Valentino "sheik" craze. The rich score included "The Riff Song" and "One Alone," as well as the comic song "It," referring to Clara Bow.

Hammerstein would handle book and lyrics alone for his next project with Jerome Kern. It would be his most passionate attempt yet at integrated story and song and would result in a theatre classic. *Show Boat* (1927) was neither musical comedy nor operetta. It was the first musical play and it broke rules as quickly as it set up new standards. Edna Ferber's book, a sprawling epic filled with racial conflicts, unhappy marriages and gambling addiction, hardly seemed promising musical theatre fare. But Hammerstein crafted the piece into a taut, powerful drama and, together with Kern, heightened that drama with the musical score. *Show Boat* produced six song standards ("Make Believe," "You Are Love," "Can't Help Lovin' Dat Man," "Why Do I Love You?," "Bill" and "Ol' Man River") but the entire score was superior and has not lost any of its strength over the decades. (It must be noted that the lyric for "Bill" was by P. G. Wodehouse, and Charles K. Harris' "After the Ball" was interpolated into the show.)With *Show Boat* Hammerstein finally created a musical that could hold its own as drama. He wanted to develop the musical play even further but the next sixteen years would be difficult ones. Although *Show Boat* was a tremendous hit, it seemed to have little immediate impact on the Broadway musical. Revues, musical comedies and operettas would continue to dominate Broadway, and the new genre introduced by *Show Boat* would only be intermittently seen during the next two decades.

The New Moon (1928) is considered the last of the great American operettas. Hammerstein contributed to the book and lyrics and Sigmund

Romberg wrote the music. "Stouthearted Men," "One Kiss," "Softly, as in a Morning Sunrise" and "Lover, Come Back to Me" are still heard, but the plot of *The New Moon* was closer to *Rose-Marie* than *Show Boat*. In his shows that followed, Hammerstein tried for a more substantial storyline. But *Rainbow* (1928), despite Vincent Youmans' jazz-influenced score, and *Sweet Adeline* (1929), with Jerome Kern's music, both failed to imitate *Show Boat*'s integrated score.

The number of Broadway offerings dwindled after the stock market crash, so Hammerstein and Romberg agreed to go to Hollywood. But film audiences became disenchanted with movie operettas and Hammerstein was back in New York. In 1932 he wrote *Music in the Air*, an attempt to capture the simplicity of the earlier Princess Theatre shows. Jerome Kern wrote the music and, with "The Song Is You" and "I've Told Ev'ry Little Star" in the score, *Music in the Air* was a hit. *May Wine* (1935) with Romberg music was a modest success as well, but Hammerstein's contribution to both shows was not the essential ingredient. A series of Broadway failures and a fruitless return to Hollywood left Hammerstein's career at an all-time low point. There was plenty of evidence that his lyric powers were still acute—*Very Warm for May* (1939) with Kern had a fine score (including the memorable "All the Things You Are"), and Hammerstein's lyric for "The Last Time I Saw Paris" won the Academy Award in 1941—but it was clear that Hammerstein, only forty-six years old, was a has-been; as outdated and forgotten as the old European operettas he sought so much to replace.

The story of how *Oklahoma!* came to be is one of accidents, surprises and long shots. Hammerstein thought the Lynn Riggs' 1931 play *Green Grow the Lilacs* would make a good musical and suggested to Kern that they collaborate. Richard Rodgers had the same hunch and approached his partner Lorenz Hart. Both Kern and Hart didn't like the idea, so when Rodgers mentioned it to Hammerstein, and he immediately accepted, the new team was born. To theatre insiders it was a teaming that forebode disaster. Rodgers had never collaborated with anyone but Hart, whose witty, urbane lyrics gave their shows a sassy verve that everyone loved. To team Rodgers with the unclever, sentimental Hammerstein, who had years of Broadway and Hollywood flops to his credit, did not seem a promising undertaking. Riggs' play did not appear to be likely musical theatre material, and the producers, the Theatre Guild, had had a very unsuccessful track record of late. Everyone expected another failure for Hammerstein and a rare flop for Rodgers.

The two men were not attempting to revolutionize the musical theatre when they worked on *Away We Go!*, as it was then called. They were just trying to tell a simple, direct story in musical terms. Rodgers enjoyed Hammerstein's homespun, honest lyrics (in contrast to the showy, dazzling ones by Hart), and Hammerstein enjoyed working with Rodgers, whose musical ideas quickly blossomed from a simple phrase or character trait. They knew what they were doing was different but they never suspected just how different. *Oklahoma!*'s quiet, gentle opening scene, the down-to-earth characters, the absence of a chorus line, and the celebration of simple pleasures such as a picnic or a ride in a surrey—all of these rule-breaking devices were not intended to change musical theatre history. But when *Oklahoma!* opened these modest innovations did just that. For twenty years American musicals would shun sophisticated wit for a more honest approach. Earthy American values would rank above educated, worldly ones. Character songs would become the expected instead of the exceptional. *Show Boat* may have influenced Broadway through a gradual rippling effect; *Oklahoma!* came on like a tidal wave.

Hammerstein's lyrics for *Oklahoma!* are among the most remembered in American popular culture. Even the character songs, such as "I Cain't Say No" and "Pore Jud Is Daid," are as familiar as the more standard hits, such as "People Will Say We're in Love" and "Oh, What a Beautiful Mornin'." With his lyrics Hammerstein created a new vocabulary for the Broadway stage: a rural, unpretentious way of expressing emotions. He proved that, indeed, "all the sounds of the earth are like music." *Oklahoma!* ran for an unprecedented 2,243 performances, produced the first original cast album, and launched a new career for Hammerstein. The musical play was here to stay.

Success had evaded Hammerstein for a long while, but now everything he touched turned to gold. *Carmen Jones* (1943), his Americanized version of Bizet's *Carmen*, opened to critical and popular acclaim. He wrote the screenplay and lyrics for the film musical *State Fair* (1945), which was not only one of the year's most popular movies, but the song "It Might As Well Be Spring" (written with Rodgers) won the Academy Award. He and Rodgers also became Broadway producers and scored hits with Irving Berlin's *Annie Get Your Gun* (1946) and a handful of non-musical plays, most notably *I Remember Mama* (1944). Hammerstein did not plan to work exclusively with Richard Rodgers; he and Jerome Kern were planning a new musical together. But with Kern's sudden death in 1945, and later Sigmund Romberg's demise in

1951, it became clear that it would be "Rodgers and Hammerstein" from now on.

Their second Broadway show as composer/lyricist-librettist was *Carousel* (1945) and, despite their worries about trying to compete with the astounding success of *Oklahoma!*, it received raves by critics and audiences alike. Again the Theatre Guild produced, and again it was based on an earlier Guild-produced play, *Liliom* by Ferenc Molnar. Hammerstein's transposing the action from Hungary to New England while maintaining the spirit of the original is a good example of his stagecraft. He did change the play's ending, but everyone, including Molnar, liked the "You'll Never Walk Alone" conclusion. *Carousel* ranks as highly as *Oklahoma!* in terms of character, integrated songs and thematic consistency. It is more solemn than the team's previous work, but it has integrity. It was a daring task to fashion a musical around a disreputable character like Billy Bigelow. Hammerstein solved the problem by developing Billy's character lyrically, especially in the brilliant "Soliloquy," one of the most intricate and absorbing character studies to be found in any musical. (Rodgers and Hart's earlier *Pal Joey* was centered around a heel, but one never gets inside Joey in the same way as with Billy.) *Carousel* has its share of song standards, "If I Loved You" in particular, but once again it is the score as a whole that one remembers. (At the end of his career Rodgers stated it was his favorite of the team's scores.)

With his confidence at a high point, Hammerstein then proceeded to write his most ambitious and personal work. *Allegro* (1947) was an original musical not based on anything but Hammerstein's beliefs and fears. It was innovative, uncompromising, even harsh; and it was, of course, a commercial failure. *Allegro* was ahead of its time, although no modern revival would be free of its shortcomings. A cross between *Everyman* and *Our Town*, the plot explores the life of a small-town doctor from his birth, through his schooling and young romance, to his capitulation to money and society, and then his final recognition of life's true values. Parts of it are as pretentious as it sounds but there are sections of raw power. Hammerstein takes a psychological approach to plot and character and even uses a modern Greek chorus and stream-of-consciousness techniques. There are scenes and lyrics that are unlike anything Hammerstein ever did before or after: vicious scenes of self-deception and betrayal, greedy people manipulating shallow people, satirical moments that are painfully exact. The story concludes with

Hammerstein's usual affirmation of life, but what has preceded it haunts the ending.

Among the many reasons for *Allegro*'s failure were the production values. This was a conceptual musical that needed an original, innovative director. (Jerome Robbins, for example, might have been able to pull it off.) But instead *Allegro* got gentle Agnes de Mille making her directorial debut. The show's large advance allowed *Allegro* to break even, but the audiences didn't like it. Neither did Richard Rodgers, whose tastes were growing conservative. He made sure that never again would a Rodgers and Hammerstein show get so "experimental." *Allegro* ends the team's period of growth and discovery. From that point on they would stick to the same formula that worked in the past and never stray from it. Their craftsmanship would usually remain high and they continued to present quality products, but their influence on the musical ended. They would continue, along with everyone else, to imitate the genre they had invented.

The rest of Hammerstein's career is mostly familiar. *South Pacific* (1949) was a smash hit. Joshua Logan coauthored the libretto, and Hammerstein revealed a talent for adult humor in his lyrics. *The King and I* (1951) was also a sensation. For the first time Rodgers and Hammerstein attempted a musical that was not American in character or setting. But their Broadway version of the Orient was as tasteful as it was exotic, and the result was very moving. *Me and Juliet* (1953) was only a modest success. Again Hammerstein wrote a completely original story, this time set backstage in the world of the musical theatre. But it was a lackluster script and the lyric work was competent but forgettable. The team's shortest Broadway run was *Pipe Dream* (1955), a musical even Rodgers and Hammerstein fans forget about. Based on John Steinbeck's *Cannery Row*, it was not suited to the musical stage nor to Hammerstein's talents. The television musical *Cinderella*, originally broadcast in 1957 with Julie Andrews in the title role, was a quality piece of work that offered no surprises. *Flower Drum Song* (1958) was a commercial, if not a critical, success, and boasted a lively score.

With *The Sound of Music* (1959) the team again had a knockout hit. For the first time Hammerstein did not write the libretto. Howard Lindsay and Russel Crouse's story, based on the actual Trapp family, was set in the romantic Austrian Alps; it resembled the old operettas in more than setting. To many *The Sound of Music* represents all that is saccharine and sentimental about Rodgers and Hammerstein. Much of that feeling is due to the phenomenally popular film version. On the stage, *The Sound of Music* has some bite to it (some of the political motivations, for example, are softened into romantic ones in the film) and Hammerstein made some discerning points in his lyrics for "How Can Love Survive?" and "No Way to Stop It," both of which were cut from the movie. Much of what is simple became simpleminded in *The Sound of Music*, but it has a score with strengths of its own.

Hammerstein was ill during most of the preparation for *The Sound of Music*. He knew he was dying, so, with his work done, he returned to his Bucks County farm. During rehearsals it was decided that another song was needed for the Trapp family to sing at the music festival. Hammerstein provided "Edelweiss," the last lyric he ever wrote. Like the best of his work, it is simple, eloquent and potent. It is about a flower and yet about so much more. Oscar Hammerstein died in 1960 and, for the first time in history, every light on Broadway and in London's West End was blacked out in tribute.

The young Stephen Sondheim once asked Hammerstein why he didn't write sophisticated shows. "What do you mean by sophisticated?" Hammerstein asked. "About people who live in penthouses? Those people don't interest me."[1]

What interested Hammerstein was much closer to the ground. Although born and raised in an urban, intellectual environment, he quickly grew to appreciate the rural, unaffected life that he later adopted himself. What appealed to him were, to most others, clichés: the dignity of man, truth, honest values, peace. All lyricists have attempted these at some time in their careers but Hammerstein believed in such values implicitly. This is not to say that Hammerstein was some form of saint; his own life had its share of indignity, self-deception and quarrels. But he always kept sight of certain ideals and was never embarrassed about expressing them in song. Because of his unconditional sincerity most of Hammerstein's lyrics ring true. The anticipation of riding in "The Surrey with the Fringe On Top" is not forced or corny because the excitement the lyrics generate is heartfelt. Nellie sings "I'm in love with a wonderful guy" over and over again. She has no clever way of expressing herself because she is not clever; she's in love and repetition is her only literary device.

Because what "interests" Hammerstein is so uncompromising, the subject matter available to him might seem rather limited. But Hammerstein applied the same values to any situation, no matter how foreign to him, and let the sincerity of his emotions carry the song. He knew nothing of royalty or Asian culture, yet everything the King sings in *The King and I* sounds right. A Siamese man who believes what Hammerstein believes would reason as he does in "A Puzzlement." Hammerstein's treatment of the King, as his depiction of Oklahoma cowhands, New England fishermen, Polynesian natives and Mississippi River dockworkers, is not condescending because he finds dignity in all men. He may have sometimes been clumsy in capturing their phraseology or a little pretentious in his imagery but he never faked the values behind them.

While some see Hammerstein as a naive dreamer or an impractical idealist, he was, in fact, very shrewd, rational and pragmatic. Unlike the safe and conservative Rodgers, Hammerstein believed in experimentation. But he experimented in order to see what worked, not to prove theories. From early on he believed that music and story should integrate completely. But he knew it would be successful only when the audience said it was. Hammerstein never felt superior to his audience but accepted their decisions. When he poured his soul into *Allegro* and gave them a Greek chorus, time and space distortions, and a plotless, conceptual approach to character, they didn't like it. So he didn't try anything so unusual again. He stuck to the formula the audience understood and tried to develop new ideas within it. Later, in *The King and I*, he attempted a modified version of *Allegro*'s techniques in "The Small House of Uncle Thomas" sequence. This time it worked (thanks to Jerome Robbins' staging), and Hammerstein knew it because the audience said so.

Few lyricists are as practical about the singer's voice as Hammerstein. He always considered what words would sound the most comfortable when the music made demands on the singer. When Jerome Kern handed him the music for a song for *Sunny* in which the singer had to start with a B natural and hold it for nine beats (and repeat this feat five times later in the song), Hammerstein experimented and came up with the single-word solution "who." The lyric "Who . . . . stole my heart away" not only fits the difficult music but it rescues the singer. Hammerstein always regretted the flat, blunt words he used at the end of each refrain of "What's the Use of Wonderin'?" Because the singer could not hold the final "that" and "talk," the song was difficult to sell. Although it is appropriate for the character of Julie to end her statements so abruptly ("that's all there is to that"), the practical Hammerstein promised himself never to do it again.

If he was practical about his audiences and his singers, he was no less so about his characters. Since it was usually his own libretto that the lyrics had to blend with, Hammerstein was very demanding about their appropriateness. The vocabulary of the lyrics must be consistent with the vocabulary of the characters, he felt. If one finds few clever or sophisticated lyrics in his works it is because few of his characters can be described as such. On those rare occasions when the educated or witty characters appear (such as Max and the Baroness in *The Sound of Music*, Sammy in *Flower Drum Song*, the wealthy Chicagoans in *Allegro*), the lyrics adjust accordingly. If we think all of Hammerstein's characters believe "You'll Never Walk Alone," that you should "Climb Ev'ry Mountain," and that "ev'rythin's goin' my way," we are ignoring the darker side of his dreams. Few lyrics have the bitterness of Lieutenant Cable's "You've Got to be Taught," the creepy desolation of Jud Fry's "Lonely Room," the self-deceptive cockiness of Billy Bigelow's "(Let Me Be Judged by) The Highest Judge of All," or the resigned ache of Joe's "Ol' Man River." For a man who limited himself to only what interested him, Hammerstein's scope was considerable.

Hammerstein's lyric craftsmanship has always fascinated other lyricists because his is a very subtle craft. He sought to avoid all the recognizable lyric techniques that other writers took such pride in. If a phrase or a rhyme drew attention to itself and away from the character, Hammerstein rejected it. He never wanted his audience to hear lyrics, only characters speaking. He achieved this effect only through careful and exacting study. His introductory essay, "Notes on Lyrics," which he wrote in 1949 for a collection of his lyrics, reveals much of the scrupulous workmanship that went into his writing. The simplest phrase or the least conspicuous word is the result of trial and error. He labored so that his words would seem uninvented. Consequently, he made lyricwriting seem easy.

Hammerstein was very particular about his use of rhyme. He felt that rhymes that grab attention usually distract from the meaning of the lyric. Also, a rhyme, by its very nature, leads the ear to expect the next rhyme. So one should use rhymes infrequently or only when the music demands it; and even then they should be used carefully and subtly. A standard example of Hammerstein's almost subliminal use of rhyme can be found in the verse for "People Will Say We're in Love."

Why do they think up stories that link my name with yours?
Why do the neighbors gossip all day behind their doors?
I have a way to prove what they say is quite untrue;
Here is the gist, a practical list of "don'ts" for you . . .

This traditional AABB rhyme scheme ends with the masculine rhymes "yours/doors" and "untrue/you"; but it is also filled with subtle internal rhymes. The "think" and "link" in the first line, the "way" and "say" in the third line, and the "gist" and "list" in the last one are all easy to spot on the page but they quietly support the music when the song is performed. More hidden is the "neigh-bor" and "day" internal rhyme in the second line. Internal rhyme is a device that is hardly unique to Hammerstein; most lyricists (Cole Porter and Lorenz Hart, in particular) use such rhymes to add a witty bounce to their lines. Internal rhymes are one of lyricwriting's more clever effects. But Hammerstein uses internal rhymes, as he does all rhymes, in a less assertive manner. He is the Master because he displays utmost restraint in rhyming, an area in which lesser lyricists cannot resist showing off.

Hammerstein also likes to use identities or repeats. These almost-rhymes are an effective way to produce a rhythm but not punctuate the ends of lines with a hard rhyme. "Ol' Man River" is a masterpiece of controlled rhyming. To give the song a steady, rolling feel, Hammerstein softens the rhymes except at the end of each completed thought.

Ol' Man River,
Dat Ol' Man River,
He mus' know sumpin'
But don' say nuthin',
He jes' keeps rollin',
He keeps on rollin' along.
He don' plant taters,
He don' plant cotton,
An' dem dat plants 'em
Is soon forgotten,
But Ol' Man River,
He jes' keeps rollin' along . . .

Rhymes like "cotton/forgotten" rest easy on the ear. Identities, like "sumpin'/nuthin'" and repetitions like "He don' plant taters/He don' plant cotton" all blend together, and the result is a powerful, eloquent lyric that allows an uneducated character to express himself with dignity.

This subtlety in technique, combined with consistency in ideals, makes Hammerstein the least compromising of lyricists. His personal vision is so strong that it saturates everything he touches. But there are some

undesirable side effects to such a vision. Hammerstein's tone is sometimes so consistent it is predictable. One anticipates the statement being
made before the drama has a chance to develop it. Many of his shows,
particularly the later ones with Rodgers, take on a solemnity that weakens
the dramatic impact. The formula, once they invented it, could not remain
fresh for as many times as they insisted. They created a new genre and
then exhausted it.

The true musical play that Hammerstein first introduced with *Show
Boat* and perfected with *Oklahoma!* is a major turning point in the history
of the musical theatre. It raised the level of characterization, it presented
thematic values, and it allowed story and song to coexist. More significantly, it provided the pattern for musicals for the succeeding decades
and still dominates our musical theatre. Yet, while the Broadway musical
gained all this it also lost something. The Hammerstein lyrics and librettos eliminated much of what was vigorous and startling on Broadway.
When musicals became "art," they sacrificed some of their theatricality.
Ethan Mordden, in his study of the musical theatre, accurately points
out that the rise of the musical play meant the fall of the great comics,
the vaudeville-type specialties, and the non-integrated musical comedies
that were tailored to the talents of extraordinary performers.[2] Something
disappears when one gets "class," and no one brought more class to the
musical than Oscar Hammerstein.

Which brings us back to the conflicting views people have toward
the Master. Irving Berlin once stated that of all the Broadway lyricists,
Hammerstein was the only one who was a poet. How one accepts
Hammerstein depends on whether one sees him as a good poet or
an inferior one. He is definitely the most influential poet the musical
theatre has yet seen. Broadway followed Hammerstein's lead, and the
result was a series of Rodgers and Hammerstein–like shows that were
only occasionally of the same quality. Does being the most powerful
lyricist/librettist make Hammerstein the best?A true evaluation of Oscar
Hammerstein must take in consideration the experimental nature of the
man himself. History has played a sly joke on us by allowing the Rodgers
and Hammerstein model to last so long. Hammerstein was the last person
to accept the status quo situation of the theatre quietly and he would be
appalled that some artists are still trying to write a *South Pacific* kind
of musical in the 1990s. His vision of the musical theatre was one
of continual testing. He himself experimented for forty years and still
thought there was a distance yet to go. If Hammerstein's work today

seems antiquated and sentimental to some it is probably because too much of what can still be found on Broadway is alarmingly out of date. The great Hammerstein musicals should be revived on occasion because they are a vibrant part of our musical heritage and they still give great satisfaction; but they should not be resuscitated in order to serve as blueprints for how musicals ought to be constructed today.

Hammerstein is the Master, the great teacher and mentor. But many of the students have not heeded what he taught. Stephen Sondheim, who was taught directly by Hammerstein, does not attempt to repeat the Master's style or construction. He has moved on. Oscar Hammerstein is our most important lyricist because he was always moving on. He lifted the Broadway musical out of the make-believe world of operetta and vaudeville. It is only right that others continue to carry it forward.

NOTES

1. Craig Zadan, *Sondheim and Co.* (New York: Harper and Row, 1986), p. 4.

2. Ethan Mordden, *Broadway Babies: The People Who Made the American Musical* (New York: Oxford University Press,1983), pp. 70-71.

6

Of Words I Sing: Ira Gershwin

Standing in the shadows of colorful artists and celebrated musical hits was the quietly efficient and dedicated lyricist Ira Gershwin, who played an essential part in the development of the musical, but would never get too close to the limelight. Throughout his long career he worked with the best. The list of the composers he collaborated with, for example, is a Who's Who of popular music: Vincent Youmans, Harry Warren, Jerome Kern, Vernon Duke, Arthur Schwartz, Harold Arlen, Aaron Copland, Burton Lane, Kurt Weill and, of course, his brother George. In every production he worked on, Ira Gershwin would lend support and inspiration to more notable talents, all the time striving to retain his own individual style and a distinctive voice.

Ira Gershwin was born in Brooklyn in 1896; George was born in 1898. Because George showed a musical talent early on, Ira avoided any competition and tended toward the literary: light verse and humorous short pieces for newspapers and magazines. But Ira Gershwin was drawn to the musical theatre, and when he started getting work as a lyricist he used the pen name Arthur Francis in order not to capitalize on his brother's name. George's "Swanee" (with lyrics by Irving Caesar) became a resounding hit when Al Jolson interpolated the song into his 1918 show *Sinbad*. Ira's success would not come until 1924's *Lady, Be Good* and then, as often was the case, he would have to share it with George. Arthur Francis became Ira Gershwin, but it was still a George Gershwin show.

A similar situation could be found in the brothers' personal lives. George was the life of the party, the center of attention, the subject of newspaper columns and the society page. His tragically short life was filled with energy, bright talk and amorous adventures. Ira was not a partygoer by nature; he was quiet, methodical, shy even. He married at the age of twenty-nine and settled down to a productive career that lasted until he retired in 1954. The photos of the Gershwins tell the whole story: George with a big smile for the camera, the bespectacled Ira reticently looking on. Ira Gershwin's thirty-six-year career would be mostly remembered for the nineteen years he collaborated with George. This is not such a great injustice since Ira's best work was done as part of the Gershwin team. But it is slighting a superb talent to dismiss Ira Gershwin as the man who merely wrote the words for George Gershwin. Ira had just as much to do with the Gershwin spirit.

Ira's first full score to be heard on Broadway was *Two Little Girls in Blue* (1921), with music by Vincent Youmans and Paul Lannin. The lyrics by Arthur Francis, as he was still calling himself, already showed a talent for the irreverent and the playful. "Who's Who with You?" and "Oh Me! Oh My! (Oh You!)" foreshadowed the Ira Gershwin style. More Arthur Francis lyrics appeared in various Broadway and London shows, but true recognition didn't come until the 1922 edition of George White's *Scandals*, with the song "(I'll Build a) Stairway to Paradise." George Gershwin's unique jazzy approach made the song a hit, but Ira's lyric (written with B. G. De Sylva) demonstrated the carefree optimism ("with a new step ev'ry day") that would earmark the lyricist's best work.The first Broadway score by both Gershwin brothers together (the Arthur Francis was dropped by this time) would also be their biggest hit yet. *Lady, Be Good* (1924) contained "Fascinating Rhythm," "Oh, Lady Be Good," "Little Jazz Bird" and "(The You Don't Know) The Half of It, Dearie, Blues," but the score's finest song was "The Man I Love," which was dropped before the opening because it was slowing down the show. The Gershwins' next offering, *Tell Me More* (1925), was to have been called *My Fair Lady* (it was the title of one of the songs), but the producers dropped the name because it didn't sound commercial enough. *Tell Me More* was a modest success and did produce the lively "Kickin' the Clouds Away" (lyric help again by De Sylva).

The Gershwins struck gold three times running with *Tip-Toes* (1925), *Oh, Kay!* (1926) and *Funny Face* (1927). The songs from these three shows demonstrate the wide range of the brothers' talent, from the romantic ("That Certain Feeling" and "He Loves and She Loves") to the rousing ("Clap Yo' Hands") to the giddy ("Do Do Do" and "'S Wonderful"). For these shows Ira wrote the first of his wistful ballads ("Someone to Watch Over Me") as well as his first successful attempts at satire ("These Charming People" and "The Babbitt and the Bromide"). The brothers also provided songs for two Ziegfeld productions: *Rosalie* (1928), a vehicle for Marilyn Miller that introduced "How Long Has This Been Going On?," and *Show Girl* (1929), a Ruby Keeler showcase that included George's tone poem "An American in Paris." Even the unsuccessful *Treasure Girl* (1928) produced such quality work as "Feeling I'm Falling," "I Don't Think I'll Fall in Love Today" and "I've Got a Crush on You."

With *Strike Up the Band* (1930) the brothers moved in a different direction. Morrie Ryskind's script, a tight, bouncy political satire, allowed Ira to explore non-traditional lyricwriting. An earlier *Strike Up the Band* had closed in Philadelphia in 1927, but this time they got it right and the result, while not as cohesive and sparkling as the later *Of Thee I Sing*, was still one of the more provocative musicals of the era. *Girl Crazy* (1930) was more conventional, but it did have newcomer Ethel Merman and more individual song hits than any other Gershwin musical: "Bidin' My Time," "Embraceable You," "Could You Use Me?," "I Got Rhythm," "Sam and Delilah," "Boy! What Love Has Done to Me" and "But Not For Me."

With such success it was inevitable that Hollywood would beckon, and the brothers went west in 1931. But the resulting film, *Delicious* (1931), was not a success, and many of Ira's lyrics were dropped when the songs were turned into background music. "Blah, Blah, Blah" did remain; it was Ira's gentle spoof on romantic lyricwriting. But the song and the movie were quickly forgotten and the brothers were back on Broadway with *Of Thee I Sing* (1931). Ryskind again wrote the libretto (with the incomparable George S. Kaufman), but what had been touched on in *Strike Up the Band* was realized and perfected in *Of Thee I Sing*. It is not only the Gershwins' best musical comedy; it is a landmark in Broadway history. Using extended musical sequences instead of individual songs, Ira utilized a free-flowing sort of rhymed recitative that had rarely been heard on Broadway before. His gifts for ridiculous word play, outlandish rhymes, and unbridled enthusiasm all came together in *Of Thee I Sing*. While some individual songs became popular ("Love Is Sweeping the Country," "Because, Because," "Who Cares?" and the title song), it was the whole that mattered. The work has aged poorly and revivals tend to be on the camp level, but *Of Thee I Sing* was important for showing Broadway what musical comedy could do.

The sequel, *Let 'Em Eat Cake* (1933), was not a success despite the efforts of the same creative team and even the same characters played by the original actors. The plot, about a fascist dictatorship in America, went further than the audience, now in the depths of the Depression, cared to venture. (Martin Gottfried has described the show as "the Marx Brothers gone Brechtian.")[1] Recently a great deal of attention has been given to *Let 'Em Eat Cake*, and many are now agreeing with the Gershwins, who thought it a better work than *Of Thee I Sing*. The music has been clearly underrated until now, and the recovery of the complete score reveals a new masterwork in George Gershwin's repertoire. But Ira's lyrics, while just as clever as those in *Of Thee I Sing*, have such a harsh, macabre quality that they, and the heavy-handed book, still keep most from embracing *Let 'Em Eat Cake*. The one song standard to come out of the show in 1933, "Mine," is still the best song, with its lyricized counter-melody and its unique blending of romance and wry commentary.

Porgy and Bess (1935) would be George Gershwin's last work for the stage and a high point for the careers of both brothers and DuBose Heyward, librettist and co-lyricist. Much discussion still continues over just what *Porgy and Bess* is exactly: opera? operetta? musical play? (The creators called it an American "folk opera.") It is clearly not a conventional opera libretto. While there are long extended musical sequences and much use of recitative, these are definitely musical theatre lyrics with all the essential qualities that musicals demand of the words. *Porgy and Bess* is a masterpiece, if ever America has produced a musical masterpiece, and the lyrics play an important role in that distinction. DuBose Heyward's popular 1925 novel *Porgy* and subsequent dramatic version were the basis for *Porgy and Bess*, and Heyward wrote most of the lyrics for the piece. But it is Ira Gershwin's contribution, seen in such songs as "There's a Boat Dat's Leavin' Soon for New York" and "It Ain't Necessarily So," that gives the work a cynical, sassy tone that mixes so well with Heyward's more painful, haunting temperament. (DuBose Heyward is discussed further in Chapter 11.)

Porgy and Bess was only a qualified success (it was greeted with respect, but it lost money), and the brothers were off to Hollywood again. George would never return, but before his untimely death from a brain tumor in 1937, he and Ira wrote the scores for three films: *Shall*

We Dance? (1937), *Damsel in Distress* (1937) and *The Goldwyn Follies* (1938). It is not the purpose of this book to concentrate on film musicals, but one cannot ignore the brothers' work in Hollywood. Both were at the peak of their powers and the songs, while all in the conventional mode, are among the finest they ever wrote. "They All Laughed," "A Foggy Day (in London Town)," "I've Got Beginner's Luck," "Love Walked In," "Things Are Looking Up," "Let's Call the Whole Thing Off," "Nice Work If You Can Get It," "They Can't Take That Away from Me," " (Our) Love Is Here to Stay" and others constitute a body of work outstanding for any composer/lyricist's lifelong achievement; yet the Gershwins wrote them all in less than a year.

Some thought that the death of George Gershwin would signal the end of Ira's career. Emotionally, it was more than the end of a partnership and the loss of a brother; it was the end of an era. The Gershwin years, as many call them, were over. It was four years before Ira returned to work. It was not his anxiety over working with a different composer that had detained him so long; during all those years of Gershwin hits Ira had occasionally written with others. In 1934 he and E. Y. Harburg did the lyrics for Harold Arlen's *Life Begins at 8:40*, and in 1936 Ira wrote the words for Vernon Duke's songs in the *Ziegfeld Follies* and came up with "I Can't Get Started with You." But the loss of George was very complex. In some ways Ira lived through George. The Gershwin magic had always had George as its representative. Ira doubted that he could take on that role. So when he did return to work he usually remained in the shadow of those he collaborated with.

Playwright Moss Hart revived Ira Gershwin's career by convincing him to do the lyrics for his experimental musical about psychoanalysis, *Lady in the Dark* (1941). In its own way, *Lady in the Dark* was as much a landmark as *Of Thee I Sing*. It had less music than most shows and, despite its complex libretto, less plot. Filled with dream sequences and an expressionistic approach to character development, *Lady in the Dark* looked like no other musical. Kurt Weill's music was alternately frolicsome and disturbing. The lyrics were double-edged and the words actually became clues in discovering the title character's persona. The recurring theme song, "My Ship," was suggested rather than displayed; it was the key to her "problem" and it was revealed to the audience in a unique way. In some respects, *Lady in the Dark* accomplished what George Gershwin had always dreamed about: pushing the confines of musical theatre further than ever before. He did it musically;

Hart/Weill/Gershwin did it thematically. Like *Of Thee I Sing*, *Lady in the Dark* is dated and rarely revived. But both shows opened up possibilities for Broadway that would not be fully realized until the 1950s with the early conceptual musicals like *West Side Story*.

Ira Gershwin's final two Broadway musicals (*The Firebrand of Florence* in 1945 again with Kurt Weill and *Park Avenue* in 1946 with music by Arthur Schwartz) contained some exceptional lyric work, but both shows were unsuccessful, and the rest of Ira's career would be spent in Hollywood. Some of the films are easily forgotten: *North Sea* (1943) with music by Aaron Copland, *Give a Girl a Break* (1953) with a Burton Lane score, and *The Shocking Miss Pilgrim* (1946) in which Ira set lyrics to unused George Gershwin "trunk" tunes. But there were notable films as well: *Cover Girl* (1944) with music by Jerome Kern, *The Barkleys of Broadway* (1949) with a Harry Warren score, and *A Star Is Born* (1954) with music by Harold Arlen.

Although he never returned to the theatre after 1946, Ira Gershwin's greatest Broadway success came in 1983, a few months before he died. *My One and Only* used most of the songs from the original *Funny Face* and some from other shows by the Gershwins, but the libretto by Peter Stone and Timothy S. Mayer was new. While most of the Gershwin musicals are difficult to revive because of the flimsy or outdated books (*Porgy and Bess* is the exception), Stone and Mayer came up with a breezy storyline set in 1927 that complemented Ira's words beautifully. *My One and Only* ran for 767 performances, longer than any other Gershwin show, and not only contained some old favorites, but allowed audiences to rediscover such forgotten songs as "He Loves and She Loves," "Blah, Blah, Blah," "Soon," "Kickin' the Clouds Away" and the title song.

There is a paradox to be found in Ira Gershwin's work. His lyrics can be very highbrow. His vocabulary is wider than that of most lyricists and the structure of his songs is methodically arrived at. Yet, at the same time, his lyrics can be very lowbrow. His use of slang, idiom and purposely bad grammar ("I got rhythm" instead of "I have rhythm"—the difference makes the song work) creates a streetwise kind of sound. The way he combines both the high- and lowbrow in one song has a great deal to do with his charm.

Ira Gershwin was not highly educated (he was a slack student and never finished college) but he loved words and studied them like a fanatic collector. Linguistic derivations, origins of slang, various forms of rhyme, disparate pronunciations and periodic changes in word definitions all fascinated him. Like some dedicated philologist, he actually spent time calculating what words were the most often used in songdom and what were the most frequently recurring rhymes. His collection of lyrics, *Lyrics on Several Occasions*, is filled with such observations and provides one of the few opportunities for a lyricist to discuss his craft at length. The impression one gets from reading his "many informative annotations and disquisitions," as he states it, is one of listening not to a dry linguist, but to an avid devotee of the language. As Betty Comden and Adolph Green, who worked with Ira Gershwin in Hollywood, have said, he was "a word lover with an encyclopedic knowledge of the intricacies and subtleties of the language."[2]

Perhaps it was this confidence in knowing his own language that allowed Gershwin to mix his educated phrases with all those "sweetie pies" and "dearies." His playfulness with words is a calculated kind of lunacy. They sound flip and easy, but are actually the result of exacting work. If Hammerstein labored to achieve sincerity, Gershwin labored just as hard to look impudent. And he usually succeeded. The ease with which the lyric develops is often deceptive. The more frolicsome the lyric the easier it is to take for granted. The refrain of "Who Cares?" is used in *Of Thee I Sing* as a glib putdown for the press, sung by President Wintergreen, but also as a sincere declaration of love.

Who Cares
If the sky cares to fall in the sea?
Who cares what banks fail in Yonkers
Long as you've got a kiss that conquers?
    Why should I care?
Life is one long jubilee
So long as I care for you—
And you care for me.

Gershwin's use of slang is one of his most recognizable characteristics. Adding "baby" to the patriotic phrase "of thee I sing" is a daring and joyous risk that pays off. Using "sweetie pie" in such a gentle lyric as "I've Got a Crush on You" gives it its distinction. Colloquial expressions that writers shy away from in prose take on power in a song if the expression is supported by a fresh approach in the lyric. "Bidin' My Time," "Let's Call the Whole Thing Off," "I've Got Beginner's Luck," "Nice Work If

You Can Get It" and other Gershwin songs that use familiar expressions avoid the trite or routine because they develop the familiar and make it unique.

Gershwin not only used everyday phrases in his lyrics, but sometimes devised his own. Who ever thought "embraceable" or "all a-quiver" would sound right in a song lyric? "It Ain't Necessarily So" is filled with linguistic concoctions such as "zim bam boddle-oo." "'S Wonderful" invents a language of its own ("'s marvelous . . . 's awful nice . . . 's paradise") and "Do, Do, Do" takes a simple sound and turns a word into a musical instrument. All the laughing "he, he, he's" and "ho, ho, ho's" in "They All Laughed" turn words into sound effects. And who else but Gershwin could build a song on a matter of differing pronunciation, as in "Let's Call the Whole Thing Off"?

The spirit in Ira Gershwin's work goes beyond such technicalities. Thematically the songs have a confident and exuberant attitude that is the heart of this spirit. Like Cohan and Hammerstein, Gershwin wrote optimistic lyrics. They are eager, alive and expect the best of every situation. Cohan used pride and patriotism. Hammerstein found a deep appreciation of life. Gershwin celebrated. Whether singing about love, London Town, the weather, or candidate Wintergreen, the lyrics are decisively positive. One doesn't describe or relate emotions in a Gershwin song, one acclaims them. Even the gentle love songs ("Mine," "Love Walked In," "Long Ago and Far Away") have a winner's pride about them.

Since Ira Gershwin was such a craftsman with words, his rhymes, puns and comic turns have served as a high standard for other lyricists' work. "Don't Be a Woman If You Can," "A Weekend in the Country" and "These Charming People" are not the most well known Gershwin songs, but they are models of musical comedy charm songs. "A Rhyme for Angela," a comic love song from the forgotten *The Firebrand of Florence*, is a virtuoso performance as the lyricist goes through all the rhymes he can think of for other women's names ("Olivia/trivia . . . Irma/terra firma . . . Chloe/snowy . . . Margot/embargo") but can't find a suitable one for his beloved Angela. Gershwin's celebrated "story" songs, such as "The Saga of Jenny" from *Lady in the Dark* and "Sam and Delilah" from *Girl Crazy*, are wonderfully self-contained and have been successfully revived in a variety of entertainment avenues. No less impressive are his ensemble songs. Gershwin was one of the few lyricists who wrote comic lines for the chorus that actually came across to the audience. Because clarity and comic nuance often suffer in the voices of many, this is no easy task. But *Of Thee I Sing* and *Let 'Em Eat Cake* are filled with group numbers that sustain effective comedy.

Politics is a noticeably recurring theme in Ira Gershwin's work. He managed to combine politics and lyricism in a handful of his shows; after all, as he saw it, both were often a matter of words used effectively. The political satires (*Strike Up the Band*, *Of Thee I Sing* and *Let 'Em Eat Cake*) brought out Gershwin's most wry sense of humor. Although it is one of the shortest lyrics in all songdom (according to Gershwin, who researched the matter), "Wintergreen for President" is still one of the most effective musical satires.

Wintergreen for President!
Wintergreen for President!
He's the man the people choose;
Loves the Irish and the Jews.

What "Blah, Blah, Blah" is to the love song, "Wintergreen for President" is to the political rally song. Both are pure Gershwin.

To describe Ira Gershwin as word crazy gives only a part of the picture. He set standards in lyricwriting that Cole Porter, Lorenz Hart and others felt compelled to live up to. The man in the shadows ended up being very influential in the long run. He moved lyricwriting further away from the confines of operetta even as he helped push musical theatre closer to opera. His idioms and optimism, along with George's soaring music, lifted theatre songs from the ordinary to the jubilant. His lyrics came from his own individual language, a language Alan Jay Lerner later called "slangy sentimentality."[3] For a man who stood quietly by as the more conspicuous ones had their say, Ira Gershwin always kept his own voice. Lerner described this voice accurately when he noted that Ira's lyrics "were more redolent of the entire jazz era than the work of any other lyric writer. You can feel the twenties in his lyrics as much as in the verse of Dorothy Parker and some of the writings of Scott Fitzgerald. He even gave 'baby' and 'sweetie pie' respectability."[4] Only a man who loved words could do that.

NOTES

1. Martin Gottfried, *Broadway Musicals* (New York: Harry N. Abrams, Inc., 1980), p. 229.

2. Ira Gershwin, *Lyrics on Several Occasions* (New York: Viking Press, 1959), p. vii.

3. Alan Jay Lerner, *The Musical Theatre: A Celebration* (New York: McGraw Hill Book Co., 1986), p. 80.

4. Lerner, p. 80.

7

Anything Goes: Cole Porter

What is it about Cole Porter? Two songwriters who can agree on nothing else will concur that Porter is "the top." Musical theatre fans and critics agree. Not only do they love a Cole Porter song, but they actually know that it is a Cole Porter song. People who mix up a Berlin ballad with a Gershwin torch song somehow instinctively know a Cole Porter number when they hear it. Porter is unique among the great songwriters, in a world apart from the others. He is also one of the least influential. There are book songwriters, Tin Pan Alley songwriters, concept songwriters; then there is Cole Porter.

The lyrics of Porter create a world as fanciful as that of Damon Runyon, Lewis Carroll or L. Frank Baum. The Cole Porter world is the sleek, art deco cosmos of millionaires cruising through tropical seas in the moonlight. New York penthouses glow with witty and sophisticated people who use allusions to Greek mythology and French vernacular to make their point. Tuxedoed playboys combine sexual innuendo with Ivy League slang to win their girls. Everyone speaks in internal rhymes and even gangsters sound clever. It is a world fashioned through Porter's music and lyrics rather than the librettos that were almost always written by someone else. The shows are mostly forgotten; the songs survive and keep the Cole Porter world alive.

Modern audiences approach Porter's work with nostalgia; "they don't write them like that anymore." Yet this illusionary world was as foreign to the original audiences as it is to us. Porter made his name, and did his best work, during the Depression years. It was fantasy, not nostalgia, that those audiences wanted. Most of the thirties musicals were escapist, but none more so than Porter's. As Cole Porter historian Robert Kimball put it, "his was a message of civilized cheer."[1] While other artists envied Porter, they did not dislike him. He came from another universe, so comparisons with themselves were meaningless. Porter left a body of work that can only be evaluated on its own terms. He is the least influential of major theatre lyricists because he was never directly involved with the development of the musical theatre. Where he came from, what he did, and what he accomplished is a separate chapter in Broadway history. There were no Cole Porter–like artists before him and none has existed since him. Does this make him the best? Probably not. He was an excellent craftsman and a superb creator of illusion. But what he was the best at was being Cole Porter.

He was born in 1891 on his family's large farm in Peru, Indiana. Porter's grandfather had made his fortune in lumber and saw to it that the boy received a quality education befitting a future lawyer: Worcester Academy, Yale and Harvard. But Porter was writing songs by the age of ten and had his first musical produced on Broadway when he was only twenty-three. The rest of his long life was spent on Broadway, in Hollywood and traveling around the world in high style. Porter's career spanned five decades and resulted in over eight hundred songs written for twenty-six Broadway shows and another eighteen films. He wrote both music and lyrics for all of them. Thanks to well-documented scrapbooks and archival collections, Porter's work is more fully recorded than most who started when he did in the 1910s. It is possible to look at his lyrics as a whole, and the picture is a fascinating one. While there is some obvious development from the collegiate humor of his student shows at Yale to the peak of his adult work in the 1930s to his occasional hits at the end of his career, the most interesting revelation is the lack of change. The quality of the lyricwriting varies from year to year, from show to show (and often from song to song in the same show), but the major impetus behind it all is consistent, even rigid. For a man whose philosophy was that "anything goes," it seems the things that went were mostly the same.

This is not to say there is no variety in subject matter, mood or character. But the tone of voice and the perspective never change. The songs written in the Roaring Twenties have the same point of view as those from the lean Depression years, the frantic war years, and the booming post-war years. The world of Cole Porter operated so independently of the real world that it is no wonder that songs from the early shows could be so easily interpolated into revivals of the later ones. A Cole Porter song is a Cole Porter song. It is that rare constant in an art form too often at the mercy of changing trends.

Charting the highs and lows of Porter's career reveals an astonishing number of good and bad songs in each period. When the Porter magic worked, it worked regardless of libretto, stars or box office success. Given a stellar cast and a solid libretto for *Anything Goes* (1935), Porter came up with "All Through the Night," "You're the Top," "I Get a Kick out of You," "Blow, Gabriel, Blow" and the title song. Yet later that same year, given an unpromising cast and a weak script called *Jubilee*, Porter provided "A Picture of Me Without You," "Just One of Those Things" and "Begin the Beguine." Many feel that Porter's 1937 horse riding accident, which left him crippled for the rest of his life, was the turning point in his work. Yet the two shows subsequent to the accident, *You Never Know* and *Leave It To Me* (both in 1938), seem to pick up right where he left off. Unlike most songwriters whose changes in their personal life are subtly suggested in their writing (Lorenz Hart being a prime example), Porter's world revolves independently of outside forces.

Even as his career waned, this consistency was evident. The last shows—*Out of This World* (1950), *Can-Can* (1953) and *Silk Stockings* (1955)—are considered sub-standard Porter. Yet they produced such gems as "From This Moment On," "All of You," "I Love Paris" and "It's All Right with Me," all of which would have been very much at home in his heyday shows. And when one keeps in mind that from 1929 to 1960 Porter kept up a second career writing songs for Hollywood films, the consistency is all the more remarkable.

By the late 1940s, when most thought Porter was past his prime, the pattern was temporarily broken. Bella and Samuel Spewack, who had written Porter's earlier *Leave It To Me*, had to convince him to do the score for their play-within-a-play version of *The Taming of the Shrew*. Porter argued that Shakespeare wasn't his style. Judging from everything in his past, he was right. The resulting musical, *Kiss Me, Kate* (1948), isn't his style, but is terrific. It is the finest book score Porter wrote and, while it did not break new ground in terms of ideas or execution, it is one of the best examples of its genre. Porter's score for *Kiss Me, Kate* so closely integrated with the story, characters and dual milieu (modern backstage mixed with anachronistic Elizabethan) that it is surprising that the songs are so well known. "Another Op'nin', Another Show," "Always True To You in My Fashion," "Brush Up Your Shakespeare" and "So In Love" are musical theatre standards even if they don't transfer well to the radio. Even the pseudo-Elizabethan songs taken from Shakespeare's lines ("I've Come to Wive It Wealthily in Padua," "Were Thine That Special Face" and "Where is the Life that Late I Led?") have a memorable quality to them. Only Porter's mock Viennese waltz, "Wunderbar," is not essential to the whole and could have been lifted from any other Porter show. *Kiss Me, Kate* surprised everyone, including Porter himself. Not until the situation demanded it did he discover that he was a playwright as well as a songwriter.

Keeping in mind the exceptional case of *Kiss Me, Kate*, one comes back to the unusual consistency of tone found throughout Porter's career. To discover the nature of this charmed point of view it is best to look at the songs rather than the shows. The individual lyrics reveal an education, a sense of wit as well as humor, and a high level of sophistication. But is that all? Others have been clever and sophisticated, but others are not Cole Porter.

The essence of Porter's sophistication is its sincerity. His world may have been a fantasy, but it was a fantasy he totally believed in. As Stephen Sondheim has pointed out, Porter "believed in what he wrote . . . in gossamer wings. No man on earth can write 'gossamer wings' except Cole Porter, and nobody has been able to imitate Porter successfully because they don't believe what he believed."[2] Porter may have sometimes mocked true love or friendship or moonlit romance in his songs, but he still believed in them. One doesn't think of his work as corny or sentimental, but the subtext beneath many of his songs is full of corn and sentiment. We subconsciously respond to that subtext and feel for the millionaire playboy standing on the veranda with his heart breaking.

There is a foreign, distant feel to much of Porter's lyrics. While most Broadway songwriters had roots in Europe and strove to write American-sounding songs, Porter was purebred American and wrote his songs with foreign sounds and exotic images. The librettists for his shows saw this clearly and set the Porter musicals in such places as Panama, Russia and (his favorite setting) Paris. When he wrote about his own country it was usually New York City, the only American milieu for the Cole Porter fantasy world. But travel is more than a mere recurring motif. Porter's songs have a restless feel to them, a wandering or searching impulse that is their driving force. Very rarely do images of settling down, of stability, or of permanence come up. Home, family, contentment and stability are not normally in the Porter repertoire. ("You'd Be So Nice To Come Home To" is a notable exception.) This restless, yearning quality to his work makes Porter's poignant songs all the more powerful. "Night and Day" is filled with such themes.

Day and night, why is it so
That this longing for you follows wherever I go?
In the roaring traffic's boom,
In the silence of my lonely room,
I think of you night and day.
Night and day under the hide of me
There's an, oh, such a hungry yearning burning inside of me . . . .

The traveling image ocassionally loses its glamour; the restlessness goes deeper. In songs like "All Through The Night," "Ev'ry Time We Say Goodbye," "In the Still of the Night," "Down in the Depths," "I Concentrate On You," "Make It Another Old-Fashioned, Please" and "Begin the Beguine," the musical situation is much the same: the world has stopped moving for a moment and the pain is worse because of it. These two ideas—a sense of constant restiveness and a sincere approach to even the most flippant emotions—could make for maudlin lyricwriting if it weren't for Porter's facility with words and his superb craftsmanship.

Consider his dexterity with rhymes. Cole Porter rhymes are justly famous. They are more than clever; they are playful. He enjoys the hard masculine rhymes for comic effect ("Strauss/Mickey Mouse") as well as the more rhythmic feminine rhymes that sneak up on you ("Colosseum/Louvre Museum"). This playfulness can also be seen in his use of internal rhymes. For example, in "Where Is the Life That Late I Led?" the internal rhyming is straightforward and obvious ("You gave a new meaning to the leaning tow'r of Pisa") whereas in "You Do Something To Me" it gets downright silly ("Do do that voodoo that you do so well"). Few lyricists have had as much fun with arch rhymes, those false rhymes that purposely draw attention to their ridiculousness. "Brush Up Your Shakespeare" is full of them: "Othella / helluvafella . . . flatter'er / Cleopaterer. . . . heinous / Coriolanus." Even identities, considered the least effective form of rhyming, become magical in Porter's hands. "Let's Not Talk About Love" consists of lists of identities such as "avidity, turbidity, Manhattan and viscidity."

Another area in which Porter's craftsmanship is exceptional is his verse. The use of a verse to introduce the refrain (the main body of the song) has just about disappeared from contemporary songwriting, but it was expected format in Porter's day. Most lyricists do not write the verse until the refrain is completed; the verse is often the throwaway part of the lyric. But Porter loved writing verses and excelled at it. The verse for "I Get a Kick Out of You" may be one of the finest ever written:

My story is much too sad to be told,
But practically ev'rything leaves me totally cold.
The only exception I know is the case
Where I'm out on a quiet spree
Fighting vainly the old ennui
And I suddenly turn and see
Your fabulous face.

I get no kick from champagne . . .

The verse not only sets up the song's situation, but it creates a mood and sense of longing that is lost when the refrain is sung without it.

Porter's list songs deserve special mention. List songs are sometimes the refuge of lyricists with nothing to say. Such songs rarely move forward, they simply catalogue until they wear themselves out. Porter wrote the most effective list songs because their energy was matched by their cleverness. "You're the Top" is considered Porter's (or anyone else's) best list song. The enthusiasm for describing the person who is "the top" moves from the silly to the sublime and back again, but it all works. To call one the Nile, Mickey Mouse, cellophane, a turkey dinner, an Arrow collar or broccoli may not pass as a compliment in prose, but Porter turns all of these into good-natured acclamations by lining up the list in the right way. All other list songs must tip their hat to "You're the Top."

Cole Porter's craftsmanship is not as precise in his chorus numbers and act finales. Lyrics are often lost when sung by a group and Porter, like most songwriters, adjusts himself accordingly. But one often finds Porter's words for these ensemble numbers sloppy or derivative. Such songs, by their nature, could never be hits, but they should still retain the character and milieu of the show. Too many of Porter's throwaway lyrics are characterless. When one sees how much effort Ira Gershwin or Oscar

Hammerstein put into their ensemble lyrics, one cannot help noticing the lack of such effort in Porter's work. The same bloodlessness can be found in some of his solos and duets as well. Because Porter stuck to such a narrow range of subjects, the same images and ideas tend to recur over and over again. For every "Night and Day" or "It's De-Lovely" there are a half dozen pale imitations that do not sustain themselves. Near the end of his career these imitations outnumbered the real thing. The Cole Porter fantasy world was, alas, as limited as any other world.

So, in the end, what has Cole Porter left us besides a collection of songs with a consistent tone of voice? Is his life's work one long list song, often endearing but ultimately going nowhere? For an artist who did little to change the direction of the musical theatre, Porter did trailblaze in some areas of lyricwriting.

Despite his recurring battle with censors, he showed that lyrics could be more overt when it came to sexual matters. Porter is the first songwriter to combine love and sex in a lyric. Romance in a Porter song usually has its tactile aspects. But pressures from without forced him to be more subtle than he probably would have wished. Even so, certain words, sometimes whole lines, and often entire verses were omitted from songs such as "I Get a Kick Out of You," "But In the Morning, No" and "By the Mississinewah." "Love for Sale," a not-so-subtle paean sung by a prostitute in *The New Yorkers* (1930), was banned from radio play for decades. Such restrictions led Porter and other songwriters to pursue the double entendre. Later lyricists, such as E. Y. Harburg, would push the parameters even further until songwriters, such as Fred Ebb and Stephen Sondheim, would have total freedom in their lyric subjects. But Porter had to be content to leave everything open to the most prudish interpretations. Everyone knew that "Let's Do It, Let's Fall in Love" and "My Heart Belongs to Daddy" were not about romance among the species or fatherlove. But the lyrics left open that possibility and got the songs past the censors.

A less controversial form of trailblazing on Porter's part was his ability to instill a sense of anticipation in his lyrics. Audiences became anxious to hear the words in a Cole Porter show and he tried not to disappoint them. In a way, Porter taught the audience to listen for lyrics. Even more so than Wodehouse and Berlin before him, Porter made lyrics fun for the audience. Lorenz Hart and others would build on this further, but it was Porter who first stimulated this joyous feeling of anticipation. Once the music of a Cole Porter song begins there is an expectancy that wonderful words are coming. This talent for creating such an anticipation may be, historically speaking, Porter's greatest gift. It is a talent that cannot be underestimated. It may be the most real thing in Cole Porter's fantasy world.

NOTES

1. Robert Kimball (ed.), *The Complete Lyrics of Cole Porter* (New York: Alfred A. Knopf, 1983), p. xviii.

2. Otis L. Guernsey (ed.), *Playwrights, Lyricists, Composers on Theatre* (New York: Dodd, Mead and Co., 1974), p. 79.

8

On His Toes: Lorenz Hart

When Lorenz Hart was at his best he was America's most ingenious and inspired theatre lyricist. It's that simple. How often he was at his best is something far less simple. Hart had more talent than any of the early lyricists, but his was a sporadic talent: unreliable, inconsistent, unexplainable. He was capable of writing a lyric that outmatched the studied and labored efforts of all the others. Yet Hart was just as capable of sloppy, derivative and uninspired nonsense. He worked less and, particularly in his last years, he cared less than the others. But when he was on his toes, Lorenz Hart surpassed all of them.

A brilliant Hart lyric heard is rarely forgotten. But what is it that is so memorable about his words? Surely Cole Porter was better at the sophisticated wit. Ira Gershwin mastered the slang. Irving Berlin was unrivaled in the simple, straightforward emotions. And Oscar Hammerstein outshone them all when it came to warmth and a sense of character. But what about Lorenz Hart? What was his specialty? We hear a lyric like "My Funny Valentine" or "I Could Write a Book" and we realize no one else writes this way so well. But what way is it? That Hart's work is so difficult to define is part of his genius and part of his problem. He has no clearly distinct style; he sometimes stumbles onto a combination of words that defies categorical definition. Stumble may be too harsh a word; Hart's flair for lyricwriting was not accidental. But his lack of discipline made his talent as elusive to him as it seems to us. When a lyric worked he knew it. But Hart was no more capable of recreating the process than he was of explaining it. He seems to have had no more control over his lyricwriting than over his personal life. It was a sad life punctuated with loneliness and bitterness, but Hart's best work went beyond even his aspirations.

One cannot discuss Lorenz Hart without speaking first of Rodgers and Hart. The title does more than acknowledge composer and lyricist. Rodgers and Hart were the first true songwriting duo in the American musical theatre. Never before had one man's words matched another's music so well. Remarkably, their songs didn't sound like a team; they had the cohesiveness found only in the one-man songwriting dynamos. Today we look back over a half dozen successful and inspired songwriting teams and we take their special collaboration for granted. But the effect of Rodgers and Hart in the 1920s was unique and exciting. George M. Cohan used to refer to them sarcastically as "Gilbert and Sullivan." He was more correct than he ever realized; their talents were that well matched. Apart from a few early efforts, Hart worked exclusively with Richard Rodgers during his entire career. Not until he met Rodgers and the two of them began to work together did each of their talents truly surface. Because Rodgers later had a second and very different career with Hammerstein, one is likely to dismiss Hart as the less important of the Rodgers and Hart team. But the fact is, without Hart even Rodgers could no longer produce that special kind of song. He moved in a different direction with Hammerstein, knowing that it was the Rodgers and Hart team that had created the magic.

Lorenz Hart was born in 1895 in New York City. He showed literary promise at a young age and, after an education at Columbia, he made his living writing and translating. When Hart first met Rodgers in 1918 (he was Rodgers' senior by seven years) they were both young, ambitious and shared plenty of ideas about the musical theatre. Jerome Kern was Rodgers' idol, Hart admired Wodehouse, and the Princess Theatre shows were their models. A year later the first Rodgers and Hart song heard on Broadway, "Any Old Place with You," appeared in a forgotten musical called *A Lonely Romeo*. With such unpredictable rhymes as "Portugal/court you, gal . . . cheerier/Lake Superior . . . go to hell for ya/Philadelphia," the Hart touch was already evident. A series of Columbia Varsity Shows and songs interpolated into others' Broadway shows led to the first hit musical of their own, *The Garrick Gaieties* (1925), produced by the Theatre Guild. While most of the songs from the satirical revue seem rather collegiate and silly now, the show was a breath of fresh air at the time, poking fun at the heavy European dramas the Guild usually presented. And there was one song, "Manhattan," taken from an earlier unproduced musical, that was quite effective. It still is to this day.

Still in their twenties, Rodgers and Hart settled down to a long career as Broadway's foremost songwriting team. It would be more correct to say that Rodgers settled down. He married in 1930 and retained a businesslike approach to turning out at least one Broadway score each year. As for Hart, he was far from settled. Constantly haunted by his small stature (he stood less than five feet tall), his less-than-dashing features and his lack of success with the women he adored, Hart's social drinking increased. Hart was a homosexual, but an uncontrollable romantic about certain women. His love songs would reflect this bittersweet dilemma more and more as the years went on.

Before Rodgers and Hart went to Hollywood in 1931, they wrote the scores for or contributed to fourteen Broadway shows, the most memorable being *A Connecticut Yankee* (1927), which contained the delightful "Thou Swell." The other pre-Hollywood shows are easily forgotten, but they did produce some song standards less easy to forget: "My Heart Stood Still," "You Took Advantage of Me," "With a Song in My Heart" and "Ten Cents a Dance." Rodgers and Hart would return from Hollywood in 1935, leaving behind them a few forgettable films and one early musical classic, *Love Me Tonight* (1932). The next five years on Broadway would be the team's most productive period and represent their finest work. *Jumbo* (1935) was staged at the Hippodrome, but even the elephants and circus acts couldn't bury such songs as "Little Girl Blue," "My Romance" and "The Most Beautiful Girl in the World." *On Your Toes* (1936) had a book by George Abbott and a score that included "There's a Small Hotel," but the show is equally famous for George Balanchine's choreography, the ballet "Slaughter on Tenth Avenue" in particular. *Babes in Arms* (1937) introduced a young cast full of future Broadway stars, a libretto this time by Rodgers and Hart themselves, and a score that contained more hits than any other show of the decade: "My Funny Valentine," "The Lady is a Tramp," "Way Out West," "Johnny One Note," "Where or When" and "I Wish I Were in Love Again." *The Boys From Syracuse* in 1938 would be no less of a success. "Falling in Love with Love," "Dear Old Syracuse" and "This Can't Be Love" would stand out in a score filled with memorable songs.

The team reached the climax of their career in 1940 with *Pal Joey*. This show would prove to be their most important contribution to the development of the musical theatre and Hart wrote his most powerful score. In addition to some song hits ("Bewitched, Bothered and Bewildered" and "I Could Write a Book"), the score revealed Hart's talent for capturing the seamier, more offbeat side of life. Hart knew the milieu well: cheap nightclubs, cynical third-rate performers, disillusioned lovers. The nightclub songs enhanced the "Den of Iniquity" setting, but also reflected the jaded temperaments of the characters. *Pal Joey* was, in some ways, the forefather of *Cabaret*.

By this time Hart's drinking, his unexplained absences, and his lack of interest in work were chronic. In frustration Rodgers started looking for another collaborator, and when Hart turned down the idea of a musical version of *Green Grow the Lilacs*, Rodgers went to Hammerstein. Contrary to rumor, Hart was still alive in 1943 when *Oklahoma!* opened and even attended the first performance. Rodgers and Hart's last show, a revised version of their earlier *A Connecticut Yankee*, opened later that same year. Hart disappeared the night of the opening and was later found in an advanced state of inebriation and pneumonia. He died three days later at the age of forty-eight. The last lyric he wrote, "To Keep My Love Alive," was as fresh, sassy and good natured as the boyish "Any Old Place with You" written twenty-five years earlier.

Lorenz Hart loved the theatre, but hated the process of creating theatre. While lyricists like Hammerstein and Gershwin meticulously labored over their words, Hart often procrastinated, disappeared, reappeared, then quickly dashed off a lyric in a matter of minutes. Dozens of stories have survived about Hart's speed in lyricwriting. When asked once what his source of inspiration was, he pointed to his pencil.

Just as Hart needed to be pressured or threatened into writing, his lyric ideas needed similar prodding. Once a word, a phrase or concept struck him (or was given to him), he could then proceed, and the result was quickly achieved. Consider the many Hart songs that hang on a simple turn of phrase or a catchy juxtaposition of words. The idea of a "funny" Valentine (Val was the character's name), as opposed to a more typically romantic one, sets up the song's premise. (Hart continues to avoid the expected by describing Val as "unphotographable" with a figure "less than Greek.") A slangy term mixes interestingly with a formal one in "Thou Swell." The expression "Ladies of the Evening" becomes intriguing when the lyric considers what happens to them "in the morning." "He Was Too

Good to Me" adds a new level of insight to an old expression when it cryptically concludes "he was too good to be true." Sometimes the melody would suggest a lyric idea to Hart (Rodgers often wrote the music first) and other times an out of the ordinary concept would challenge him. The image of a disillusioned dance hall hostess becomes "Ten Cents a Dance." The winter solstice provides the romantic idea for "The Shortest Day of the Year" because such a phenomenon causes "the longest night of the year." Even the quirky sensation of déjà vu becomes enchanting in "Where or When."

Because Hart was bored by the ordinary and commonplace, he went to great lengths to avoid the expected. A lover could not simply admit "I love you." Instead he'd proclaim "It's Got To Be Love" (because it "couldn't be tonsillitis") or "This Can't Be Love" (because "I feel so well"). When a lyric must describe love's sensation it does so with new images ("Bewitched, Bothered and Bewildered"), with candor ("You Took Advantage of Me"), or with seeming off-handedness ("I Could Write A Book"). Hart purposely shunned the most popular romantic devices. When a movie producer kept rejecting Hart's lyrics for a song for *Manhattan Melodrama* because he wanted something more commercial, Hart angrily wrote "Blue Moon" for him as an act of sarcasm. It became one of the team's most popular songs, but Hart hated it.

Hart takes many different approaches to the age-old problem of writing love songs. Take, for example, the various ways he explores sudden love: "All at Once," "My Heart Stood Still," "I Didn't Know What Time It Was," "Have You Met Miss Jones?" and "You Took Advantage of Me." Hart is equally adept at the less violent, more comfortable kind of love: "Mountain Greenery," "The Blue Room," "My Romance" and "There's a Small Hotel."

But where Hart excels is in his love songs that reveal a painful subtext. He was a romantic, but often a cynical one. Many of his songs of unrequited love are not-so-subtle revelations of his own loneliness and anger. They are more than mere torch songs; they paint a romantic picture and then puncture it with icy commentary. "Where's That Rainbow" asks "where's that lining they cheer about?" and concludes that everything will be "just dandy for ev'rybody, but me." "A Ship Without a Sail" describes the situation of the rejected lover who is "all alone, all at sea." "Spring Is Here" but there is no joy because "nobody loves me." The lesson taught in "Little Girl Blue" is to "count the raindrops" that fall on you because they are the only thing you *can* count on. Perhaps Hart's most effective song of unrequited love is "Glad To Be Unhappy." The surface is controlled, even flippant; the subtext is heartbreaking.

Fools rush in, so here I am,
Very glad to be unhappy.
I can't win, but here I am,
More than glad to be unhappy.
Unrequited love's a bore
And I've got it pretty bad.
But for someone you adore,
It's a pleasure to be sad.

If Hart could find wry humor in such heartbreak then it is no surprise that his comic or charm songs are delightful, and the Rodgers and Hart shows have some delicious comic treasures. *Babes In Arms* has "The Lady Is a Tramp" and "Way Out West." *On Your Toes* has "Too Good For the Average Man" and "The Heart Is Quicker Than the Eye." *Pal Joey* has "Zip" and *Too Many Girls* (1939) has "Give It Back to the Indians." *The Boys From Syracuse*, being a farce, has several including "Oh, Diogenes," "I Had Twins" and "What Can You Do With a Man?" But the best may have been the last: Morgan Le Fey's solo "To Keep My Love Alive" from the 1943 revival of *A Connecticut Yankee*.

I married many men,
A ton of them,
And yet I was untrue to none of them
Because I bumped off ev'ry one of them
To keep my love alive.
Sir Paul was frail;
He looked a wreck to me.
At night he was a horse's neck to me.
So I performed an appendectomy
To keep my love alive . . .

Sir Athelstane indulged in fratricide;
He killed his dad and that was patricide.
One night I stabbed him at my mattress side
To keep my love alive.

These are the bright moments when Hart was on his toes. But what of the rest? It is not difficult to notice the times he lost his balance. There are the comic songs that simply aren't funny ("The Greeks Have Got the Girdle") or that pander to the audience for cheap laughs ("He and She"). If indications of the mature Hart can sometimes be seen in his early lyrics, the juvenile efforts of a beginner can sometimes be seen in his later work.

The most recurring fault to be found in the substandard Hart repertoire is sloppiness. It is often amazing to think that he wrote so quickly; at other times, it's more than believable looking at the result. Too often a lyric was written at the last possible moment and was accepted regardless of its quality. And Hart wasn't one to go back and fix up lyrics he was unhappy with (as Ira Gershwin often did); he was usually already behind on his next project. This sloppiness can be seen most clearly in the verses. If the refrains were written in haste, one can only imagine how the verses, the less important part of the lyric, were thrown together. There are, of course, some excellent Hart verses ("Ten Cents a Dance," "My Funny Valentine" and "Where or When" come to mind immediately), but most are weak. Too often they clumsily approach the song subject and end with a limp joke. Moon/June rhymes, the kind that Hart would disdain using in a refrain, show up in the verses frequently. Some superior Hart songs, such as "There's a Small Hotel" and "I Could Write a Book," are diminished by their inferior verses.

Because the Rodgers and Hart scores were rarely integrated closely with the plot and characters (*Pal Joey* is the obvious exception), Hart was able to get away with many weak lyrics. A Hart lyric had mood, passion, humor and occasionally a dramatic situation; but it usually operated independently of the libretto. Since most of the team's librettos were superficial, a weak lyric here or there was not catastrophic. And one must remember that Rodgers' music during this period was rarely routine. What one team member lacked, the other sometimes compensated for.

Lorenz Hart's story is a sad one, but the fruits of his unhappiness are undeniably moving at times. He may have felt that "unrequited love's a bore," but boring is not a word that describes Hart's lyrics, good or bad. Hart was intriguing. Those who knew him had plenty of opportunity to be annoyed, furious and disgusted with him. But very few people disliked him. The same can be said for Hart's lyrics. There is a youthful, "bad-boy" charm about even his least impressive work. As even he admitted, his was a talent largely wasted. Imagining what Hart could have accomplished had he lived differently and longer can be very disconcerting. We can only take comfort in realizing how remarkable it was that he manged to accomplish as much as he did.

9

On and Off the Band Wagon:
Howard Dietz and
Dorothy Fields

Lyricists Howard Dietz and Dorothy Fields did not work together, but their careers parallel each other. Both made names for themselves on Broadway in the late 1920s and continued with long careers in the musical theatre and in Hollywood. But lyricwriting was only their part-time occupation; Dietz was also a prominent movie studio executive and Fields was one of Broadway's most successful librettists for other songwriters. But both always returned to lyricwriting and contributed many memorable songs over the decades. Each maintained their double careers with resilient prowess. For two writers continually jumping on and off the lyric band wagon, Howard Dietz and Dorothy Fields kept their balance very well.

With Irving Berlin, Howard Dietz and his collaborator Arthur Schwartz wrote the finest scores for the musical revue. That genre, in its original form, is long gone now, but the outstanding songs from those revues do resurface on occasion and remind us of what we are missing. Like Berlin, Dietz and Schwartz also moved into the realm of the book musical, but their best songs would always be those individual triumphs that were written to be enjoyed without benefit of plot.

Howard Dietz was born in 1896 in New York and raised in various neighborhoods throughout the city. He attended Columbia at the same time that Oscar Hammerstein II and Lorenz Hart were students. Drawn more to writing than performing, he submitted light verse to the popular magazine columns of the day and was even printed in Franklin P. Adams' *The Conning Tower* under the pen name of Freckles. When he won a $500 prize for an advertisement he entered in a Fatima cigarettes contest, the advertising agency doors opened up for him and Dietz became a successful publicist. (He developed the Leo the Lion trademark for the new Goldwyn Pictures Corporation as well as their "Ars Gratia Artis" slogan.) After Dietz served in the Navy during the First World War, he returned to advertising and in 1924 became the head of publicity for the newly formed Metro-Goldwyn-Mayer company. He remained at MGM as a top executive for over thirty years.

Dietz's other career developed almost as rapidly. He had been composing lyrics since his college days, and in 1923 a song he wrote with Arthur Samuels, "Alibi Baby," was interpolated into the W. C. Fields vehicle *Poppy*. Jerome Kern, who had read Freckles' verses in *The Conning Tower*, approached Dietz about doing the lyrics for his next show. The result, *Dear Sir* (1924), was not one of Kern's better efforts, but Dietz's work was very promising. In one song, "A Houseboat on the Harlem," he displayed a tongue-in-cheek sense of sarcasm and, in "If We Could Lead a Merry Mormon Life," he comically extolled the virtues of polygamy (which he rhymed with "make a pig o' me").

Dietz's first show with composer Arthur Schwartz was *The Little Show* (1929), one of the most successful (and fondly remembered) revues of the 1920s. While there were some outside interpolations, most of the lyrics and sketches were by Dietz. He patterned the musical on the small but vigorous 1925 Rodgers and Hart revue, *The Garrick Gaieties*. While that show contained a good deal of collegiate humor, *The Little Show* was very urbane and its satire was more mature. For audiences used to the lavish Ziegfeld spectaculars, this intimate revue filled with elegant wit was a refreshing surprise. The superb score contained the satiric "Hammacher Schlemmer, I Love You," the haunting "Moanin' Low" (music by Ralph Rainger), and the airy "I Guess I'll Have to Change My Plan." *The Band Wagon* (1931) was the best of the Dietz/Schwartz revues and, in the opinion of many, the greatest of all American revues. Dietz did all of the lyrics and, with George S. Kaufman, the sketches. *The Band Wagon* was on a larger scale than their earlier revues (twin revolving stages were used to dazzling effect) but it retained the intimate, engaging quality that Dietz and Schwartz were known for. The revue opened with the cast assembling on stage as an opening night audience and demanding "It Better Be Good." There was the foot-stomping "I Love Louisa" and the playful "Hoops." "Dancing in the Dark" and "High and Low" were the romantic offerings. And the jubilant "New Sun in the Sky" set a gaily debonair style that Fred Astaire would forever be associated with. *The Band Wagon* was a treasure chest of riches and few musical revues have ever rivaled it.

Just as the Depression was sealing the fate of operetta, the musical revue seemed to be in its waning days as well. Everyone was turning to the book musical, so Dietz and Schwartz did also. The result, *Revenge With Music* (1934), was popular enough to run, but the libretto, based on a Spanish folk tale, did not provide the right background for their talents. Two romantic ballads from the score were exceptional ("You and the Night and the Music" and "If There Is Someone Lovelier Than You") but were peculiarly un-Spanish in tone. The team returned to the revue format with *At Home Abroad* (1935), and Dietz, who did all the lyrics and some of the sketches, used the framework of a world tour to hold the show together. The superior cast included Ethel Waters, who presented Dietz/Schwartz's comic "Hottentot Potentate" and the moving "Thief in the Night," and Beatrice Lillie, who delivered the sly "Get Yourself a Geisha" in the Japan segment where "it's better with your shoes off." Their second attempt at a book musical, *Between the Devil* (1937), had libretto problems again but the Dietz/Schwartz score had three superb numbers: "Triplets," "By Myself" and "I See Your Face Before Me."

In the 1940s Dietz teamed up with Vernon Duke for four shows. In each case a weak book diminished the score, and many felt that Dietz without Schwartz was less impressive. Reunited with Schwartz for the 1948 revue, *Inside U.S.A.*, Dietz provided far better lyrics. The premise for the revue was a tour of the country with songs and sketches about the different states, Mardi Gras, Pittsburgh, Churchill Downs and cowboys. Most of the evening was comic (Beatrice Lillie sang "Song to Forget," about being pursued by Tchaikovsky, Chopin and Liszt, and two Indians touted "We Won't Take It Back") but there was one memorable Dietz/Schwartz ballad, "Haunted Heart," that ranks with their finest torch songs. Other projects away from Broadway occupied Dietz during the 1950s, but by the sixties Dietz was back on Broadway as he and Schwartz once again pursued the book musical. *The Gay Life* (1961) was based on Arthur Schnitzler's *Anatol*, but the librettists Fay and Michael Kanin could not capture the appropriate European flavor of the tale. None of the Dietz/Schwartz songs became popular, but it was a high-quality score with such effectual numbers as "For the First Time," "Magic Moment" and "Something You Never Had Before." Their 1963 venture, *Jennie*, also failed.

With the revue format long forgotten and the musicals of the mid-1960s moving in disparate directions, there seemed to be no place for Howard Dietz. Suffering from Parkinson's disease, he retired from MGM and lyricwriting and even had to give up his avocation of painting. But the team of Dietz and Schwartz came to new life in 1974 when MGM celebrated its fiftieth anniversary and the film anthology *That's Entertainment* was released. The title song, which they had written for the movie version of *The Band Wagon* (1953), became one of the most recognized songs across the country, temporarily supplanting Berlin's "There's No Business Like Show Business" as the unofficial anthem for the entertainment business.

For a man who specialized in revue lyrics and interpolated songs, Dietz had as fine a grasp of dramatic lyricwriting as the book musical writers. Schwartz's music contributes much, of course, but the lyrics themselves have an intriguing sense of drama. They rarely develop a story but they do dramatize a situation. And since they do not have to conform to a libretto with specific characters and setting, they create a vague, rough-sketch situation with just enough detail to keep things in focus.

For example, in "By Myself," a song powerful in its ambiguous attitude about love, the point of view is that of a forsaken lover. Instead of a torch song approach, the lover breezily and rationally decides to "go my way by myself." We know nothing of the lover or the details of the situation, so the lyric allows for some mysterious ambiguity. Dietz's songs are often filled with such deliberate vagueness. One cannot say exactly if the lover in "I See Your Face Before Me" is joyous or in agony over the fact that he "can't erase" the image of his lover's face. "Haunted Heart" has a similar ambiguity. A Dietz lyric often describes an inescapable feeling vividly but has mixed emotions about whether one wishes to escape or not. Even the popular love songs ("Dancing in the Dark," "Something to Remember You By" and "You and the Night and the Music") have a bittersweet quality to them. For each acclamation of love there is a question: will this last? what will the morning bring? what happens when the music ends? is this real or only a dream? Hart's love songs have a painful subtext; Dietz's have a sense of mystery. Hart foreshadows heartbreak and despair; Dietz looks to the future wistfully.

Dietz did not make the important innovative contributions of Berlin or Hart, but he did have an individual voice of his own. He was more limited and produced much mediocre work (especially in some of the misconceived book musicals), but his was a talent respected by the best of the other writers because they knew an exceptional lyric when they heard one. Because the book musical, which Dietz never successfully conquered, became the predominant Broadway product, his lyrics are not heard in revival productions but, instead, reappear much as old Tin Pan Alley hits do. Regardless, his are musical theatre lyrics in the fullest sense and are vital evidence of the once-flourishing Broadway musical revue at its best.

Dorothy Fields' career, from 1929 to 1973, was not only one of the longest in musical theatre history, but also one of the most varied. A successful lyricist and librettist both on Broadway and in Hollywood, Fields is one of the few who have made the crossover from one medium to another and from one decade to another so effortlessly. Like Hammerstein, Dorothy Fields came from a famous show business family. Her father was Lew Fields, of the ingenious Weber and Fields team, who later became a solo star and producer on Broadway. Her brother, Herbert Fields, was a librettist who had a string of hits with Rodgers and Hart, Irving Berlin, Cole Porter and others. Her other brother, Joseph Fields, was a playwright and librettist as well. Dorothy Fields was born in 1904 at the family's summer home in Allenhurst, New Jersey. She started to write light verse and lyrics while at school and later convinced composer Jimmy McHugh to collaborate with her. Together they provided the songs for a series of Cotton Club Revues. Their first Broadway effort, *Blackbirds of 1928*, ran for an astonishing 518 performances. *Blackbirds* had an all-black cast featuring Adelaide Hall and newcomer Bill "Bojangles" Robinson. Fields did the lyrics as well as some of the sketches. The outstanding score included three hit songs: "Diga, Diga, Do," "Doin' the New Low Down" and "I Can't Give You Anything But Love." Also in the show was a song called "Porgy," a musical capsulization of the 1927 drama of the same name. (This was six years before the Gershwin folk opera version.) Fields and McHugh immediately followed this with a series of forgotten book musicals and revues but one of them, *The International Revue* (1930), introduced one of the decade's biggest hit songs, "On the Sunny Side of the Street."

The Depression was taking its toll on Broadway but Hollywood beckoned. Fields would stay in Tinseltown for ten years and collaborate with

various composers on a repertoire of movie song standards. During this
stay, and subsequent shorter ones, Fields wrote "The Cuban Love Song,"
"I Feel a Song Coming On," "I'm in the Mood for Love" and others with
McHugh. She teamed up with Jerome Kern for five films and produced
such memorable songs as "I Dream Too Much," "A Fine Romance," "Let
Me Look at You," "The Waltz in Swing Time," "The Way You Look
Tonight" (an Oscar winner) and "Lovely to Look At" (with McHugh
and Kern). Returning to Broadway in 1939 with *Stars in Your Eyes*,
Fields worked with composer Arthur Schwartz for the first time. The
score was not memorable but Fields and Schwartz liked working together
and would reunite again in the 1950s when he returned from Hollywood.
Teaming up with her brother Herbert, Fields wrote the librettos for three
Cole Porter hits: *Let's Face It* (1941), *Something for the Boys* (1943) and
Mexican Hayride (1944). She provided book and lyrics (with Herbert
again) for the unlikely hit *Up in Central Park* (1945). The music was
by Sigmund Romberg, whose career seemed quite over. But the strong
story about the Boss Tweed ring in 1870 New York and the graceful
lyrics supported Romberg in one of his few non-operetta scores. Songs
such as "It Doesn't Cost You Anything to Dream," "April Snow" and
"Close as Pages in a Book" made the show charmingly effective. In 1946
Dorothy and Herbert Fields wrote their most famous libretto, *Annie Get
Your Gun*. Not only did it provide Irving Berlin with his best book for
a musical but it showed Fields' librettist skill at its peak. *Arms and the
Girl* (1950), for which Dorothy Fields co-authored the book and wrote
the lyrics to Morton Gould's music, is remembered for making Pearl
Bailey a star. She was helped by two delightful Fields lyrics: "Nothin'
for Nothin'" and "There Must Be Somethin' Better Than Love."

Reteaming with Arthur Schwartz for *A Tree Grows in Brooklyn* (1951),
Fields wrote her most heartfelt score. Betty Smith and George Abbott's
libretto, based on Smith's best seller, provided a more solid dramatic
framework than Fields had been offered previously. Her lyrics for *A Tree
Grows in Brooklyn* were simple, colloquial and moving. She developed
character lyrics in a way not yet seen in her work, and the score had
many poignant songs: "Make the Man Love Me," "Love Is the Reason"
and "I'll Buy You a Star." Fondly remembered and raised to cult status
by some, *A Tree Grows in Brooklyn* marked a turning point in Fields'
already twenty-two-year-old career. *By the Beautiful Sea* (1954) also had
music by Schwartz. Fields did the book and lyrics with brother Herbert
but, despite some good songs ("I'd Rather Wake Up by Myself" and

the unusual "Alone Too Long"), it was disappointing, and only Shirley Booth's performance kept the show running for 270 performances. Another star, Gwen Verdon, would save *Redhead* (1959). Albert Hague composed the music and Fields provided the lyrics and co-authored the book. The brightest songs ("Pick-Pocket Tango" and "The Uncle Sam Rag") were fodder for Verdon's dancing talents and there was a lovely number for her called "Merely Marvelous." *Redhead* was unimpressive but managed to win the Tony Award in a very lean year for musicals.

Sweet Charity (1966) would bring a new (and much younger) composer collaborator for Fields. Cy Coleman's music was the music of the sixties: bright, brassy, irreverent. Fields' lyrics, helped by Neil Simon's libretto, captured that tone. "Big Spender" and "There's Gotta Be Something Better Than This" had the appropriate sarcasm and "Baby, Dream Your Dream" and "Where Am I Going?" had the right pathos for the characters. And "If My Friends Could See Me Now" showed that Fields could still write an upbeat hit like "On the Sunny Side of the Street." The libretto for *See Saw* (1973), by director Michael Bennett, Neil Simon (uncredited) and William Gibson, was not as strong, but Fields and Coleman came up with another exceptional score. *See Saw* was as much about New York City as it was about the two mismatched lovers, and Fields' lyrics caught the verve of the city in the 1970s. "My City" and "Poor Everybody Else" were as contemporary-sounding as any new lyricist could provide; Fields, who was sixty-eight years old, sounded fresher than ever. *See Saw* again gave her the opportunity to write character lyrics ("Nobody Does It Like Me," "Welcome to Holiday Inn" and the title song) but the hit song was again an optimistic rouser, "It's Not Where You Start (It's Where You Finish)." Unfortunately, *See Saw* finished in the red but it was a well-beloved show and still has many admirers.

Dorothy Fields died in 1974 but she indirectly had another Broadway hit in 1979. *Sugar Babies*, a nostalgic tribute to the early burlesque revues, revived such Fields/McHugh favorites as "Exactly Like You" and "I Can't Give You Anything But Love." This last song was also featured in the 1978 revue *Ain't Misbehavin'*. From *Blackbirds of 1928* to *Sugar Babies*, it was a remarkable career. And one that started and finished, as the song says, on top.

Few lyricists have the talent Dorothy Fields had for writing words that sit so well on the music. Just reading her lyrics one can see the music rise and fall. One of her earliest lyrics is a good example: "I can't give you anything but love . . . baby!" Or later in the same song: "Gee, but it's tough to be broke . . . kid." Her words not only fit the music, they confidently ride on top of it. Perhaps Lehrman Engel put it best when he said Fields' lyrics "dance."[1] The song "If My Friends Could See Me Now" is filled with "pow" and "wow" and "holy cow" to accent the music. In a more subtle song, "I Dream Too Much," Fields repeats the words "dream," "we" and "me" over and over to match the lulling rhythm of the music.

This gift for writing melody with words is matched by her sense of the character's rhythm. Charity, Gittel, Johnny Nolan, Sissy or other characters each has an individual vocal pattern. This pattern is independent of the music, yet the two must coexist effortlessly or the song falls apart. For a lyricist who started out writing for revues, Fields soon learned the power of character lyrics. A Brooklynite sings "love is the aspirin you buy" or "when there's no magic in the words: Make Believe." A modern Manhattanite sings "remember the guy's preempted by me." A dance hall hostess sings "there's gotta be something better than this." One has only to read the lyrics aloud and the vocal pattern appears. One of Fields' most remarkable lyrics is *Sweet Charity*'s "Big Spender." There is a bitter but resigned attitude to be found in the chorus of weary dance hostesses. They call their prospective customers men of "distinction" but even the customers know the girls are lying. The cynicism of "I don't pop my cork for ev'ry guy I see" is obvious. And the real kicker—"wouldn't you like to know what's going on in my mind?"—can be interpreted as disgust. These girls lie and they lie badly.

Dorothy Fields perfected the character lyric to a level beyond that of many better known songwriters. Whether the song was an elegant ballad for a romantic Hollywood film or a streetwise character song for a musical play, Fields wrote with a precision found only in the best lyricists. The fact that she was able to sustain this precision for over forty years makes her unique in a way rarely seen on Broadway.

NOTE

1. Lehrman Engel, *Their Words Are Music* (New York: Crown Publishers, 1975), p. 81.

10

Yip's Rainbow: E. Y. Harburg

One might expect rather somber work from a lyricist who proudly believes that "the purpose of a musical is to make people think."[1] But never was there a lyricist less gloomy than E. Y. Harburg. He is the American musical theatre's master of fantasy, satire and passionate dreams. He was also one of the most consistently experimental and adventurous of Broadway's writers. What Harburg did—use comedy to explore deadly serious matters—was not a new idea, as even he admitted. "For me, satire has become a weapon . . . the way Swift used it in prose, Gilbert in his verses, Shaw in his drama," Harburg said at the end of his career. "I am stirred and my juices start flowing more when I can tackle a problem that has profundity, depth, and real danger . . . by destroying it with laughter."[2]

What was new about Harburg was his use of musical comedy for such devastating satire. The Gershwins had done it to some degree in *Strike Up the Band* and *Of Thee I Sing*; but those were light-hearted spoofs with familiar targets. *Let 'Em Eat Cake* was more vicious but still vague in its philosophy. Marc Blitzstein also tried, but his work was more preachy than entertaining. Harold Rome's *Pins and Needles* was a good-natured satire on labor and management, but it was performed for an audience already converted. Harburg, on the other hand, dealt with specific social issues—racism, women's rights, poverty, the effects of war—and focused in on the problems with deliberate persistence even as he entertained. He often used fantasy to explore what was so prevalent in reality. Harburg was a dreamer who was willing to deal with the world's nightmares.

Edgar Y. Harburg was born of Russian immigrant parents in 1898 in a poor neighborhood on the East Side of Manhattan. As a boy he worked as a streetlamp lighter and sold newspapers. While in high school he wrote light verse for the school newspaper and was encouraged to enroll at City College. One of his classmates there was Ira Gershwin and together they wrote a column for the college newspaper. Like Howard Dietz, Harburg also submitted material to Adams' *The Conning Tower*, where his work was published under his nickname "Yip." After graduation he traveled and worked abroad; when he returned he went into the electrical supply business. But Harburg hated it and was more than happy when the crash of 1929 destroyed the firm and he was free to write fulltime.

Ira Gershwin introduced him to composer Jay Gorney and they collaborated on five songs interpolated into *Earl Carroll's Sketch Book* (1929). Harburg also collaborated with composer Vernon Duke on a series of revues in the early thirties. *Americana* (1932) introduced Harburg and Gorney's "Brother, Can You Spare a Dime?" which swept the nation. It is a brilliantly subdued song of protest that has not lost any of its impact over the years.

Once I built a railroad,
Made it run,
Made it race against time.
Once I built a railroad,
Now it's done.
Brother, can you spare a dime? . . .

Once in Khaki suits,
Gee, we looked swell,
Full of that Yankee Doodle-de-dum.
Half a million boots went sloggin' thru Hell,
I was the kid with the drum.

Say, don't you remember,
They called me Al.
It was Al all the time.
Say, don't you remember
I'm your pal!
Buddy, can you spare a dime?

The shifting from noble, bold accomplishments ("Once I built a railroad") to a humble plea ("Brother, can you spare a dime?") gives the lyric its distinction and power. This is not a maudlin request for sympathy but a personal plea by a man who still believes in America. "Brother, Can You Spare a Dime?" became the watchcry for many Americans during the Depression. Gorney went out to Hollywood after *Americana*, so Harburg collaborated with Harold Arlen on the song "It's Only a Paper Moon" (lyric help by Billy Rose), which was used in the non-musical play *The Great Magoo* (1932). The song was written to be sung by a Coney Island barker in the play, and the imagery is not only appropriate but brutally realistic: "It's a Barnum and Bailey world . . . it's a honky-tonk parade." Yet the song is also curiously romantic, stating that all the phony make-believe could be real "if you believed in me." It was becoming clear that Harburg's approach to a lyric was more elaborate than most.

Harburg's first important book musical, and one that foreshadowed his talent for fantastical satire, was *Hooray for What!* (1937). Howard Lindsay and Russel Crouse's libretto, about an inventor who tries to end wars with his new laughing gas, was rich with social commentary but much of it got toned down when the show became a vehicle for Ed Wynn. All the same, the Arlen/Harburg score is daring and vibrant. "God's Country" is a silly flag-waver in which Popeye and Gypsy Rose Lee are touted as American role models, "Moanin' in the Mornin'" is about romantic disillusionment, and "Down With Love" is a rejection of the highly lyrical, Cole Porter kind of love song. *Hooray for What!* was definitely ahead of its time (it even alluded to the atom bomb) and served as a preview for Harburg's experimental musicals of the forties and fifties.

In 1938 Harburg went to Hollywood, where he contributed to a handful of films, including the songs with Arlen for *The Wizard of Oz* (1939), arguably the finest original score ever written for the movies. Back on Broadway, Harburg collaborated with composer Burton Lane on the score for *Hold on to Your Hats* (1940), a satire on radio westerns in which Martha Raye stole the show with her two numbers: "Life Was Pie for the Pioneer" and "She Came, She Saw, She Can-Canned." Arlen and Harburg reteamed for *Bloomer Girl* (1944), a slice of Americana that was much more than frolicsome. The Sig Herzig/Fred Saidy libretto was about a headstrong girl, Eveline, in 1861 Cicero Falls, New York, who rebels against her manufacturer father and joins her radical Aunt Dolly, who advocated bloomers rather than hoop skirts. Aside from the obvious women's rights issues, *Bloomer Girl* also dealt with racial equality (pro-abolitionist Eveline falls in love with a Southern slave owner). *Bloomer*

Girl was highly anticipated as another *Oklahoma!*; Celeste Holm, Joan McCracken, choreographer Agnes de Mille, and much of the staff for *Bloomer Girl* had been involved with the Rodgers and Hammerstein hit. What audiences found instead was a deeply disturbing musical that was more serious than Harburg's other work. The score has several exemplary songs, though none of them became popular because they were too closely knit into the Civil War–era story. The opening number, "When the Boys Come Home," is a pretty and engaging song with an air of frustration behind it. "Right As the Rain" is a pleasing ballad and "Eveline" is a fun duet with the lovers moving on two different tracks of mind. "It Was Good Enough for Grandma" is a feminist lament ("but it ain't good enough for us") and "Sunday in Cicero Falls" is a sly chorus number bemoaning the piety of small towns. "T'morra, T'morra" is a lazy but rebellious solo ("why is t'morra better than today?") and "The Eagle and Me" is a simple plea for freedom (sung by Dooley Wilson). *Bloomer Girl* was no *Oklahoma!* but it did run for 654 performances and was an important step for Harburg and Broadway.

It was with Burton Lane that Harburg scored his most successful musical, *Finian's Rainbow* (1947). Some of the same social concerns from *Bloomer Girl* reappeared in *Finian's Rainbow* but this time the approach was fantasy. Set in "Missitucky, USA," the story (by Harburg and Saidy) followed the adventures of two recent arrivals to America: the Irishman Finian and Og, a leprechaun who is losing his powers and becoming more human every day. Subplots regarding Finian's daughter, a bigoted senator (who is turned into a black man), local sharecroppers, and a pot of gold all blend together beautifully. The score for *Finian's Rainbow* is unquestionably one of the best in the history of musical theatre. The bouncy "If This Isn't Love," the wistful "How Are Things in Glocca Morra?" and the hypnotic "Old Devil Moon" all became hits, but the score is filled with wondrous songs. David Wayne's leprechaun sang the playful "Something Sort of Grandish," a comic song filled with Ira Gershwin-like word play and rhymes: "So bride-and-groomish/so love-in-bloomish . . . so adorish/toujour l'amourish." The tender "Look to the Rainbow" is balanced by the sassy "When the Idle Poor Become the Idle Rich" and "Necessity." The spirited "That Great Come-and-Get-It Day" is complemented by the mock-spiritual "The Begat." And perhaps the cleverest of all is "When I'm Not Near the Girl I Love," a brilliant comic song that Stephen Sondheim has called "one of the five or ten best lyrics ever written."[3]

Oh, my heart is beating wildly,
And it's all because you're here,
When I'm not near the girl I love
I love the girl I'm near.
Ev'ry femme that flutters by me
Is a flame that must be fanned;
When I can't fondle the hand I'm fond of
I fondle the hand at hand.
My heart's in a pickle,
It's constantly fickle
And not too partickle, I fear.
When I'm not near the girl I love,
I love the girl I'm near . . .

Finian's Rainbow was the high point of Harburg's theatre career. It was a bold, joyous experiment and it worked. The musical boasted the first fully integrated chorus in Broadway history; Harburg's ideas were more than academic. *Finian's Rainbow* is still potent. (Even in the 1970s the musical and the film version were not allowed in South Africa.) It is the pot of gold at the end of Yip's rainbow.

Harburg's fantastical view of the world reached some kind of crazy peak with *Flahooley* (1951). The libretto was again by Harburg and Saidy, but this time modern consumerism, the McCarthy witch hunts and big business were the targets. The outrageous plot concerned a laughing doll named Flahooley, an Arabian princess with a magic lamp, a genie, and a reactionary group called the Capsul-anti. Unlike *Finian's Rainbow*, the whole thing did not come together and audiences were confused more than disturbed. Yma Sumac, with her abnormally-ranged voice, was the princess who sang three songs with no lyrics. But much of the rest of the score (music by movie composer Sammy Fain) is daring and charming in an off-beat way. "He's Only Wonderful" is a conventional love song and "The World Is Your Balloon" is a sprightly piece of romantic joy, even if it is partially sung by puppets. "Here's to Your Illusions" is an oddly engaging lyric about love midst the "sweet confusions" of reality. "The Springtime Cometh" is a comic number for the genie that utilizes "eth" endings as the leprechaun uses "ish" words in "Something Sort of Grandish." The song that best summarizes *Flahooley*'s weird wisdom is "You Too Can Be a Puppet," a highly satirical plea for conformity: "Be a puppet instead of an also-ran."

Jamaica (1957) had a Harburg/Saidy script about a poor Caribbean fisherman who eschews modern life in America for a simple, more noble existence. The musical lost much of its impact when producer David Merrick cast Lena Horne in a secondary role and the focus shifted to her, but the Arlen/Harburg score still contains some evidence of the original concept. "Push de Button" is a calypso number that mocks the up-to-date life style of the American cities, "Cocoanut Sweet" is a lovely lullaby, "For Every Fish" is a sardonic look at the balance of nature ("man, he eat barracuda . . . .little worm eat the man"), and "Monkey in the Mango Tree" is a tongue-in-cheek view of Darwin's evolution theory. Aristophanes' anti-war, feminist comedy *Lysistrata* became the musical *The Happiest Girl in the World* (1961) when Harburg wrote lyrics to familiar melodies by Jacques Offenbach. The result was less than memorable. Then Harburg teamed up with composer Jule Styne for *Darling of the Day* (1968), a musicalization of Arnold Bennett's novel *Buried Alive*. There were severe book problems (Nunnally Johnson worked on the libretto but the show opened with no author credited) but the Styne/Harburg score was not without merit. *Darling of the Day* ran for only thirty-two performances and Harburg, who hadn't had a hit on Broadway for twenty years, retired. The musical theatre was then being inundated with shows about civil rights, feminism, anti-war sentiments and all the other subjects Harburg had pioneered. But rarely were they done with any subtlety, charm or humor. Harburg, who had spent most of his career being ahead of his time, died in 1981, considered by some to have been old-fashioned and behind the times.

Yip Harburg was a difficult paradox that show business had trouble living comfortably with. He was obviously left wing, very opinionated, even dangerous. But he was also charming, magical and beloved in the business. When he was blacklisted in the fifties, his Hollywood career suffered, so Harburg returned to Broadway, where there was somewhat more open-mindedness. But even as late as 1968 Styne had to threaten and plead with producers to hire Harburg for *Darling of the Day*, promising that he wouldn't let Yip slip any messages into the score.

This paradox of being dangerous but loved can also be applied to his work. Harburg wrote about the most uncomfortable subjects but, because of his charm and humor, audiences usually listened. His use of fantasy was more than a personal whim; it was a pragmatic means to an end. "I don't believe the theatre is a place for photographic reproduction," he once said. "That's why I'm attracted to fantasy, to things with a poetic quality. Through fantasy, I feel that a musical can say things with greater effectiveness about life. It's great for pricking balloons, for exploding shibboleths."[4] E. Y. Harburg was that unique thing in any art form: a dreamer without compromises, a meticulous craftsman who was all heart. Today's theatre despises both dreamers and failures. Perhaps it is best that Harburg lived and worked when he did. For forty years he wrote slyly but vividly about unspeakable things. Today one can write about anything, but Harburg's lyrics often make our theatre seem mute in comparison. The musical theatre has found other craftsmen, other poets, even other experimenters. But who else has had the talent to laugh at our fears?

NOTES

1. Stanley Green, *The World of Musical Comedy* (New York: A. S. Barnes & Co., Inc., 1980), p. 187.

2. Max Wilk, *They're Playing Our Song* (New York: Atheneum, 1973), p. 232.

3. Otis L. Guernsey (ed.), *Playwrights, Lyricists, Composers on Theatre* (New York: Dodd, Mead and Co., 1974), p. 80.

4. Green, p. 187.

11

Also in the
1920s and 1930s

Musicals being plentiful on Broadway during the second and third decades of the century, there are many other lyricists from the period who are worth noting. The craftsmanship and output of many of these writers were usually substantial.

Although prominent for only a few years during the second half of the 1920s, the team of De Sylva, Brown and Henderson quickly established themselves as one of the most successful songwriting forces on Broadway. By 1931 they had split up to move in different directions, but they left behind them some of America's most popular pre-Depression songs. "Buddy" George De Sylva and Lew Brown collaborated on the lyrics set to Ray Henderson's music. De Sylva, the coordinator of the trio, had an impressive career as a Broadway lyricist before the team's formation and continued to make important contributions on Broadway and in Hollywood after the team disbanded. He was raised in California and attended the University of Southern California, where he played ukelele and wrote lyrics for the college shows. One of his lyrics, "Chloe," was somehow brought to the attention of Al Jolson, who provided music and put it in his Broadway musical *Sinbad* (1918). The royalty check for "Chloe" convinced De Sylva to move to New York, where he befriended lyricist Arthur Jackson; together they provided the lyrics for *La, La, Lucille* (1919), the first musical scored by George Gershwin. De Sylva also worked with Jerome Kern on *Sally* (1920), writing the lyrics for two of that show's most popular songs: "Whip-poor-will" and "Look for the Silver Lining." For Al Jolson's 1921 *Bombo* two interpolated songs with De Sylva lyrics became standards, "April Showers" (music by Louis Silvers) and "California, Here I Come!" (with Joseph Mayer and Jolson). De Sylva worked again with George Gershwin on *George White's Scandals of 1922*, writing lyrics (with Ira Gershwin) for "(I'll Build a) Stairway to Paradise." One of the unusual features of that year's *Scandals* was an innovative idea by De Sylva. "Blue Monday," a twenty-five minute tragic jazz opera with a libretto by De Sylva and music by George Gershwin, was a challenging piece that foreshadowed Gershwin's later *Porgy and Bess* in subject, style and sound. ("Blue Monday" was too heavy for the frolicsome *Scandals* and was withdrawn by producer White after a few performances.) De Sylva and Gershwin collaborated on succeeding *Scandals* but when Gershwin gave up the series in 1925 to pursue book musical comedies, George White brought in Brown and Henderson to work with De Sylva.

Lew Brown was born in Odessa, Russia, and immigrated as a boy to New Haven and then New York. He left high school to pursue a career on Tin Pan Alley and hit it lucky when he met veteran composer Albert von Tilzer. Tilzer and Brown collaborated on a handful of popular songs, some of which were interpolated into Broadway musicals: "I Used to Love You," "Oh, by Jingo" and the memorable World War One ballad "I May Be Gone for a Long, Long Time." The new team of De Sylva, Brown and Henderson, created by White, provided the score for his 1925 *Scandals*. Although it contained two lovely songs ("What a World This Would Be" and "I Want a Loveable Baby"), it was no match for the previous Gershwin scores and no one thought very highly of the new team. But their score for the 1926 edition of the *Scandals* was a sensation. Many feel that it was the finest score to come from any of the annual shows. There was the sentimental love song "The Girl is You and the Boy is Me," the lively "Lucky Day," the Charleston-inspired "Black Bottom," and the unforgettable "The Birth of the Blues." There were comic songs to augment the skits, as well as a delicious satire, "A Western Union," about Irving Berlin's recent marriage to telegraph heiress Ellin MacKay. The 1926 *Scandals* was the longest running of the series' shows and it made the careers of De Sylva, Brown and Henderson.

Good News! (1927) rivals *No, No, Nanette* as the most often produced twenties musical comedy. It was the team's first book musical (De Sylva coauthored the libretto with Laurence Schwab) and was filled with contagious, sophomoric nonsense. The setting was collegiate (fictional Tait College) and the plot revolved around young love and football. The De Sylva-Brown-Henderson score introduced five song standards: "Lucky in Love," "Just Imagine," "The Varsity Drag" (another Charleston variation), "The Best Things in Life Are Free" and the title song. *Good News!* ran for an impressive 557 performances and put the team at the forefront of musical comedy.

De Sylva, Brown and Henderson scored a handful of less memorable musicals in the late twenties, presenting such perennial song favorites as "You're the Cream in My Coffee," "I Could Give Up Anything But You," "Button Up Your Overcoat" and "My Lucky Star." But by 1930 the team members separated when De Sylva went to Hollywood. Brown and Henderson collaborated on the 1931 *Scandals* without De Sylva and introduced "Life Is Just a Bowl of Cherries." But the glory days were over and the Jazz Age came to an end with the Depression. The collaboration of De Sylva, Brown and Henderson was one of the shortest in musical theatre history (five years) but certainly one of the most memorable.

Irving Caesar was a man of considerable talents: lyricist, composer at times, often a librettist and performer as well. He collaborated with some of the era's brightest composers—George Gershwin, Louis Hirsch, Sigmund Romberg, Ray Henderson, Rudolf Friml—but Caesar is best known for the two songs he wrote with Vincent Youmans for *No, No, Nanette* (1925). "I Want To Be Happy" was a showstopper in the original production and had audiences cheering again during the popular 1971 Broadway revival. But "Tea for Two" is the better known song from that show; in fact, it is still one of the most easily recognized songs in American popular culture. Caesar's lyric for "Tea for Two" was never intended to be heard by the public. He wrote it as a dummy lyric; that is, a slapdash refrain to be used temporarily to pinpoint the music until the lyricist had time to go back and write the polished lyric. But Youmans loved the dummy lyric and put it in *No, No, Nanette* as it stood. The almost idiotic simplicity of the "Tea for Two" lyric is what makes the song soar. All the optimism and light-heartedness of the twenties are captured in that song. Caesar contributed lyrics to some two dozen Broadway musicals between 1918 and 1943, including *Hit the Deck* (1927) and several editions of *The Greenwich Village Follies* and *George White's Scandals*. Caesar is also remembered for providing the lyrics for "Swanee," George Gershwin's single biggest hit song.

Also known for their carefree twenties musical comedies are lyricists Gus Kahn and Bert Kalmar. Kahn's greatest success was *Whoopee* (1928) with composer Walter Donaldson. In that show Eddie Cantor introduced "Makin' Whoopee" and Ruth Etting first sang "Love Me or Leave Me." But Kahn spent most of his career in Hollywood, where he collaborated on the scores for *The Jazz Singer* (1927), *Flying Down to Rio* (1933) and many other film musicals. Among his individual song hits are "Pretty Baby," "Ain't We Got Fun?," "My Buddy," "Carolina in the Morning," "Yes, Sir, That's My Baby," "Toot Toot Tootsie, Goodbye" and "I'll See You in My Dreams." Bert Kalmar usually collaborated with composer Harry Ruby, and together they scored such 1920s Broadway favorites as *The Ramblers* (1926), *The Five O'Clock Girl* (1927) and *Animal Crackers* (1928), which offered the merry "Hooray for Captain Spaulding." Broadway lost Kalmar and Ruby in 1930 when the Marx Brothers took the team with them to Hollywood.

Another lyricist who personified the attitudes of the Roaring Twenties was Noble Sissle, the first black lyricist to be represented on Broadway. Sissle and composer Eubie Blake wrote the landmark *Shuffle Along* (1921), the longest running book musical produced, written, directed and performed by black artists. At first *Shuffle Along* was merely a curiosity, but soon it gained the patronage of the mainstream Broadway audience and ran for 504 performances. Sissle's lyric work throughout *Shuffle Along* is exceptional. The high-stepping "I'm Just Wild about Harry" is the score's most well known song, but just as accomplished are the spirited dance number "The Baltimore Buzz," the infectious love song "Honeysuckle Time," the winning ballad "Love Will Find a Way," the racy chorus number "Bandana Days" and the entertaining solo "I'm Craving for That Kind of Love," in which the singer wants a Romeo, "not a phoneo." Sissle and Blake came back to Broadway with the less popular but equally vibrant *Chocolate Dandies* in 1928. "Have a Good Time Everybody" is a jubilant number and "Dixie Moon" is still quite effective. In "Sons of Old Black Joe" the lyric boasts of a pride in a heritage that many considered merely a cliché. There were new editions of *Shuffle Along* in 1933 and 1952 but they did not compare favorably with the original. Sissle and Blake stopped collaborating too soon in their careers and, with all the racial barriers they had to overcome, they could never fulfill the promise shown in these early musicals. But Sissle's deft lyricwriting must be acknowledged not only for its own high quality but for the groundwork it laid for later black songwriters.

Few have enjoyed such an auspicious theatrical debut as composer/lyricist Harold Rome had with *Pins and Needles* in 1937. The topical musical revue ran for four years in its various versions. A good deal of the score still holds up; not because labor-management concerns still exist but because the personal, detailed aspects of the lyrics are still accurate. Rome was educated at Yale, where he studied architecture. During the summers he worked at Green Mansions, an adult camp in the Adirondacks, writing songs and sketches for camp revues. When the International Ladies Garment Workers Union's entertainment division was preparing a musical revue, they hired Rome based on those summer camp songs. *Pins and Needles*, as it was called, had a cast made up entirely of ILGWU members and was scheduled to run weekends only. Despite lackluster reviews and skepticism about the non-professional performers, audiences cheered, and word of mouth turned *Pins and Needles* into a surprise hit. While the sketches in the show covered familiar labor-management territory and global politics, it was the songs that raised the revue above the ordinary. Rome's score was topical but, more importantly, it was also romantic, honest and sometimes self-mocking. The songs are never patronizing but seek to see the political and social issues in a personal light. "Sing Me a Song of Social Significance," the signature song for the revue, is straightforward and clear. "We want a ditty with heat in it," the lyric demands. Yet the reasons are personal: girls only love men who care about important matters. This is a protest song to enjoy. "One Big Union for Two" is about collective bargaining but is delivered like a love song. "It's Better with a Union Man" and "What Good Is Love" are similarly personal. Rome employed elaborate rhyming in "It's Not Cricket to Picket," "Four Little Angels of Peace" portrayed the schemes of world dictators and "Doing the Reactionary" turned left wing politics into a new dance. But the songs from *Pins and Needles* that have held up the best over the years are the bittersweet character studies: "Nobody Makes a Pass at Me," about a girl who uses all the beauty products advertised on the radio but the men still don't notice her; "Chain Store Daisy," about a Vassar graduate who works in a big department store selling ladies' foundation garments; and "Sunday in the Park," a dreamy ballad about how the working-class man spends the "only day I can call my own."

Rome followed *Pins and Needles* with other revues, the most memorable being *Call Me Mister* (1946), a musical about military personnel returning to civilian life after World War Two. In the 1950s he began to score book musicals, some of which were very popular. *Wish You*

Were Here (1952) was a light-hearted musical set in an adult Jewish summer camp much like Rome's old Green Mansions. *Fanny* (1954) was a romantic musicalization of Marcel Pagnol's film trilogy that leaned toward the operatic. *Destry Rides Again* (1959) was a raucous musical western with a less-than-impressive score. With *I Can Get It For You Wholesale* (1962), Rome returned to urban working class characters of the Depression years. The story of a brash young opportunist who makes his way through the cutthroat world of the New York garment district was unromantic, cold and uninvolving. But the songs were honest and insightful and Rome's witty lyrics for "Miss Marmelstein" provided an unforgettable vehicle for Barbra Streisand in a supporting role.

Comparisons between E. Y. Harburg and Harold Rome are unavoidable. Both made a name for themselves writing songs for topical revues in the 1930s and 1940s before moving on to book musicals. And both dealt with social and economic subjects with a leftist point of view. But there are significant differences as well. Rome abandoned much of the sociopolitical lyrics as he expanded into book musicals, while Harburg sharpened his intensity and used libretto and lyrics working together to present his ideas. Rome's strength was realism while Harburg's was fantasy; yet Rome's satire was lighter and less piercing than Harburg's deadly accurate humor. Most importantly, Harburg attempted issues that were deeply controversial and not easily solvable, while Rome's targets were often one-sided and safe. It takes less courage to lampoon Hitler or sneer at anti-unionists, as Rome did, than to confront contemporary bigotry and capitalism, as Harburg did. Rome was a man of strong and sincere beliefs, but he usually preached to the converted and his songs made people laugh freely. Harburg presented unpopular ideas, guised them in fantastical satires, and the audience laughed nervously. But when it came to portraying the working class man or woman, Harold Rome was about the best in the business. Within that narrow range he was another Hammerstein.

Some might categorize Marc Blitzstein's work for the theatre as opera. Being a classically trained composer, Blitzstein employed various kinds of music in his shows; but his lyrics are firmly rooted in the American musical theatre tradition. *The Cradle Will Rock* (1937) was a blistering socialist piece that utilized spokesmen more than fully developed characters. But that didn't make the lyrics less vivid. Two artists caught in the paradox of wealthy patronage complain about "The Rich." A prostitute sings the pragmatic "Nickel Under the Foot" and a father and son are confronted with mobster violence in the musical sequence "The Drugstore Scene." Blitzstein's *Regina* (1949), a musicalization of Lillian Hellman's 1939 drama *The Little Foxes*, is very passionate on a more personal level. The familiar story about a greedy Southern family doesn't always adapt well to the musical stage but much of the lyric work is powerful. To want and to take, one character professes, is "The Best Thing of All", while "Birdie's Aria" is a tender and pathetic look at an opposite view of life. Blitzstein's *Juno* (1959), based on Sean O'Casey's *Juno and the Paycock* (1924), underwent numerous revisions and revivals but it never quite worked, although the ballad "I Wish It So" is memorable. Blitzstein's most enduring work is his adaptation/translation of *The Threepenny Opera* that he did for the 1954 Off-Broadway production. Bertolt Brecht's libretto and lyrics were loosely interpreted by Blitzstein and resulted in the first successful American production of the musical. Many have since written more faithful or more graphic lyrics for Kurt Weill's music for *The Threepenny Opera* but none has approached the lyricism and magnetism of Blitzstein's version.

Some mention must be made about another collaborator of Weill's: the verse playwright Maxwell Anderson. The author of several successful history plays and social dramas, Anderson provided lyrics for two unforgettable Broadway musicals. *Knickerbocker Holiday* (1938) was a lighthearted look at dictatorship in the personage of Peter Stuyvesant of seventeenth century New York City. The story is playful, the subtext is a bit alarming, and the lyrics are very exacting. The popular "September Song" is a wistful treatment of an old man's wooing a young wife. The song's lyrics are subtle and slyly alluring. The refrain avoids rhyme for the most part and uses soft identities and repetition to maintain its flowing rhythm. "September Song" compares favorably with Hammerstein's "Ol' Man River" in terms of such lyric craftsmanship. Also of note in *Knickerbocker Holiday* is the ballad "It Never Was You," the comic "All Hail the Political Honeymoon" and the witty "How Can You Tell an American?" Anderson's other Broadway musical was *Lost in the Stars* (1949), a powerful version of Alan Paton's novel *Cry, the Beloved Country* about racial strife in South Africa. Working with Weill once again, Anderson provided a libretto and lyrics that were stirring and understated. "Thousands of Miles," "Train to Johannesburg" and the title song are simple but eloquent reflections on a painful situation, and "Trouble Man" is a potent lament with expert lyric work.

Finally, one must not leave the thirties without acknowledging DuBose Heyward and the important role he played in bringing *Porgy and Bess* (1935) to the musical stage. Heyward was a Charleston-born novelist and poet whose *Porgy* (1925) was a best-selling book. Heyward and his wife Dorothy dramatized the story for the 1927 Theatre Guild production. When the Gershwins got involved in a musical version, Heyward was slated to write the libretto only. But during the long preparations of *Porgy and Bess* he turned his poetic talents to lyricwriting for the first time and provided most of the songs in Act One and about half of those in Act Two. Not to belittle Ira Gershwin's contribution to this landmark musical (Heyward wrote his lyrics under Ira Gershwin's tutelage), Heyward's words for *Porgy and Bess* place him with the finest lyricists of his era. The Gershwins had hoped to work again with Heyward and some projects were proposed; but George Gershwin died in 1937 and Heyward in 1940.

12

Almost Like Being in Love: Alan Jay Lerner

While Rodgers and Hammerstein dominated the musical theatre during much of the 1940s and 1950s, the genre found its greatest moments of romance and fantasy in the works of another favorite songwriting team. Alan Jay Lerner and Frederick Loewe wrote seven Broadway scores together and, like the finest collaborative teams, they excelled because of their unexplainable talent for blending words and music together so effectively.

It is rare for the lyricist to get top billing in a collaboration, but Lerner was a rare individual who dominated the duo in spirit, ego and originality. He always wrote both the libretto and the lyrics for his shows and, rare for Broadway, many of his scripts are original stories not based on previous sources. While Lerner's subject matter varied greatly (ESP, the California gold rush, the Paris fashion world, American history, World War Three), his approach was always a romanticized one. His talent for mixing romance with an intelligent wit is unique in postwar musicals. He was able to go further, romantically speaking, than most because he always displayed passion with brains; he gave class to unbridled sentiment. Lerner himself was a thorough romantic (any man who marries eight times must be incurably romantic) but he was also a deliberate craftsman and acute perfectionist. He wrote ninety-one separate lyrics for "On A Clear Day You Can See Forever" before he was satisfied. Lerner was fragile and insecure and went through great anxiety over each of his shows.

He needed all the elements around him to be working well in order to do his best. One of those elements was Frederick Loewe. Although they often quarreled, they brought out the best in each other. When Loewe retired, Lerner collaborated with a series of talented composers but the combinations never worked as well. Yet he continued. Lerner could no more stop writing for Broadway than he could stop breathing. But the spirit and the inspiration were gone. Only his remarkable talent for lyricwriting remained. Broadway abandoned him but Lerner, ever the romantic, continued on even as show after show failed. Another marriage, another production, another chance for romance.

Alan Jay Lerner was born in 1918 in New York City into a wealthy family. His father had made a fortune as founder of a chain of women's clothing stores, the Lerner shops. The family saw to it that Lerner received the best education: exclusive private schools in England and the United States, Juilliard, Harvard, Oxford. Few men of the theatre were better educated. Lerner knew at an early age that he wanted to write for the theatre and never wavered from his decision. He wrote music and lyrics for the Hasty Pudding shows at Harvard and after graduation worked as a radio scriptwriter. He contributed songs to the revues put on by the Lambs Club, where he met Frederick Loewe. Loewe was very different from Lerner in background and temperament. He was born in Berlin to a musical family and became a child prodigy, playing piano with the Berlin Symphony at the age of thirteen. At fifteen he wrote a song called "Katrina," which became one of the most popular songs in Europe. When he was twenty Loewe traveled to America to make his fortune in the New World but met with bitter disappointment. His musical abilities were not recognized, so to survive he worked as a nightclub pianist, a boxer, a busboy, a cow puncher and even a gold prospector. He was Lerner's senior by fourteen years and was desperate to salvage his music career when their partnership was formed in 1942.

What's Up? (1943), their first Broadway production, was an inauspicious debut. Lerner wrote the lyrics and, with Arthur Pierson, the libretto, which was about a sultan who travels to America and mistakenly ends up in a girls' school. The show was even less entertaining than it sounds and was soon forgotten after its sixty-three performance run. *The Day Before Spring* (1945) ran a bit longer and the score attracted some attention. Although no popular songs emerged from the musical, it was clear that two bright talents were at work. The plot of *The Day Before Spring* concerned the reunion of former lovers and had its share of merriment and pathos. Lerner's lyric work in the score reveals the influence of Lorenz Hart and Ira Gershwin ("A jug of wine, a loaf of bread and thou—baby!") but at the same time there are indications of the Lerner style. The verse and first refrains of "My Love Is a Married Man" illustrate the influences working on Lerner and the unique way he utilizes them.

My lonely bitter heart has needed him to make it sweeter;
He came he saw he conquered and then sic transit Peter.
And now I shouldn't cry, I should be brave instead;
But bravery is cold in bed.

My love is a married man;
I'm a marital also-ran;
Though I love him so,
Does he love me? No!
I'll never enter his life
Because he's true to his wife.
My love is a married man.

How often I dream and plan
That he'd climb on my caravan.
I'm a childish dope;
Will it happen? Nope!
He's not that kind of married man.

My dreams abundant
Are redundant
And they fall very short.
The ship I hoped for,
Sat and moped for,
Docked in someone else's port.

The idea that "bravery is cold in bed" reminds one of Gershwin's torch songs, and there is a Hart feeling to "I'm a childish dope." But much of the lyric is pure Lerner: romantic but self-aware, sentimental but smart.

The promising work in *The Day Before Spring* was fulfilled with *Brigadoon* (1947). Lerner admired the work of J. M. Barrie, and there is plenty of the Barrie whimsy and charm in this fantastic tale of a Scottish village that appears every one hundred years. Lerner wrote his first cohesive libretto and, with Loewe, created one of Broadway's most memorable scores. Structurally, *Brigadoon* has more in common with

Oklahoma! than Scotland: the rustic setting, the two pairs of lovers (one romantic, the other comic), the impassioned villain who dies, and so on. They even got Agnes de Mille to choreograph. But *Brigadoon* leaves the down-to-earth approach of *Oklahoma!* and pushes romanticism as far as it can go. The real "miracle" of *Brigadoon* is that it works so well when the whole thing could so easily have become mawkish drivel. Lerner's lyrics throughout are wonderfully quaint (except for "Almost Like Being in Love," the American's song that brings a slick Broadway touch to Scotland) and quite droll for a folktale. "Come to Me, Bend to Me" and "The Heather on the Hill" are reminiscent of Hammerstein's elegant simplicity. The haunting title song and the ballad "There But For You Go I" are moody but appealing. The comic "My Mother's Wedding Day" has a great deal of fun with Scottish names and the lighthearted "The Love of My Life" shows Lerner's gift for song narrative.

Brigadoon put Lerner and Loewe at the forefront of musical theatre teams, but neither of them considered working exclusively with the other. In 1948 Lerner collaborated with composer Kurt Weill on *Love Life*, the most experimental show of the lyricist's career and one of Broadway's first conceptual musicals. Lerner's libretto was an expressionistic chronicle of the United States as seen through one married couple who progress through the centuries without aging. Just as Hammerstein had attempted a theatrical approach to explore his personal beliefs in *Allegro* the year before, so Lerner constructed an avant garde piece about marriage in which the story was interrupted by vaudeville acts that commented on the action. (The same device was later used in *Cabaret*, *Follies* and *Chicago*.) *Love Life* is unmistakingly pretentious at times but Lerner's lyric work is exemplary. As Weill was able to do with so many others, he brought out the social consciousness in Lerner, and the lyrics are more stinging and less romanticized than in the other Lerner musicals. "Progress" is a jaunty vaudeville number that mocks its own optimism: "Progress . . . where ev'ry man can be a king." "Economics" is a witty satire that repeatedly acknowledges that what's good for business is "awful bad for love." And in "This Is the Life," Lerner cleverly works out an extended musical sequence that foreshadows his lyric work in *My Fair Lady*'s "You Did It!"

Because of the success of *Brigadoon*, the inevitable call from Hollywood came and Lerner went west to work on two films. *Royal Wedding* (1951) was a disappointment but it gave him the opportunity to work with composer Burton Lane for the first time. Their score for the film contains the silly "How Could You Believe Me When I Said I Love You When You Know I've Been a Liar All My Life"—surely some sort of record when it comes to song titles. Lerner did much better with the second film: *An American in Paris* (1951). He wrote an original screenplay utilizing several songs by the Gershwins and won an Academy Award for his efforts.

When Lerner reteamed with Loewe for *Paint Your Wagon* (1951) the result was quite different in temperament from *Brigadoon*. An original tale about a father and daughter during the California gold rush, *Paint Your Wagon* was raucous and jubilant. Many of the songs have such authentic-sounding folk melodies and words that they hardly seem like musical theatre numbers. But *Paint Your Wagon* is pure Broadway and quite good Broadway at that. The tender ballad "I Talk to the Trees" and the surging "They Call the Wind Maria" both became popular, but just as effective were the touching "I Still See Elisa," the comic "What's Goin' on Here?" and the rousing "I'm on My Way." The signature song for the show was the simple but elegant "Wand'rin' Star," which tied the musical together. *Paint Your Wagon* was a moderate hit (289 performances) and would enjoy more revivals today if it were not for the tasteless and annoying movie version (1969). Lerner constructed one of his better librettos for *Paint Your Wagon* and, with its sparkling score, it will someday be restored to its rightful place.

Disappointed by the lukewarm success of his last two Broadway efforts, Lerner decided that their next project should be based on an existing work with a strong story. George Bernard Shaw's *Pygmalion* was offered to Lerner and Loewe after several others had turned it down. Lerner had so much trouble trying to open up the story that he abandoned it for a while. But once he and Loewe stopped trying to force Shaw's work to conform to standard musical comedy structure, the whole thing fell into place rather quickly. Of the many things that can be said about *My Fair Lady* (1956), it must be noted that it shouldn't have worked. The musical breaks most of the rules set up by the genre and then triumphs all the same. *My Fair Lady* has no overt love story or love songs. The action is that of a drawing room comedy. There is too much talk and too little dancing. The humor comes from the principal characters (Higgins, Eliza, Doolittle) rather than the supporting players (Freddie, Pickering, Mrs. Higgins). And, most unusual, there is absolutely nothing American about it. *My Fair Lady* is not only one of the best musicals ever written but it is possibly one of the bravest.

Of course the show did work and still does. In terms of both its libretto and lyrics, it is Lerner's masterpiece. Every song is excellent and, more difficult, memorable. "Wouldn't It Be Loverly?," "I'm an Ordinary Man," "Just You Wait," "Show Me" and "A Hymn to Him" (more familiarly known as "Why Can't a Woman Be More Like a Man?") are among the finest character songs ever. "With a Little Bit of Luck" and "Get Me To the Church On Time" are in the British music hall style but are contagiously fun for any audience. "I've Grown Accustomed to Her Face" is a brilliant piece of restrained romance; Higgins sings the song but he is unaware that it's a love song. The two biggest hits to come out of the show were "On the Street Where You Live" and "I Could Have Danced All Night," yet they are the least Shavian songs in the score. Both are solid, engaging musical comedy numbers but they lack the precision of the other songs. (Lerner always despised the "my heart took flight" phrase in "I Could Have Danced All Night" and one tends to agree with him.) An evaluation of the lyric work in *My Fair Lady* must consider the libretto as well because rarely have book and score blended so perfectly. The fact that one cannot tell where *Pygmalion* stops and *My Fair Lady* begins is a credit to Lerner's talent. One of the reasons each lyric works so effectively is the support it gets from the libretto. "The Rain in Spain" is the best example. The lyric itself is playful but hardly inventive. But given the context in which it appears and the expert way in which Lerner sets up the song, "The Rain in Spain" becomes explosively joyous. Lerner's Anglo-American background and his erudite (even Shavian) temperament made him the perfect lyricist for this musical, but the success of *My Fair Lady* would haunt Lerner and Loewe for the rest of their careers; all of their succeeding work would have to suffer comparisons with it. Very wisely they did not attempt another Broadway show right after *My Fair Lady* but instead took an offer to score a film musical. *Gigi* (1958) is to Hollywood what *My Fair Lady* is to Broadway: an exquisite period musical that breaks rules and still conquers. Lerner wrote the screenplay based on Colette's novel about the grooming of a young Parisian courtesan—hardly promising material for a film, no less a musical. The casting was inspired, Vincente Minnelli's direction was stylish and the Lerner and Loewe score turned out to be one of filmdom's best. (The movie won nine Oscars, two for Lerner.) The vocal patterns of Higgins can be found in Gaston's lyrics ("It's a Bore," "She's Not Thinking of Me" and the title song) but Lerner fashioned a very distinct character who captured the French romantic spirit just as Higgins had embodied

Shaw's disposition. The songs for Maurice Chevalier ("Thank Heaven for Little Girls," "I'm Glad I'm Not Young Anymore") were inspired by the strong personality of the actor. Gigi herself is not as well developed lyrically. In fact, Gigi's "Say a Prayer for Me Tonight" was written for Eliza Doolittle but cut before *My Fair Lady* opened. The most charming lyric in *Gigi* is "I Remember It Well," a lovely duet that comes closest to the temper of Colette's writings.

Lerner and Loewe's return to Broadway in 1960 was the eagerly awaited *Camelot*. A record advance of over two million dollars awaited the musical while it struggled through its out-of-town engagements. *Camelot* had one of the most grueling of all pre-Broadway tryouts: script problems, technical snafus and illnesses (including Lerner's burst ulcer and director Moss Hart's heart attack). Lerner's libretto, based on parts of T. H. White's *The Once and Future King*, seemed to be torn between a frolicsome medieval fantasy and a dark drama of ideas. The score also wavered between two distinct styles, and songs were added and dropped even after the Broadway opening. With such high expectations from the public and critics it was impossible not to disappoint. *Camelot* was the work of gifted artists at their peak but it was a disappointment all the same. Over the years public opinion has shifted and today *Camelot* is in the repertoire of often-produced musical favorites. But many of the script problems were never solved, and Lerner found himself making further changes when he wrote the screenplay for the 1967 film version.

While the songs in *Camelot* do not have the consistency of style and high level of characterization found in the team's best work, there are some exceptional individual numbers. "If Ever I Would Leave You" became the musical's hit song but it is one of the least impressive lyrics in the show. It succumbs to a false, operetta generality that Lerner usually avoids. The title song is also a bit more flowery than necessary; that same sense of fanciful idealism is what turned the song into a national hymn when used to signify the Kennedy years. Much finer lyric work can be found in Guinevere's self-mocking "The Simple Joys of Maidenhood" and the simple but evocative "Before I Gaze at You Again." The Lerner wit can be found in Lancelot's "C'est Moi" and Mordred's "The Seven Deadly Virtues." "How to Handle a Woman" seems too simpleminded for a character as complex as Arthur but the Arthur-Guinevere duet "What Do the Simple Folk Do?" is very bright with a painful subtext.

The rigors of preparing *Camelot* convinced Frederick Loewe to retire. Lerner's career after *Camelot* would be a series of disappointments.

Without Loewe, his lyric work would manage to remain competent and occasionally excellent; but his librettos would diminish in quality and show after show would fail to take off. Lerner's first collaborator after Loewe retired was Richard Rodgers. Hammerstein had died in 1960 and Rodgers was not about to retire, so it was inevitable that the two surviving members of Broadway's greatest teams should consider working together. But the Rodgers-Lerner collaboration lasted only a few months; the two strong personalities were incompatible and their work habits too fixed to change, so they eagerly parted company. Lerner then turned to Burton Lane whom he had worked well with in Hollywood but who hadn't been represented on Broadway since *Finian's Rainbow* nineteen years earlier. *On A Clear Day You Can See Forever* (1965) was such a jumble of ideas that the story, an original one inspired by Lerner's belief in ESP, was intriguing but curiously unsatisfying. The setting was contemporary with flashbacks to the eighteenth century; neither era was very convincing. The show ran for only 280 performances but "Come Back to Me" and the title song enjoyed some popularity. The score is enjoyable but lacks consistent style. The title song, though, is a wonderful blending of Lane's soaring music and Lerner's wide-eyed lyrics, perhaps his most optimistic ever.

Coco (1969) had an even less involving libretto by Lerner (based on the career of Paris fashion celebrity Coco Chanel), but the presence of Katharine Hepburn allowed the musical to run. Andre Previn provided the lackluster music and even Cecil Beaton's costumes were uneventful. But Lerner's lyric work in *Coco* is noteworthy. There is a slyness at work throughout the score, particularly in "When Your Lover Says Goodbye," "That's the Way You Are" and "The Money Rings Out Like Freedom." Rock music had successfully invaded Broadway by the time *Coco* opened and there was a wry subtext to Lerner's lyrics for "The World Belongs to the Young" that reveals a bitterness about the new sound ("salute and praise them or hold your tongue") and a fatalistic conclusion ("we shall see"). Lerner's next project, *Lolita, My Love* with movie composer John Barry, never made it to New York but closed in Philadelphia in 1971. In 1973 Loewe came out of retirement briefly to write four new songs with Lerner for the stage version of *Gigi*. The new songs (with the exception of Gigi's "In This Wide, Wide World," which replaced "Say a Prayer for Me Tonight") were forgettable and even the old favorites couldn't keep the Broadway production running for any more than 103 performances.

Continuing with adaptations of unlikely works of literature, Lerner then adapted Antoine de Saint-Exupéry's short fantasy *The Little Prince* into a film musical in 1974. He even convinced Loewe to collaborate on the songs but, according to Lerner, director Stanley Donen changed the music's tempo, deleted musical phrases and distorted the "intention of every song until the entire score was unrecognizable."[1] The film was a critical and artistic disaster. Sadly, it contained the last music Frederick Loewe ever wrote. For the bicentennial in 1976 Lerner wrote an original libretto for *1600 Pennsylvania Avenue*, a chronical of the presidency from George Washington to Teddy Roosevelt. Like *Love Life* it was ambitious storytelling; but unlike the earlier experiment, there is little of value in it. Leonard Bernstein composed some warm melodies but Lerner's lyrics fall short of adequacy. *1600 Pennsylvania Avenue* lasted only a week on Broadway. Lerner himself later referred to it as "the *Titanic*."[2]

Reteaming with Burton Lane once again, Lerner wrote a conventionally satisfying score for *Carmelina* (1979). His libretto, co-authored with Joseph Stein, was based on the 1969 film *Buona Sera, Mrs. Campbell*, which did not lend itself to the stage nor to the musical form. But the score recalled the earlier romantic songs of Lerner and Loewe with such lovely numbers as "It's Time for a Love Song," "Someone in April" and "One More Walk Around the Garden." The lyrics for Georgia Brown's solo "Why Him?" were top-notch as well. But *Carmelina* could not survive its ineffectual book and unlikeable characters and lasted only seventeen performances. For *Dance a Little Closer* (1983) Lerner chose a better source to adapt: Robert Sherwood's 1939 play *Idiot's Delight*. But in his efforts to update the story to the eve of World War Three his libretto lost most of the charm of the original. Lerner's collaborator this time was Charles Strouse, who provided a very tuneful score. Lerner's lyric work was his best in over a decade: sharp, engaging and memorable. "No Man Is Worth It" is a delightful solo in which the character contradicts herself within the lyric. "He Always Comes Home to Me" is an interesting mini-drama and "There's Always One You Can't Forget" is touching and knowing. On the lighter side is the enjoyable "It Never Would Have Worked" and the title song. The heroine's ambitious solo "Another Life" best illustrates Lerner's resiliency. *Dance a Little Closer* is filled with energy and a youthful vigor that is admirable coming from a man with years of flops to his credit.

After six major disasters, Lerner proved that his lyric powers were still acute. But *Dance a Little Closer* would fare worse than any of them. With Lerner as librettist, lyricist and director (and his wife Liz Robertson as the leading lady), there was little opportunity for him to evaluate the production's progress objectively. *Dance a Little Closer* closed on opening night. It was the last Lerner musical to open on Broadway.

Although in ill health and beset by financial troubles, Lerner outlined the libretto and wrote several of the lyrics for his proposed musical version of the 1936 film *My Man Godfrey*. As his physical condition worsened, even that project was postponed. Then Andrew Lloyd Webber asked Lerner to write the lyrics for his musicalization of *The Phantom of the Opera*. The highly romantic approach that was proposed was perfect for Lerner's talents, but he had to decline the offer for medical reasons. How ironic that Lerner was deprived of having a West End and Broadway hit at the end of his career. And how much richer lyrically *The Phantom of the Opera* would be had he worked on it. Lerner died in 1986. His career of four decades made him one of the most respected men in the musical theatre; yet during the last twenty years of that career he was a commercial failure. His librettos had failed him, his instincts had failed him, Broadway had failed him. Only his lyric craftsmanship survived.

The words of Alan Jay Lerner are known for their romantic style, but it is worth exploring just how romantic those words actually are. Rarely do his lyrics conform to the standard categories of love songs. Very rarely do they even use the word *love*. Part of the rapturous quality of Lerner's writing is his ability to avoid direct love proclamations. The young Lerner befriended Lorenz Hart during his last years and became something of a protégé of the older lyricist. There is some of the Hart sarcasm in Lerner's work, but the more outstanding feature that the two share is their aversion to saying "I love you" or anything close to it. It is not just Higgins who cannot say anything more rhapsodic than being "accustomed to her face." Lerner is just as reticent. As idealistic and passionate as he was, his lyrics describe a sensation that is "almost like being in love."

Lerner's scores are considered romantic, yet they usually contain more comic songs than serious love songs. Lehrman Engel has pointed out that *My Fair Lady* has more comedy numbers than most any other musical.[3] One thinks of *Brigadoon* with all that heather on the hill and "Come to me, bend to me"; but just as prominent in that score are the comic songs of Meg and Charlie. This tendency toward comedy rather than serious, poetic writing is consistent with Lerner's vision of himself. He did not consider himself a songwriter but, rather, a playwright. (He disliked the term "librettist" because of its old operetta connotations.) Many of his librettos were flawed but in his lyrics he was indeed a skilled playwright.

Like Frank Loesser, Fred Ebb and Stephen Sondheim, Lerner understood the dramatic possibilities of a song. Each of his musical numbers is a drama first, a lyric second. Song after song illustrates this, from the intricate storytelling in "You Did It" to the simple evocation of the past in "I Still See Elisa."

This dramatic approach to songwriting is supported by Lerner's superb lyric structure. His songs are constructed like precise little plays and he builds them as a playwright does with character and plot. Consider the alternating verses of conflicting emotions found in "I'm an Ordinary Man" where the violent and tranquil aspects of Higgins coincide with great comic effect. A similar dramatic situation can be found in the song "Gigi," with Gaston arguing with himself the case of Gigi the girl versus Gigi the woman. Songs like "If Ever I Would Leave You," "The Heather on the Hill," and "Camelot" use a seasonal sequence. A similar use of nature and natural progression is evident in "They Call the Wind Maria" and "Without You." A different form of organization can be found in the Lerner songs that develop an idea by conjuring up a series of images, usually three in number. Arthur and Guinevere wonder what the simple folk do and provide three possible answers: they sing, dance, and wonder what royal folk do. Tommy explains the different images of loneliness he has seen by describing three desperate men in "There But For You Go I." None of these devices is unique to Lerner. They are old tried and true methods of lyric construction. But few use them as expertly and as effortlessly as he does. Singers will attest that Lerner's songs, despite their unusual length at times, are easy to memorize and retain because there is always an internal progression of the character in the lyric. Like a well-structured monologue that flows logically, Lerner's words are a joy to deliver as well as receive.

In many ways the death of Alan Jay Lerner in 1986 signaled the end of an era of romanticism in American musical theatre. Few current lyricists have taken up the idealized point of view that Lerner pursued. Sondheim has Lerner's literate wit but not his utopian vision. Perhaps the contemporary theatre doesn't want such fantasy and romance in its musicals—although the success of the Andrew Lloyd Webber shows seems to indicate otherwise. Lerner's talent was a unique one and he was unusual for his time; a contemporary Lerner would be similarly unusual. But it takes an odd, out-of-the-mainstream talent to do the exceptional. A *My Fair Lady* or a *Brigadoon* cannot be manufactured by conventional methods, for neither show was conventional in its day.

A future Lerner will need to come from off center: someone who can romanticize the world without losing his or her intelligence.

NOTES

1. Alan Jay Lerner and Benny Green (eds.), *A Hymn to Him: The Lyrics of Alan Jay Lerner* (New York: Limelight Editions, 1987), p. 205.

2. Alan Jay Lerner, *The Street Where I Live* (New York: W. W. Norton & Co., 1978, p. 253.

3. Lehrman Engel, *Their Words Are Music: The Great Theatre Lyricists and Their Lyrics* (New York: Crown Publishers, 1975), p. 150.

13

Two on the Aisle: Betty Comden and Adolph Green

The team of Comden and Green is not only the longest collaboration in musical theatre history but also one of the closest. For over fifty years one has never written without the other. They have collaborated with a number of different composers on Broadway and in Hollywood; sometimes they write the libretto or screenplay, sometimes the lyrics, sometimes both. But the one constant is that they always work together. Another unique aspect to the careers of Betty Comden and Adolph Green, and an important one when considering their lyrics, is the fact that they are both performers as well as writers. They bring an actor's point of view to lyricwriting and, with their background in satiric musical revues, they have created some of Broadway's most memorable specialty numbers: those self-contained songs that provide a showcase for a performer. Most of Comden and Green's lyrics have been written for stars; few lyricists are more qualified for the task. It's a case of performers writing for performers. Comden and Green may not be the most inspired lyricists in the musical theatre (and they are certainly not the most versatile), but they always deliver on a prodigious level and have provided more fun than a handful of more talented artists.

Betty Comden and Adolph Green were both born in 1915 in New York City. They both attended New York University, joined the Washington Square Players, and then started writing revue sketches and songs for clubs and small Greenwich Village theatres. Their goal was to become musical comedy performers; the writing was a way to get topical material that displayed their performing talents. They formed a group, the Revuers, and by 1938 were appearing in more prestigious nightclubs and Off-Broadway houses. "Variety Says," a song that survives from those early revue days, is typical of the Comden and Green style: contemporary, satirical, eager, full of name dropping and, most significantly, about "show biz." The song makes fun of the abbreviated lingo of *Variety* ("Show Biz Fizz . . . Buff on Cuff . . . Pop Op Flop . . . Hix Nix Six Pix") as it picks up on the fast, urban temperament that is so characteristic of their many New York City songs. Comden and Green brought this irreverent, flippant kind of writing with them when they eventually worked on Broadway.

Leonard Bernstein, Green's old school roommate, saw the team perform their own material at the Blue Angel and approached them about writing the libretto and lyrics for a musical based on Jerome Robbins' ballet of Bernstein's "Fancy Free." *On the Town* (1944) was a smashing Broadway debut for Comden, Green, Bernstein and Robbins (as choreographer). Its vibrant, sassy score and the mesmerizing dance sequences made *On the Town* refreshingly original. While most musicals were set in the past in order to capture a romantic setting, *On the Town* was brazenly contemporary and celebrated the romance of the city itself. Comden and Green's lyrics in *On the Town* still sound fresh and contemporary. From the high-spirited "New York, New York" to the mellow, engaging "Some Other Time," the lyric work is exceptional. The comedy numbers ("I Get Carried Away," "Come Up to My Place" and "I Can Cook, Too!") would not be out of place in a Greenwich Village revue. But even these specialty songs are consistent with the characters and seem comfortably at home in the thinly plotted story. For the ballads "Lonely Town" and "Lucky to Be Me" the lyrics are simple and not at all gimmicky; it is Bernstein's music that raises them to a near-poetic level. (It must be pointed out that Bernstein wrote the lyrics for "I Can Cook, Too!" and contributed to other songs in the show as well.)

Both Comden and Green appeared in major roles in *On the Town*, but the success of the musical made it clear their future lay in writing. They were soon represented on Broadway again with their libretto and lyrics for *Billion Dollar Baby* (1945), a forgettable show with composer Morton Gould about gangsters in the 1920s. *Bonanza Bound* (with music by Saul Chaplin) did not even make it to Broadway but closed in Philadelphia. It seemed as if Comden and Green had hit it lucky with *On the Town*; the

Broadway offers dried up. But Hollywood was willing to give the team a try and they were asked to script the film version of *Good News!* (1947). Three more movie assignments came in 1949: scripts for the musicals *Take Me out to the Ball Game* and *The Barkleys of Broadway* and the film version of their own *On the Town*. Although Comden and Green returned to New York in 1951 they would often return to Hollywood and script other musicals, most memorably *Singin' in the Rain* (1952), *The Band Wagon* (1953) and *Bells Are Ringing* (1960). *Two on the Aisle* (1951) not only marked the team's return to Broadway but it provided a new impetus for their careers: it was their first of nine musicals with composer Jule Styne. *Two on the Aisle* was a musical revue, though on a much grander scale than their old Greenwich Village shows. Bert Lahr was the star and Comden and Green provided him with some knockout sketches. But Dolores Gray sang the two best songs in the revue: "Give a Little, Get a Little Love" and the delightful "If You Hadn't, But You Did" in which she outlined all the reasons why she bumped off her husband.

Comden and Green reteamed with Leonard Bernstein in 1953 and wrote their finest score: *Wonderful Town*. The libretto by Joseph Fields and Jerome Chodorov (based on their 1940 play *My Sister Eileen*) was intended as a vehicle for Rosalind Russell's return to Broadway. But *Wonderful Town* was much more than a vehicle. The plot, about two sisters trying to find love and success in New York, tends toward the episodic and is not so easily revived today, but the score is thrilling. The specialty number "One Hundred Easy Ways (To Lose a Man)" was Russell's only solo in the musical, but it was a brilliant showcase for her comic (and limited singing) talents. The lilting "(Why Did We Ever Leave) Ohio" is a captivating character song. There is also the lovely ballad "A Quiet Girl," the joyous "It's Love" and the cynical "What a Waste." "Conga!," a comic dance number, has delicious rhymes ("rhythm bands . . . monkey glands . . . hot-dog stands") and there are two extended musical numbers, "Conversation Piece" and "Christopher Street," that mix prose dialogue and traditional lyrics in an effective way. Comden, Green and Bernstein's playfulness reach a peak with "The Wrong Note Rag," a sly piece that incorporates nonsense lyrics ("ricky-tick-tacky") within a rag melody that purposely breaks syncopation with "that lovely wrong note." Bernstein would continue this kind of experimentation in *Candide* and *West Side Story*. Comden and Green, who unfortunately did not work with Bernstein again, never had so challenging a composer. *Wonderful Town* was their finest hour.

The team's next seven shows would be with Jule Styne, forming a close-knit triumvirate recalling the days of De Sylva, Brown and Henderson. The musical version of *Peter Pan*, with music by Mark Charlap and lyrics by Carolyn Leigh, was having trouble on the road. Styne was called in to help and, with Comden and Green providing the lyrics, added eight songs including "Wendy," "(Captain) Hook's Waltz," "Oh, My Mysterious Lady" and the show's most endearing number, "Never, Never Land." *Peter Pan* was not a great success when it opened in 1954, running for only 152 performances. But the subsequent television production and numerous revivals have made it a musical theatre favorite.

Comden and Green's biggest success, *Bells Are Ringing* (1956), was also their most conventional show. They wrote the lyrics and the libretto, about a telephone answering service, and Judy Holliday, their friend from the old Revuers team, triumphed in the leading role. She sang the show's most popular songs: "Just in Time" and "The Party's Over." Also in the score for *Bells Are Ringing* is the brassy specialty number "I'm Going Back (to the Bonjour Tristesse Brassiere Company)," the comic "It's a Simple Little System" and the winsome "Long Before I Met You." Everything in *Bells Are Ringing* seems a bit artificial today, including those two hit singles, but it pleased Broadway audiences for two years. *Say Darling* (1958) was a play with music about the making of a Broadway musical; the Styne-Comden-Green songs were inconsequential. That same year Comden and Green returned to performing with their Broadway entertainment *A Party With Betty Comden and Adolph Green*. Presenting a wide repertoire of their own songs, some going back to their Greenwich Village days, the show ran for eighty-two performances—a long run for that kind of program. (They did an updated version of the same show in 1977.)

The team's next two musicals with Styne, *Do Re Mi* (1960) and *Subways Are For Sleeping* (1961), managed respectable runs despite weak librettos and less than impressive scores. *Do Re Mi* added "Make Someone Happy" to the growing list of Comden and Green's hit singles, and there was a comic showcase number for Nancy Walker called "Adventure." New York City provided the theme and setting for *Subways Are For Sleeping* and there was the bouncy "Be a Santa" to highlight the show. "Girls Like Me," a somber song about lonely office girls, is noteworthy as well as "Ride Through the Night," an enchanted view of a subway ride. *Fade Out—Fade In* (1964) was devised to showcase the comic talents

of Carol Burnett, but the Comden and Green libretto, about Hollywood
in the thirties, was scattered. Burnett impersonated some Hollywood
favorites, and her Shirley Temple spoof "You Mustn't Be Discouraged"
was the musical's highpoint.

Hallelujah, Baby! (1967) was one of Comden and Green's more ambitious projects, but the finished product was a disappointment. Arthur
Laurents' libretto about the plight of black Americans from 1900 to the
1960s was an uneasy mixture of musical comedy and political fervor.
The Styne-Comden-Green score for *Hallelujah, Baby!* is rather lackluster.
There are some competent lyrics and pleasant melodies but each song falls
short of the hoped-for impact. "Now's the Time" has spirit but not much
originality, and "My Own Morning" has an attractive yearning quality.
After a series of near misses, the team finally had a hit again with
Applause (1970). Charles Strouse and Lee Adams did the score and
Comden and Green wrote the tight, smart libretto based on the 1950
film *All About Eve*. In 1974 they contributed lyrics for some new Jule
Styne songs for *Lorelei*, the slightly altered revival of Styne's *Gentlemen
Prefer Blondes*. The new songs were no match for the old Jule Styne-Leo
Robin favorites such as "A Little Girl from Little Rock" and "Diamonds
Are a Girl's Best Friend."

Working with composer Cy Coleman, Comden and Green had an
artistic, if not a popular, success with *On the Twentieth Century* (1978).
Their libretto, based on the 1932 farce *Twentieth Century*, was a freewheeling comic opera with wonderfully animated lyrics. Everything in
the musical was on a grandiose scale: Coleman's vivacious music, the
flamboyant performances, even the witty scenery with a train recreated
on stage. Comden and Green's lyrics matched the vigorous production.
"Our Private World" is an energetic duet that mocks operetta even as it
celebrates its lyric clichés. "I Rise Again" is a smashing egocentric solo.
"Never" and "She's a Nut" are propelling songs that echo the driving force
of the train. In flashbacks and dream sequences, the pastiche numbers
"Veronique" and "Babette" are filled with an exuberant flavor that recalls
the team's work in their two Bernstein musicals. *On the Twentieth Century* was too stylized for most audiences, and Robin Wagner's magnificent
set ran off with the show. But Comden and Green's book and lyrics
are top-notch, and the musical may someday find a following. Also
deserving of a second look is *A Doll's Life* (1982), though major script
revisions are necessary. Comden and Green's libretto is an attempt to
tell what happened to Nora after the events of Ibsen's *A Doll's House*.

The score (music by Larry Grossman) is intriguing, but the musical failed to satisfy and closed after only five performances. Comden and Green, at this writing, are far from retired and always have a project in the works. It is not unlikely that they will soon again be represented on Broadway. One has learned never to be surprised by the musical theatre's longest-running team.

Comden and Green work within a narrower scope than most Broadway writers. Musical comedy is what they love and they rarely attempted to go beyond that. They use standard musical comedy conventions for the most part but they use them well. If a Comden and Green musical is rarely innovative or challenging, it is usually not sloppy or misguided either. And even their least successful shows have one or two enjoyable numbers. One must also acknowledge Comden and Green's gift for providing tailor-made showcases for Broadway's biggest stars. Bert Lahr, Lauren Bacall, Mary Martin, Carol Channing, Phil Silvers, Rosalind Russell, Judy Holliday, John Cullum, Nancy Walker, Leslie Uggams, Carol Lawrence, Mitzi Green and Madeline Kahn are among the Broadway favorites who had some of their finest moments (and won awards for) performing Comden and Green material.

Regardless of the settings of their musicals, all the Comden and Green shows seem to exist in the same place: Broadway. There is a show business subtext to all their work. We never really believe we are in Greenwich Village or on a train; we know we are in a musical comedy. Their truth is Broadway truth. This may be their greatest limitation as writers but it is also their most attractive feature. Comden and Green are sitting on the aisle watching Broadway; with each musical we are invited to join them and enjoy. With such an approach they will never move the musical theatre forward or change its direction. But, at their best, Comden and Green remind us of what makes musicals so terrific.

14

Make a Miracle:
Frank Loesser

Although Frank Loesser was associated with only six Broadway musicals during his life, he was a much admired, very individual artist who defies simple description. Writing both music and lyrics during most of his career, Loesser has no easily identifiable style. Those six musicals do not resemble each other in subject matter, approach, character or theme. From old-fashioned musical comedy to Italianate opera, from period romanticism to contemporary satire, the musicals Loesser scored are so individual in character that no generalization about them can be made. At times it seems that there must have been several Frank Loessers.

To be eclectic is one thing; to be consistently top drawer is something even more laudable. Loesser's high level of craftsmanship, both in his music and lyrics, is the one recurring feature in all his shows. If there were more than one Loesser, they were all equally talented. Not that all of his Broadway efforts gained favor, for he continually courted disaster by moving in a new direction with each project and tried never to repeat himself. Because of his successful Hollywood career, Loesser's Broadway stay was less than thirteen years. But in such a short time he covered a lot of ground.

Frank Loesser was born in New York City in 1910. He grew up in a musical family: Loesser's father was a piano teacher and his brother Arthur later became a respected concert pianist. But Loesser was only interested in popular music, and even as a child wrote a few songs. After failing in his studies at the City College of New York, he worked as a newspaper reporter and then as a sketch writer and lyricist for vaudeville acts, radio shows and summer resorts. In 1931 he got his first song published: "In Love With a Memory of You," with lyrics by Loesser and music by the later celebrated composer William Schuman. Loesser then teamed up with Irving Actman; they contributed songs to various club shows, sometimes with Loesser performing. These songs caught the attention of the Society of Illustrators, who were putting together a musical revue. *The Illustrators' Show* (1936) only ran for five performances, but Loesser's lyrics were finally heard on Broadway. One song, "Bang—the Bell Rang," had a tricky lyric that foreshadowed Loesser's mature work. But Broadway didn't seem interested, so when Loesser and Actman were offered a Hollywood contract, they accepted. It would be twelve years before Loesser would return to Broadway.

Contributing lyrics to several movie musicals, Loesser worked with such composers as Hoagy Carmichael, Jule Styne, Burton Lane, Jimmy McHugh and Arthur Schwartz. His Hollywood songs from this period included two hits: "The Lady's in Love With You" (with Lane) and "Two Sleepy People" (with Carmichael). At the outbreak of World War Two Loesser joined the Army, where he wrote "Praise the Lord and Pass the Ammunition," his first effort at writing music as well as lyrics. The song was a sensation, and Loesser composed his own music from then on. After the war he scored several B movie musicals. Even after his return to New York Loesser continued to work for Hollywood on occasion and produced several popular songs, including the Oscar winner "Baby, It's Cold Outside." In 1952 he scored *Hans Christian Anderson*, one of the best film musicals of the decade, with such memorable songs as "Anywhere I Wander," "Inch Worm," "No Two People" and "Wonderful, Wonderful Copenhagen."

Loesser returned to Broadway with his delightful score for *Where's Charley?* (1948). George Abbott adapted the popular farce *Charley's Aunt* and directed it as well, giving Ray Bolger the best role of his career and Loesser his first Broadway hit (792 performances). Loesser's score for *Where's Charley?* is lush and romantic yet consistent with the farcical plot and characters. The duet "My Darling, My Darling" is rapturous but humorous. The ensemble number "The New Ashmoleon Marching Society and Student Conservatory Band" is rousing yet witty. The show's biggest hit was "Once in Love With Amy." The song became so popular that later in the run Bolger each evening entreated the audience to join him in singing it. Lyrically, the most accomplished song in *Where's Charley?* is "Make a Miracle." This unique duet is a love song on one level, a satire on progress on another level, and a contest of wills on yet another. The resulting number is a fully developed musical scene.

Producers Cy Feuer and Ernest Martin approached Loesser about doing the score for their musical based on a Damon Runyon story. Loesser immediately agreed, but the producers went through eleven librettists before they got the book they wanted for *Guys and Dolls* (1950). Newcomer Abe Burrows, using Jo Swerling's draft plus some characters from other Runyon stories, fashioned a very stylized "fable of Broadway" that was quite unlike anything seen before. The characters were poetic yet slangy, low-life yet literate. Loesser picked up on this unusual style and wrote one of the musical theatre's finest scores. The Bach-like "Fugue for Tinhorns" lyrically introduces the Runyon world. "The Oldest Established (Permanent Floating Crapgame in New York)" and the title song are thrilling examples of revealing character, exposition and a play's theme. The romantic songs—"I'll Know (When My Love Comes Along)," "I've Never Been in Love Before" and "My Time of Day"—are in the persuasive vein, which keeps them dramatic and funny. "Sue Me" is mock opera; "Sit Down, You're Rockin' the Boat" is mock gospel. Even the two nightclub numbers, "A Bushel and a Peck" and "Take Back Your Mink," are in the Runyonesque mold. And justly famous is "Adelaide's Lament," easily one of the best comic songs in any Broadway musical. *Guys and Dolls* marked the highpoint of Loesser's career. With Abe Burrows he created an irreverent look at New York and filled it with warmth. Never have such characters been treated with such affection. (Compare these gangsters to the ones in Porter's *Kiss Me, Kate*.) The New York of *Guys and Dolls* is a place that never was, peopled by characters who could never be. Musical theatre was the ideal medium to capture such a dream existence.

Loesser spent four years writing the score for his next project, *The Most Happy Fella* (1956). Some felt it was his masterpiece because it seemed to have "masterpiece" stamped all over it. Others were bored and kept waiting for Cleo and the other smart aleck characters to come back on. *The Most Happy Fella* was certainly a labor of love; Loesser wrote music, lyrics and libretto. With over forty musical numbers and three acts of almost continuous singing, it was labeled opera by some. Loesser insisted it was "an extended musical comedy." Whatever it is, *The Most Happy Fella* is often inconsistent and unsatisfying. The musical comedy sections make it all the more difficult to enjoy the opera-like portions of the show. Characters are developed in a grand opera manner rather than a dramatic one; the main character, for example, is colorful and passionate in opera terms, obtuse and irritating in theatre terms. The musical is based on a play, Sidney Howard's sentimental *They Knew What They Wanted* (1924), and Loesser improved on the original by adding some important secondary characters and softening some of the hero and heroine's more ridiculous actions. While *The Most Happy Fella* may contain some of Loesser's best music, his lyric work is variable. The songs in the musical comedy sections—"Big D," "Ooh, My Feet," "Standing on the Corner"—are lively and enjoyable, but they lack the inspired sparkle of Loesser's two previous shows. When the musical turns to opera the lyrics immediately flatten out. Loesser falls into the cliché that opera lyrics must be repetitive, predictable and dull. In the Italian immigrant Tony's songs, the broken English proves irresistible for Loesser and the lyrics border on the offensive. (Tony spends much of "Happy to Make Your Acquaintance" stupidly mispronouncing the word "likewise.") The best of the operatic lyrics is "Joey, Joey, Joey," a haunting song that conjures up striking visions using the simplest of images. Also effective is the "Letter Theme," a motif that recurs throughout the musical as in an opera. *The Most Happy Fella* is extraordinary at times, numbing at other times. It is the most challenging work of a man who always sought challenges.

Greenwillow (1960) also met with a mixed response. Loesser co-authored with Lesser Samuels this atmospheric story about a young man from a sleepy town called Greenwillow who fears falling in love and searches for romantic courage within himself. The musical was decidedly uncommercial and too slight for most tastes (it only ran for three months) but it had a lovely, evocative score that captured the spirit of rural America by celebrating its small-town customs. Anthony Perkins, as the young hero, sang two stirring solos: the romantic "Summertime Love" and the anti-romantic "Never Will I Marry." Also in the score is the memorable "Walking Away Whistling," a carol, "Greenwillow Christmas," and the touching "Faraway Boy." If *The Most Happy Fella* toyed with grand opera, *Greenwillow* courted chamber opera: unpretentious and endearing.

Nothing could have been further from sleepy *Greenwillow* than the contemporary urban setting of *How to Succeed in Business Without Really Trying* (1961). Jack Weinstock and Willie Gilbert wrote a comedy based on Shepherd Mead's book. Abe Burrows then turned it all into a brash, cynical, almost vicious satire about big business. *How to Succeed* is probably the most unromantic musical ever. The most heartfelt love song, "I Believe in You," was sung by the hero to his own image in the mirror. This is definitely not a boy-gets-girl show; more a boy-gets-job musical. Just as *Guys and Dolls* had created a fantasy New York of gangsters and bookies, *How to Succeed* presented a sharp, cartoonish world of office politics. There was nothing in Loesser's previous work to foreshadow such a project. The music in *How to Succeed* is not melodic but frantic, drilling and pulsating. The lyrics are funny and sly but a bit broad in character development. All of the songs support the story and theme. Even the rousing "Brotherhood of Man" at the end of the show is wry commentary after all the deception and backbiting that precedes it. Ironically, little of the score is memorable. It is literate and accomplished songwriting but the songs are truly secondary. Each musical number seems to disappear once it has served its purpose. *How to Succeed* is that rare instance in which a musical's book outshines its score. Loesser succeeded too well in *How to Succeed*. Only "I Believe in You" became popular and only when sung as a traditional love song, not the shrewd, egotistical character song it was on stage. Also, the score was so closely knit with the early 1960s temperament that some of it has dated badly, something that cannot be said about *Guys and Dolls* or even *Where's Charley?* But Loesser did get to share the Pulitzer Prize that the musical was awarded, and the show ran for 1,416 performances, the longest run of all his works.

Frank Loesser's career on Broadway was over by the mid-sixties. His musical *Pleasures and Palaces* closed in Detroit in 1965, never making it to New York. Illness forced Loesser into premature retirement and he died of cancer in 1969. In addition to his half dozen Broadway musicals and numerous movie songs, Loesser left another legacy. He founded the Frank Music Company to publish his own songs but also used it to promote young and promising talent. Richard Adler, Jerry Ross and Meredith Willson are among the songwriters he discovered, encouraged and published.

The many Frank Loessers left a distinctive mark on the musical theatre. Several marks. There is probably no such thing today as a Loesser-like musical. But many of the best songwriters admired him and were influenced enough to imitate what he did so well. There is a *Guys and Dolls* feeling, for example, in the salesmen's "Rock Island" number in *The Music Man*. Parts of *Hello, Dolly!* have the high-spirited quality of

Where's Charley? and even *The Most Happy Fella* paved the way for the later opera-like musicals such as *Sweeney Todd*. Much of Loesser's work is still fresh and challenging today. *Guys and Dolls*, in particular, is constantly revived and continually pleasing. Frank Loesser's craftsmanship is rediscovered each year. He will always be one of our most modern theatre artists.

15

Something's Coming:
Stephen Sondheim

The history of the book musical is the history of Oscar Hammerstein II and Stephen Sondheim. The careers of these two men—spanning from the 1920s up to the present day—do more than chronologically parallel the growth of the American musical. Both men were instrumental in determining the direction that growth took, and most musicals are influenced by one or the other or both. When Hammerstein was struggling through the early drafts of *Oklahoma!* on his farm in Doylestown, Pennsylvania, a frequent visitor was the thirteen-year-old Sondheim, a friend of Hammerstein's son and a precocious adolescent with a curiosity about musical theatre. Sondheim started as Hammerstein's protégé and eventually became his successor, but the connection did not end there. Sondheim has moved the musical theatre in directions as radically different as those Hammerstein pioneered with *Show Boat.* An American musical theatre without Porter or Hart would be a poorer place; one without Hammerstein and Sondheim would be unimaginable.

Stephen Joshua Sondheim was born in New York in 1930 and was educated at the George School in Pennsylvania and at Williams College. For a while he wrote scripts for the *Topper* television series. Drawn to the musical theatre from an early age, he learned the craft of lyricwriting from the Master directly. Following a course of study outlined by Hammerstein, Sondheim wrote several musical adaptations as exercises and studied music with avant-garde composer Milton Babbitt. Soon he had completed the music and lyrics for a musical called *Saturday Night*, which was slated for Broadway until the unexpected death of the producer brought the project to a halt. When the young Sondheim was added to the team putting together *West Side Story* it was as co-lyricist with Leonard Bernstein. Bernstein had planned to write all the lyrics himself (he had previously assisted with the lyrics in *Candide* and *On the Town*) but, as it was Bernstein's habit to compose the dance music and do the orchestrations for his musicals, the job of lyricwriting as well seemed impractical. As more and more of the show's lyrics were penned by Sondheim, Bernstein dropped his name from the lyricist credits and *West Side Story* opened on Broadway with "Lyrics by Stephen Sondheim."

In the years since the original 1957 production, Sondheim has often publicly stated his dislike of his lyrics for *West Side Story*. His self-criticisms are specific and incisive: the out-of-character internal rhymes in "I Feel Pretty," the miscalculated emphasis on the wrong word in "Somewhere" ("there's *a* place for us"), and the overly clever and in-audible wording in "America." But Sondheim is too hard on himself to belittle his contribution to the score of *West Side Story*. Perhaps it was Bernstein's music, the highly melodramatic libretto by Arthur Laurents, or even the nature of youth itself; but some of Sondheim's lyrics have a simple richness that traditionalists miss in his later scores. The mono-syllabic "One Hand, One Heart" is effective because it is so unaffected. The purposely awkward phrasing of "A Boy Like That (Who'd Kill Your Brother)" makes it distinctive. And few lyrics introduce a character's mood as well as "Something's Coming." While some feel that *West Side Story* is dated, the lyrics for "Gee, Officer Krupke" are as fresh as ever, and "Tonight" and "Maria" remain among Sondheim's, or anyone else's, most remembered lyrics.

Was *West Side Story* inferior Sondheim or was it indeed an auspicious debut? When one considers the new ground that *West Side Story* broke in terms of story, choreography and music, the lyrics seem rather traditional. Perhaps what bothered Sondheim so much about his work in *West Side Story* was the fact that fireworks were going off all around him but his words were routine; talented, efficient and occasionally inspired, but, in terms of later work, routine. There is one section in the score in which the lyrics do break ground: the complex "Tonight" quintet near the end of the first act. The temperaments of the gangs as they prepare for the rumble contrast with the sexually charged anticipation of Anita and then the optimistically romantic yearnings of Maria. Then they all combine to create a moment hitherto unseen in musical theatre. It's an old opera device, of course, but it took Bernstein to bring it to Broadway and it took Sondheim's lyrics to make it work.

Sondheim's next project, *Gypsy* (1959), came as a result of his work on *West Side Story*. The score for *Gypsy* had been offered to and turned down by both Cole Porter and Irving Berlin before Sondheim was suggested. But Ethel Merman refused to let an untried composer write her music, so Jule Styne was brought in and Sondheim found himself writing "lyrics only" once again. The result was a sensation. Styne wrote his greatest musical score, Merman gave the performance of her career, Arthur Laurents created one of the theatre's finest librettos, and the lyrics . . . even Sondheim hasn't bad-mouthed them. *West Side Story* called for lush, highly emotional words. *Gypsy* called for the wise-cracking, brittle dialogue of backstage. Sondheim's caustic wit shone for the first time and the lyrics vibrated with energy. Using the simple "May We/Let Me Entertain You" as a framework, the lyrics fluctuate from the tough-minded ("Some People," "Everything's Coming Up Roses," "You Gotta Get a Gimmick") to the fragile ("Small World" and "Little Lamb"). "Mr. Goldstone, I Love You" is a virtuoso lyric, sustaining the simplest premise for a song. "Together, Wherever We Go" is a contagious romp. And the whole score climaxes with "Rose's Turn," a unique solo that reveals Sondheim's talent for stream-of-consciousness approach to a lyric. Few Broadway musicals are as cohesive and integrated as *Gypsy*, and the lyrics are no small part of its success.

Sondheim finally got to write both music and lyrics for *A Funny Thing Happened on the Way to the Forum* (1962) but to most in the business he was still a lyricist. (Although *Forum* won the Tony Award for Best Musical, Sondheim's score wasn't even nominated.) Purposely breaking away from the integrated type of score that had dominated his work with Bernstein and Styne, Sondheim created for *Forum* a collection of songs rather than a unified score. More often than not the musical numbers are pleasant diversions from the story rather than continuations of it. Burt Shevelove and Larry Gelbart's book, which is based on several Roman comedies by Plautus, is such a fast-paced farce that Sondheim's songs become breathing spots. Lyrically, it was the most playful and robust work he had yet done. Filled with outrageous rhymes ("gaudy . . . bawdy . . . everybawdy . . . ") and ridiculous alliteration ("The bong of the bell of the buoy in the bay"), the whole score seems like a devilish reaction to the stiff confines of writing for Tony and Maria.

The few quiet and charming lyrics ("Your Eyes Are Blue," "The Echo Song" and "Love Is in the Air") were dropped before opening and replaced by more piquant numbers ("That'll Show Him" and "Comedy Tonight"). The temperament of the score is best illustrated in "Everybody Ought to Have a Maid," a crowd pleaser that recalls the classic clown routines of vaudeville. Sondheim's score for *Forum* is a little gem. But little gems do not make the careers of "serious" composer/lyricists. Everyone loved *Forum* and few gave Sondheim the credit. Not until the 1972 Broadway revival of the musical would critics acknowledge the words in *Forum*.

Anyone Can Whistle (1964) would become one of the decade's most controversial projects and, in hindsight, one of its most adventurous. It has an original story about lunatics, con men, miracles and politics. The fact that it only lasted on Broadway for nine performances helps to guarantee its cult status. (Martin Gottfried has noted that *Anyone Can Whistle* "would have run forever if everyone who claims to have seen it had actually bought tickets."[1] But no reconsideration or major revival of the musical has proven that this is a neglected classic. Most people blame Arthur Laurents' quirky libretto but the score, while bold and ambitious, is uneven at best. Lyrically it ranges from sardonic ("Me and My Town") to poignant ("There Won't Be Trumpets" and the title song) to commonplace ("See What It Gets You"). "I've Got You to Lean On" is a more ironic but less effective version of "Together, Wherever We Go." "Come Play Wiz Me," with its mock French 101 vernacular, draws more attention to its gimmick than to the purpose of the song. And few Sondheim lyrics have aged as badly as "Everybody Says Don't." If the score for *Anyone Can Whistle* was underrated by most in 1964 it has made up for it by being overrated by many today. The high points—and there are indeed high points—are noteworthy. The justly famous interrogation scene at the end of the first act ("Simple") is full of power and delight. The title song is restrained (especially for this show) and moving. And "A Parade in Town" deserves a better dramatic situation, to say the least. *Anyone Can Whistle* taught Sondheim (and the theatre) a great deal but it had its price.

Since Hammerstein's death in 1960, Richard Rodgers had been looking for a new collaborator. (He had written his own lyrics for *No Strings* in 1962.) Sondheim being Hammerstein's protégé and one of the hottest lyricists in town, it seemed inevitable that he and Rodgers team up. But *Do I Hear A Waltz?* (1965) was a nightmare on both sides of the footlights. Among the many problems was a growing animosity between composer and lyricist. It showed in the final product. Sondheim wrote his weakest lyrics, and Rodgers began a series of stillborn musicals that concluded his long and astonishing career. The lyrics for the title song are passable but it is Rodgers' talent for waltzes that saves it. There was some spark in "We're Gonna Be All Right" (with even a reference to homosexuality) but it was scrubbed clean by opening night. Most disappointing about the lyrics for *Do I Hear A Waltz?* are the feeble attempts at comedy. "Bargaining" is trite and obvious. "No Understand" is simpleminded. And with "What Do We Do? We Fly!" Sondheim's wit is reduced to jokes about airline food.

It would be with *Company* (1970) that all the training with Hammerstein and the innovative experience of *West Side Story* would come together and Sondheim would create the first great conceptual musical on Broadway. While there have been few shows exactly like *Company* there have been several that are derived from it. For example, without *Company* there would have been no *A Chorus Line*. *Company* showed audiences that linear plotlines were not necessary in a Broadway musical. There had always been shows without plot or characters; but *Company* was all character without plot. George Furth's libretto about a New York City bachelor and all his married friends is sharp and telling, but it is Sondheim's score that gives the show its energy and uncompromising verve. Much has been made of the telephone busy signal as a metaphor for *Company*. That insistent quality can be found in the lyrics, which use repetition creatively. The words echo with the reverberations of that insistent busy signal. "Another Hundred People" keep getting off the train long after the song ends. "Someone Is Waiting" lingers in the mind because the lyric doesn't resolve the character's situation. And has any lyric left its audience in such a beguiling state as effectively as "Sorry Grateful"?

You're sorry-grateful,
Regretful-happy,
Why look for answers where none occur?
You'll always be what you always were,
Which has nothing to do with,
All to do with her.

If *Company* lacks a story its songs do not. Sondheim has often stated that a song should be constructed like a little one-act play; *Company* is filled with such mini-dramas. "Ladies Who Lunch" is a caustic soliloquy. "Getting Married Today" is more like an episode than a song. And the technique is never more fully realized than in "Barcelona," the postcoital scene set completely in lyrics. *Company* finally brought Sondheim recognition for his composing (he won Tony Awards for his music and lyrics), but it was also his finest set of lyrics to date. Not since Cole Porter's day had audiences listened to a score in such a way.

Sondheim once called his next project, *Follies* (1971), an "embarrassment of riches,"[2] and it's an apt description. James Goldman's libretto, about the reunion of several former Follies performers, was overabundant. There were too many songs, too many characters, too many costumes and too many ideas, many of them quite good. Although *Follies* has found new life in concert and in revival, it is still overabundant. The score for *Follies* can be divided into the book numbers, which concern the characters in the present, and the pastiche numbers, which recreate and ironically comment on the musical styles of the past. Those pastiches allow Sondheim to exercise his talent for satiric imitation, especially in the lyrics. Irving Berlin's "A Pretty Girl Is Like a Melody" becomes "Beautiful Girls." Ira Gershwin's "(You Don't Know) The Half of It, Dearie, Blues" becomes "The-God-Why-Don't-You-Love-Me Blues" and innumerable Cole Porter songs are capsulated in "Live, Laugh, Love." None of the imitations is as good as the original, but as exercises in irony they are right on target. (An exception comes to mind: Sondheim's "Broadway Baby," written in the brash De Sylva-Brown-Henderson style, is better than the original model. The satire comes from the fact that in *Follies* it's sung by an old lady who belts out the song with the bravado of a young golddigger.) As for the book songs in *Follies*, they are unrelentingly painful. They have the same uncompromising attitude found in *Company* but are more fatalistic. The characters in *Company* may be bewildered or in pain but they are still in there fighting. The characters in *Follies* have lost the fight before the first song is sung. Lyrics like "The Road You Didn't Take" and "Could I Leave You?" are exposés on a life and a marriage that are already dead. The heartbreak behind the optimistic lyrics of "In Buddy's Eyes" and "The Right Girl" illustrates Sondheim's interest in subtext. All the book lyrics in *Follies* are rich, multilayered and, ultimately, numbing. Is there such a thing as being too brilliant? An embarrassment of riches indeed.

If *Follies* was a nightmare of emotions, *A Little Night Music* (1973) was a romantic dream based on the Ingmar Bergman film *Smiles of a*

Summer Night (1955). Moving into the realm of operetta, Sondheim devised a score that was elusively charming. Musically, he set it in 3/4 time; lyrically, he set it in fantasy. The pains of love, infidelity, growing up and growing old were softened. These were polite lyrics, and some audiences previously turned off by Sondheim finally embraced him. ("Send in the Clowns" would become his first and only major hit song.) On the other hand, many who had been excited and stimulated by *Company* and *Follies* felt that *A Little Night Music* was a sellout. (Hugh Wheeler's libretto actually had a happy ending for all the characters.) While the lyrics for *A Little Night Music* are softer, they are nonetheless skillful and effective. The triple-song opening ("Now," "Later" and "Soon") is a craftsman's delight but it also charms. "You Must Meet My Wife" and "It Would Have Been Wonderful" are very droll but still crowd pleasers. "The Miller's Son" is a wonderful ballad that turns a minor role into a fully realized character. The finest lyric in *A Little Night Music* is the bittersweet "Every Day a Little Death":

Every day a little death
In the parlor, in the bed,
In the curtains, in the silver,
In the buttons, in the bread.
Every day a little sting
In the heart and in the head,
Every move and every breath—
And you hardly feel a thing—
Brings a perfect little death.

The words are so knowing that, even coming from a fantasy, they move us because of their ordinary, everyday images.

Before moving on to another full score, Sondheim returned to the "lyrics only" role and supplied some new lyrics for the 1974 revival of *Candide*. Regardless of how one felt about Sondheim's next show, *Pacific Overtures* (1976), one could not say that he was playing it safe this time. John Weidman's book was an unusual attempt at dramatizing social history. Harold Prince's directorial style was Broadway/Kabuki. The music was atonal and used the Japanese pentatonic scale. The lyrics were unique and exquisite. *Pacific Overtures* is one of Sondheim's finest, most heartfelt scores. The musical attempted to tell the history of the Westernization of Japan beginning with the arrival of Commodore Perry in 1856. Director Prince told the press that *Pacific Overtures* was not about people but about cultures. Yet much of the words are very personal and deeply affecting. Using simple sentence structure, Japanese haiku, and straightforward imagery, Sondheim establishes character and mood on both a personal and cultural level. In the song "Poems," two men travel across the countryside and make up poems to pass the time. One composes

Rain glistening
On the silver birch,
Like my lady's tears.
Your turn.

The other man, who has spent some time in America, responds

Rain gathering,
Winding into streams,
Like the roads to Boston.
Your turn.

As they travel, their contrasting temperaments are revealed.

I am no nightingale,
But she hears the song
I can sing to her,
My lady wife.

I am no nightingale,
But my song of her
Could outsing the sea.
America.

By the end of the play these two men will be on opposite sides of a deadly struggle between the personal life and the social world; the lyric foreshadows the play's major theme. In "Bowler Hat," many years pass as one Japanese governor gives in to the influence (and affluence) of Westernization. He starts with a bowler hat, then an umbrella stand, then says "I visited the church beside the shrine." By the end, he is completely Westernized and has learned that "one must accommodate the times." Sondheim purposely avoids traditional rhyming in *Pacific*

Overtures except in the comic numbers such as "Chrysanthemum Tea" and "Welcome to Kanagawa." "Please, Hello" is a masterful piece of lyricwriting that wryly comments on the national personalities found in the British, American, Dutch, French and Russian ambassadors. "Pretty Lady" is the most romantic song in the show, but its tenderness is purposely offset by having it sung by three American sailors who mistake a Japanese maiden for a prostitute. And, finally, there is "Someone in a Tree," a *Rashomon*-in-miniature in which an event is recalled by contrasting viewpoints. (Sondheim has stated that he feels "Someone in a Tree" is the finest song he has ever written.) *Pacific Overtures* is not overabundant with riches. It is smaller, more simple and more direct than any previous work of his. He has never written better words.

While many considered *Sweeney Todd, the Demon Barber of Fleet Street* (1979) closer to opera than musical theatre, the creative team (Hugh Wheeler wrote the book based on Christopher Bond's play and Harold Prince directed) saw it as a melodrama with continuous musical underscoring. Although originally produced on a grand opera scale, *Sweeney Todd* was unquestionably theatre. The penny-dreadful tale of the barber/murderer in industrial England had its roots in Victorian melodrama. Because music was used to create tension throughout the play it did not sound like any other musical. The words in opera are always of secondary importance, but the lyrics in *Sweeney Todd* are literate, sometimes brutal, often engaging. Using some of the ideas of subtext that he experimented with in *Follies*, Sondheim more successfully incorporates them into *Sweeney Todd*. "Pretty Women" is musically and lyrically tender and soothing but the subtext is one of revenge; on any note Todd may slit the judge's throat. Mrs. Lovett delivers the affectionate "Not While I'm Around" as she plots the murder of the young lad to whom she is singing. The haunting "Johanna," sung with much the same passionate abandon as *West Side Story*'s "Maria," forebodes danger instead of romance. The comic numbers in *Sweeney Todd* are indeed funny but they sometimes heighten the tension instead of relieving it. "Worst Pies in London" is as crude as it is enjoyable. "By the Sea" is a quaint and silly music hall number that is also very pathetic. And the hilarious "A Little Priest" is a brilliantly sustained sick joke. *Sweeney Todd*'s score is probably Sondheim's most paradoxical: chilling and warm, sophisticated and crude, rhapsodic and deadly.

Merrily We Roll Along (1981) reunited the team that put together *Company* (book by George Furth, Prince again the director) but would result in a brief Broadway run (sixteen performances) and vitriolic reviews. The libretto, about three struggling artists, started at the end of the story and then worked backward to the characters' idealistic beginnings. Both book and direction were miscalculated blunders, but the score was one of Sondheim's most emotional. Listening to *Merrily We Roll Along* divorced from the irritating characters and story is a more satisfying theatrical experience than seeing many musicals when staged. The progression (in this case, backwards) is overwhelming. It's like watching the disillusioned characters in *Company* and then exploring all the things that made them that way. The ironic title song, juxtaposed with the optimistic and cliché-ridden graduation anthem ("The Hills of Tomorrow"), grows more potent as the score progresses. It climaxes with the three characters on a rooftop watching for *Sputnik* and the arrival of a new age. They sing "Our Time," perhaps the most optimistic lyric Sondheim has ever written:

Something is stirring,
Shifting ground . . .
It's just begun.
Edges are blurring
All around
And yesterday is done . . .

It's our time, breathe it in:
Worlds to change and worlds to win.
Our turn coming through,
Me and you, pal,
Me and you!

Years from now,
We'll remember and we'll come back,
Buy the rooftop and hang a plaque:
"This is where we began,
Being what we can."

It is a song sung by the young unaware of the future. Coming near the end of the show as it does, it is both joyous and sobering. The score for *Merrily We Roll Along* has many other lyric highpoints: a nervous breakdown on a talk show ("Franklin Shepard, Inc."), two lovely Hit Parade–type ballads ("Good Thing Going" and "Not a Day Goes By"), a musical March of Time song showing the burgeoning careers of three artists ("Opening Doors") and a sparkling finale for the first act with the whole cast offering advice to the newly-divorced hero ("Now You Know"). *Merrily We Roll Along* has been revived and revised a few times since its short Broadway run in the effort to solve the book problems; this score is too good to be denied a wider audience.

With *Sunday in the Park With George*, Sondheim started working with a different team, most noticeably playwright James Lapine, who wrote (and directed) this show and the subsequent *Into the Woods*. In many ways Lapine opened up new avenues for Sondheim and gave him even more nontraditional ideas to build on. Lapine is an exceptional idea man. It is unfortunate that he's not a better writer. *Sunday in the Park With George* must be the first Broadway musical based on a painting (Georges Seurat's *Dimanche L'Après-Midi a' L'Ile de la Grande Jatte*), but Lapine and Sondheim make the premise work for the most part; they have lots of good ideas. But Lapine's posterboard characters and lead-footed dialogue cannot carry out those ideas, whereas Sondheim's lyrics raise the ideas to thrilling heights. Within each musical number the show comes to life and the painting breathes. The words are as theatrically poetic as Sondheim has ever written. In "Color and Light," Seurat's mistress Dot ruminates to herself:

If I could concentrate—
I'd be in the Follies.
I'd be in a cabaret.
Gentlemen in tall silk hats
And linen spats
Would wait with flowers.
I could make them wait for hours.
Giddy young aristocrats
With fancy flats,
Who'd drink my health
And I would be
As hard as nails . . .
And they'd only want me more . . .
If I was a Folly girl.
Nah, I wouldn't like it much.
Married men and stupid boys
And too much smoke and all that noise
And all that color and light . . .

Later, artist George reveals his own thought process in the soliloquy "Finishing the Hat":

Mapping out a sky,
What you feel like, planning a sky,
What you feel when voices that come
Through the window
Go
Until they distance and die,
Until there's nothing but sky . . .

　　　• • •

But the woman who won't wait for you knows
That, however you live,
There's a part of you standing by,
Mapping out the sky,
Finishing a hat . . .
Starting on a hat . . .
Finishing a hat . . .
Look, I made a hat . . .
Where there never was a hat. . . .

In the second act the setting is contemporary but the lyrics do not lose any of their poetic quality. The aged Marie, supposedly Dot's daughter, sings the touching "Children and Art," which brings the whole play into focus. The modern artist George sardonically comments on the difficulties facing contemporary artists in "Putting It Together," a lyric that uses a variation on the music from the earlier "Finishing the Hat." The whole score forms an intricate tapestry quite unlike Sondheim's previous work.

Into the Woods (1987) is not nearly as accomplished, although the musical proved to be very popular. If the characters in *Sunday in the Park With George* were constructed out of posterboard, the ones in *Into the Woods* were made of crepe paper. Under the guise of a fairy tale, characters follow traditional one-dimensional paths in Act One. In Act Two they attempt to become more complex, even profound, but the writing is still one dimensional. If vibrant ideas keep *Sunday in the Park With George* alive, it is the lack of coherent ideas that deaden much of *Into the Woods*. Sondheim's score is partially to blame. He never captures a workable tone in his music or lyrics for *Into the Woods*: sometimes cheery and simpleminded ("Ever After," "So Happy" and the title song), sometimes satirical ("Hello, Little Girl" and "Agony"), and sometimes maudlin ("Moments in the Woods" and "No One Is Alone"). "It Takes Two" is one of those cute duets that you never thought you had to endure in a Sondheim show. "Your Fault" manages to be irritating (on purpose) but to no dramatic effect. The lyrics throughout are rhyme crazy but they don't have the playful self-mockery, as in *Forum*, that an audience can enjoy. How is one to take the silly lyrics ("there are bugs on her dugs") referring to a cow that we are expected later to lament in "I Guess This Is Goodbye"?

As in any Sondheim score there still are moments that soar. In *Into the Woods* those moments come at odd intervals and usually involve minor characters. Little Red Riding Hood has such a treat in "I Know Things Now," her commentary on life after having escaped death. She has experienced exciting danger as well as practical safety and concludes that there is something to be said for inexperience. Jack (of Beanstock fame) has a marvelous song, "Giants in the Sky," in which he realizes "just how small you are." Other admirable lyrics can be found in Cinderella's wistful "On the Steps of the Palace," and the finale, "Children Will Listen," is very moving despite that one is not convinced that these characters have such a depth of thought. *Into the Woods* is a disappointment in light of Sondheim's previous work but reveals a talent still at its sharpest. Future musicals—and Sondheim's new works are the most eagerly awaited in the business—will probably prove just as skillful. Sondheim's high level of craftsmanship is one of the few constants in the fluctuating world of Broadway.

More has been written about Stephen Sondheim than any other contemporary theatre songwriter and Sondheim has written or spoken about the art of lyricwriting more than most in the field. Yet with all that has been said about him or by him, Sondheim is still a puzzle for many. He is impossible to categorize for there is no clearly recognizable pattern to be found in his choice of subject matter, theme, characters or even style. Critics sometimes describe a lyric or a lyricist as being Sondheim-like but what is that? One writer's work may remind one of the acerbic *Company* lyrics; another recalls the adult romanticism of *A Little Night Music*. *Sweeney Todd* is dark, *Gypsy* is brassy, *Forum* is lighthearted. Who is to say which is the most Sondheim-like? Among the ongoing clichés regarding Sondheim is the conception that all his works are deeply pessimistic. Obviously he doesn't embrace the optimism of Ira Gershwin or Jerry Herman, but even seemingly bleak musicals such as *Company*,

West Side Story and *Anyone Can Whistle* have very life-affirming aspects to them. "You can't just tell the sunny side and have a story with any richness in it," Sondheim has said.[3] This interest in richness and ideas with some depth and texture, rather than pessimism, better characterizes Sondheim's approach.

The librettos for the Sondheim musicals offer little help in establishing a pattern in his work. Unlike Hammerstein or Lerner, who always wrote their own librettos, Sondheim has relied on librettists with talents as diverse as Larry Gelbart and James Goldman. The ideas for most of the Sondheim shows originated with someone else; Sondheim would become interested in the project and then create a fresh body of work inspired by the new premise. Because each premise had to be unusual enough to attract Sondheim, the resulting scores are as different as they are unique. No noticeable formula or model is used; style itself is dictated by the new project. Sondheim has written in the traditional mode (*Gypsy*), the thirties-style musical farce (*Forum*), the operatic style (*West Side Story*), the contemporary Frank Loesser approach (*Merrily We Roll Along*), romantic operetta (*A Little Night Music*), the Brecht/Weill music drama (*Sweeney Todd*), as well as models not yet clearly defined (*Anyone Can Whistle*, *Sunday in the Park With George*). The only consistency to be found from musical to musical is a deliberate inconsistency. It is easier to say what Sondheim is not: predictable, trendy and, alas, commercial. As Martin Gottfried describes Sondheim, "he seems incapable of the safe or conventional."[4]

Being a continual experimenter, Sondheim has had (and will continue to have) more than his fair share of failures. Each new project is a risk of several sorts: financial, popular and creative. Yet Sondheim's near-misses are bolder and more fascinating than other songwriters' successes. Gottfried again: "He might well be discouraged by the greater success of lesser shows than his or by the failure of mass audiences to respond to his major efforts."[5] Discouraged or not, Sondheim refuses to compromise. In his lyric work in particular, he remains steadfastly true to the concept being explored. The reversed plotting of *Merrily We Roll Along*, for example, has insurmountable problems but Sondheim does not abandon it for a safer, more traditional solution. Such a commitment has resulted in some glorious scores but few hit songs. Sondheim is so deeply involved with the project's characters and theme that he cannot (or will not) generalize his words so that they can travel elsewhere. Even the hugely popular "Send in the Clowns" doesn't make complete sense once removed from the play's context. (When Barbra Streisand recorded the song in 1985, Sondheim gladly honored her request that he rewrite a few lines to make the lyric more self-sufficient.)

Sondheim's use of lyrics to develop character has been justly praised. He may not be a librettist, but in his character lyrics he is a masterful playwright. He is at his peak writing lyric subtext and in revealing both the public and private personas of his characters. We can see the lies in "In Buddy's Eyes," the self-deception in "A Bowler Hat," the conniving in "Not While I'm Around" and the internal disintegration in "Rose's Turn." The soft-spoken misery in "Every Day a Little Death," "Anyone Can Whistle" or "Little Lamb" reveals deeper emotions than a more overt lyric could. Sondheim's characters are rarely one dimensional even if they are uneducated, simpleminded or exaggerated. The naive immigrant Maria in *West Side Story*, the half-witted Toby in *Sweeney Todd* and the abrasive Joanne in *Company* are all deeply felt portraits. Sondheim has admitted his fascination with "neurotic people, troubled people, people with conflicts."[6] But his lyrics are neurotic or troubled only when the character dictates such.

A common criticism of (and often a praise for) Sondheim's scores is that they cannot be appreciated on one hearing. The complexity of the music aside, the lyrics are more elaborately constructed than most, but they are written to be grasped in a theatre, not from repeated listening of a cast recording. Because Sondheim often bombards his audience with several images and ideas at once, many are bewildered by Sondheim lyrics. But the crucial information and the predominant character of the song are always readily available on a first hearing. The seemingly chaotic title song that opens *Company*, for example, explodes with vocal activity as all the couples contribute their ideas at once. But catching only small portions of their lyrics is more than enough for the audience to size up the situation and be introduced to the characters. And the whole sequence is much more effective than a straightforward choral number that states the information in unison. Because Sondheim rarely reprises his songs within a score, the audience does not get the spoon-fed kind of reinforcement that some other songwriters provide. Berlin and Rodgers were experts in marketing their songs through reprises. Sondheim shuns reprises unless the repetition is plot effective, as in his use of "May We/Let Me Entertain You" in *Gypsy* and the title songs in *Merrily We Roll Along* and *Sweeney Todd*. The Sondheim musicals demand more from the audience, but they demand nothing that is not within reason. This adult approach to an audience forces the musical theatre to grow. What Sondheim asks is no more impossible than what Hammerstein asked in *Show Boat*. Audiences have a history of surprising one; Sondheim likes to provide opportunities for such surprises.

Sondheim has been called a cult artist, appealing to a select few. There may be more to this in theory than in reality. The select few has grown in number over the years. Anticipation of a new Sondheim musical may not translate into commercial success (despite a great deal of interest, *Merrily We Roll Along* closed after sixteen performances), but it does guarantee a great deal of creative speculation and artistic stimulation. And Sondheim has become the standard by which the business judges new talent, especially in the craft of lyricwriting. The highest praise critics could heap on William Finn's score for *March of the Falsettos* was to call it Sondheim-like. But the general theatre-going public still has trouble with the Sondheim musicals. As late as 1985 Sondheim believed "I'm still essentially a cult figure. My kind of work is caviar to the general public. It's not that it's too good for people, it's just that it's too unexpected."[7]

The effect Sondheim has had on the modern Broadway musical is inestimable. Without ever having come up with a megahit, he has influenced everyone in the business. Even those who dislike him and yearn for a more traditional musical theatre have been altered by him. Today the most derivative boy-meets-girl musical has some small Sondheim touches in it. And the influence has spread past the footlights. The Sondheim musicals have taught audiences to expect more (even when they don't want more). Many hesitate to rank Sondheim with Cole Porter or Lorenz Hart. With them one knew where one stood; with Sondheim it's always a surprise—pleasant or unpleasant. Comparisons with the past are futile with Sondheim. He is an artist set firmly in the present and looking to the future. He is the best contemporary theatre songwriter because, with Stephen Sondheim, it's always "Something's Coming."

NOTES

1. Martin Gottfried, *Broadway Musicals* (New York: Harry N. Abrams, Inc., 1980), p. 319.

2. Craig Zadan, *Sondheim and Co.* (New York: Harper and Row, 1986), p. 142.

3. Al Kasha and Joel Hirschorn, *Notes on Broadway: Conversations with the Great Songwriters* (Chicago: Contemporary Books, 1985), p. 335.

4. Gottfried, p. 327.

5. Ibid.

6. Kasha, p. 335.

7. Otis L. Guernsey (ed.), *Broadway Song and Story: Playwrights, Lyricists, Composers Discuss Their Hits* (New York: Dodd, Mead and Co., 1985), p. 228.

16

Tradition: Sheldon Harnick

If Stephen Sondheim's writing represents the exciting new directions musical theatre took when it departed from the Hammerstein model, Sheldon Harnick's work is the best example of the quieter, more fragile kind of musical that adhered more closely to the Master. This is not to say that Harnick's work is unexcitedly conventional or old fashioned. Like Hammerstein, he is continually experimenting in a studious and cautious manner. Harnick gets less attention than most major songwriters since his Broadway shows are not flashy or controversial. Even *Fiddler on the Roof*, which contains Harnick's most famous lyrics, is a quiet musical. It is, in fact, one of the few quiet musicals to become a megahit. Harnick's continual search for humor and dignity in the ordinariness of human behavior is what motivates all of his writing. Lyrically, Sheldon Harnick is the truest descendant of Oscar Hammerstein: steeped in tradition and yet subtly breaking rules to achieve self-expression.

Harnick was born in Chicago in 1924. Circumstances pointed to a career as a composer/lyricist: violin lessons as a child, verse writing at school, songs composed for USO shows while in the Army, undergraduate musicals while a student at Northwestern, and work as a professional violinist for Chicago dance orchestras. He decided in 1950 to pursue a musical theatre career and moved to New York. Within two years Harnick had a few songs and sketches on Broadway in *New Faces of 1952*. He wrote both music and lyrics, as was always his intention, and one of his songs, "The Boston Beguine," was sung by "new face" Alice Ghostley and gained some attention. "The Boston Beguine" shows the influence of E. Y. Harburg, Harnick's idol and the reason he wanted to write lyrics. The naive singer searches for romance in Boston, "the home of the bean," where the "books we should have read" all have been banned. The Harburg social viewpoint and comic style can be seen in much of Harnick's early work. In the revue *John Murray Anderson's Almanac* (1953) Orson Bean sang Harnick's "The Merry Minuet," another socially conscious song about the cruelties of nature being outweighed by the threat of the atomic bomb. As in Harburg's work, the lyrics are sharp and knowing.

He finally got to meet Yip Harburg but the encounter devastated Harnick. Harburg told him to stick to lyricwriting and to find a good composer to collaborate with. Once resigned to the fact that Harburg's advice was solid, Harnick teamed up with Jerry Bock when actor Jack Cassidy introduced them in 1956. Bock had some viable experience on Broadway, having just written the music for the Sammy Davis, Jr., vehicle *Mr. Wonderful* (1956). Bock and Harnick's first collaboration together was *The Body Beautiful* (1958), a musical about boxing. It was not an exceptional score and Harnick later admitted that the subject matter was so foreign to him that he could find little to identify with. But there are three memorable songs in *The Body Beautiful*: "All of These and More" is a very romantic duet; "Summer Is" became a popular audition song; and "Gloria" is an amusing love song with the lover not quite sure Gloria is the one for him. George Abbott was impressed enough with Bock and Harnick's work in *The Body Beautiful* to recommend them to Harold Prince, who was producing a musical about New York mayor Fiorello LaGuardia. Prince asked the team to write a few songs on spec and when they presented the first one, "Politics and Poker," Prince immediately hired them. *Fiorello!* (1959) would secure Bock and Harnick's careers, running for 795 performances and winning the Pulitzer Prize. Like the previous Pulitzer musical *Of Thee I Sing* (1931), *Fiorello!* was a satirical look at American politics. George Abbott and Jerome Weidman's libretto presented a very warm and human LaGuardia but a shrewd view of New York City corruption. The musical's two best songs concern the political system rather than the mayor himself. "Politics and Poker" is a dandy waltz set to the pattern of a poker game where the politicians consider possible candidates. "Little Tin Box" is a delightful softshoe with corrupt city officials displaying shocked innocence when asked to explain their large incomes. These two numbers, as well as the comic "The Bum Won" and the slick "Gentleman Jimmy," show the continuing influence Harburg had on Harnick's lyrics. Other songs in *Fiorello!* point to the more Hammerstein-like direction he would eventually take: the touching "When Did I Fall in Love?" and the lilting "Till Tomorrow."

The same production team was reunited the next year for *Tenderloin* (1960). Abbott and Weidman's book this time was about a minister in the 1880s who tried to clean up the corrupt Tenderloin district of New York City. Although quite different in intent than *Fiorello!*, *Tenderloin* suffered from comparisons and lasted only 216 performances. But there was much to recommend in *Tenderloin*: Abbott's brash direction, Cecil Beaton's outstanding sets and costumes, and a score that almost rivaled that for *Fiorello! Tenderloin*'s opening, a juxtaposition of the religious choir's "Bless This Land" with the prostitutes' "Little Old New York (Is Plenty Good Enough for Me)," is a sensational number that sets the tone for the whole play. "Artificial Flowers" is a sentimental turn-of-the-century ballad that, in the show's context, is rather wry and mocking. "The Picture of Happiness" merrily celebrates the joys of vice, while "Good Clean Fun" is the minister's naive tribute to the good old days of "wienie roasts and treasure hunts." "My Gentle Young Johnny" is a pleasing ballad and the first of many wistful, heartfelt songs of yearning that the team would write throughout the decade. *Tenderloin* was defeated by its libretto, but it was another impressive performance by Bock and Harnick.

Harold Prince hired Bock and Harnick for the third time for *She Loves Me* (1963), a romantic musical about the employees of a European *parfumerie* in the 1930s. The story was far from an original one, being based on a Hungarian play and having been filmed twice. Joe Masteroff, in his Broadway writing debut, devised a delicately humorous libretto, and Bock and Harnick provided what is arguably their finest score. With its dozens of distinct musical numbers and its recurring motifs, *She Loves Me* is a beautifully sustained musical valentine. The score is filled with traditional theatre songs but they are surrounded by musical conversations and soliloquies. The result is highly melodic but very restrained and intelligent. Some have referred to *She Loves Me* as chamber opera, but it is traditional musical comedy with a softer touch. The recurring "Dear Friend" is a beguiling solo that musicalizes the heroine's letters to her beloved even as it reveals her own subtextual fears. "Tonight at Eight" is an exuberant song of anticipation that aches with realistic detail. "Will He

Like Me?" is a ballad filled with hope and pain. "A Trip to the Library" is a delightful comic narrative, and "I Resolve" is an entertaining character song. The ensemble numbers ("Good Morning, Good Day," "Twelve Days to Christmas" and "Goodbye, Georg") are unique in that they develop the individual characters rather than summarize a group reaction. And perhaps the most captivating song in this extraordinary score is "Ice Cream," a lyrical stream-of-consciousness number that once heard cannot be forgotten. Despite a lovely production directed by Prince, a marvelous cast, and generally favorable reviews, *She Loves Me* had limited appeal and only lasted 301 performances. The early sixties was no time for a gentle, atmospheric musical with no stars and no hit songs. (The title song did enjoy some popularity later when jazzed up by various pop singers.) *She Loves Me* is one of the most affectionately remembered of all cult musicals. Harnick's lyrics have never been better.

Fiddler on the Roof (1964) is Bock and Harnick's most popular musical and in many ways their most characteristic. It deals with issues that bring out the Hammerstein integrity in Harnick's words: the plight of a simple people who are eternally optimistic, the importance of the social unit (be it a family, a village or a common faith), and the power of tradition versus the strength needed to accept change. In *Fiddler on the Roof* all these themes take the guise of a deceptively conventional musical. Yet, like the most important works in the history of the American musical, *Fiddler on the Roof* is very daring. It shuns all the necessary ingredients for success: anti-romantic in its approach, uncommercial in its development, and modest in its scope. No one was more surprised than its creators when the musical became an international phenomenon. Joseph Stein's book, Bock and Harnick's score and Jerome Robbins' direction sought to create an ethnic musical that could be appreciated by a wider audience; they inadvertently touched everyone. Harnick's lyrics for *Fiddler on the Roof* are more homespun than those for *She Loves Me*. The parfumerie employees work in a thriving city and have some sophistication, but the villagers of Anatevka are distinguished only by their folklore sense of humor and resounding pride and dignity. When they dream ("If I Were a Rich Man" and "Matchmaker, Matchmaker") their imagery is lofty but uncomplicated. When they rejoice ("To Life" and "Wonder of Wonders") the celebration is unrestrained and never self-conscious. Sometimes sadness is mixed with joy, as in "Sunrise, Sunset" and "Far from the Home I Love." In "Do You Love Me?" the characters are uncomfortable with abstract ideas; the humor comes from practical people trying to express the impractical notion of love. The two most innovative numbers in *Fiddler on the Roof* are "Tradition" and "Tevye's Dream." While both were showcases for Jerome Robbins' imaginative staging, the lyric work in each scene is exceptional. "Tradition" breaks tradition by asking the audience to accept the village as the central character. The metaphor of the fiddler sets up the musical's unpretentious environment. Just as *Tenderloin* opens with contrasting choruses to convey the dissention in the story, *Fiddler on the Roof*'s opening conveys the balance and harmony within the village. "Tevye's Dream" is one of the musical theatre's most effective expressionistic sequences. Harnick's lyrics retain the folklore charm but there is a touch of mysticism present. Both numbers utilize Stein's dialogue throughout and the result is a powerful blending of words, music and dance.

The team's next project, *The Apple Tree* (1966), was an obvious attempt to do something not at all like *Fiddler on the Roof*. In that, they succeeded; but *The Apple Tree* did not. Writing the libretto as well as the score, Bock and Harnick adapted three very different stories into musical form: Mark Twain's "The Diary of Adam and Eve," Frank R. Stockton's "The Lady or the Tiger?" and Jules Feiffer's "Passionella." They tried to connect the three one-act musicals in subtle ways, but the links were superficial at best. *The Apple Tree* ended up being three pleasant enough little musicals that added up to one big unsatisfying musical. The Adam and Eve tale works the best and has some memorable lyrics. Much of the score for the Stockton story was anachronistic and in a mock heroic style; it was something other songwriting teams did much better. "Passionella" was the most farcical of the stories and the songs strove for a psuedo-rock/folk tone. But parody was not what Bock and Harnick were all about.

The Rothschilds (1970) once again displayed the sensitivity and humor that distinguished the team's talents. The libretto by Sherman Yellen tells the saga of the Rothschild family from its humble beginnings to its days of power and influence. Yellen kept the story on a personal level and the family unit was again central to the musical. Because the Rothschild clan was Jewish, the inevitable comparisons with *Fiddler on the Roof* arose. But *The Rothschilds* has its own admirable qualities. Harnick develops another extended musical sequence in "Sons," a number that illustrates the passing years and the education of the Rothschild sons. "One Room" contains all the simplicity and warmth seen in the best Bock and Harnick shows. "Give England Strength" is an effective hymn. There is a definite

Gilbert and Sullivan feel to some of the musical's songs, particularly "Have You Ever Seen a Prettier Little Congress?" But other songs are weak and disjointed. "I'm in Love, I'm in Love" is forced, "He Tossed a Coin" is too cute to be comfortable and "In My Own Lifetime," *The Rothschilds'* version of "The Impossible Dream," has a pretentiousness that doesn't sit well.

The Rothschilds did not have a smooth preparation period. Bock and Harnick fought with each other over various issues (particularly the re-placing of the director) and parts of it seem to reflect the lack of harmony between composer and lyricist. Regardless, *The Rothschilds* was to be Bock and Harnick's last collaboration. Bock has since worked with other lyricists, but none of the results has received major productions. Bock and Harnick still speak admiringly of each other in interviews but have never discussed publicly the reasons why their collaboration ended. As late as 1985 Harnick was quoted as saying he would like to work with Bock again someday.[1] It may happen, but with each passing year it becomes more evident that the breakup of Bock and Harnick was an unfortunate setback for our musical theatre.

Harnick's career since *The Rothschilds* has been more active than Bock's but not overwhelmingly successful. In 1976 Harnick provided the lyrics for Richard Rodgers' *Rex*, a musical about Henry VIII of England. Sherman Yellen's libretto managed to turn an overly familiar story into uneventful history. Rodgers was very ill during the production's preparation and his stroke made it difficult for him to communicate. But he and Harnick came up with a score that is occasionally noteworthy. "No Song More Pleasing" and "Away from You" are moving ballads in the Rodgers and Hammerstein mold, and "Christmas at Hampton Court" shows some vitality. *Rex* closed after forty-nine performances, the biggest flop for Rodgers in fifty years and the briefest run of Harnick's Broad-way career.

Most of Harnick's projects after *Rex* have been translations and adapta-tions of operatic works. Most notable were the English lyrics he provided for Jacques Demy's words in the Off-Broadway production of Michel Legrand's *The Umbrellas of Cherbourg* (1979), and the new translation for Peter Brook's controversial *Carmen* (1983). Harnick's theatre works since have been showcased at workshops and colleges but have not made it back to Broadway. The opera world has proven more receptive (he wrote the libretto for Jack Beeson's *Captain Jinks of the Horse Marines* and a new version of Lehar's *The Merry Widow*), and it is Broadway's loss. What would have happened had Oscar Hammerstein left the musical theatre in 1943 after the success of his *Carmen Jones*?

Sheldon Harnick is perhaps the gentlest of all American theatre lyricists. He is gentle in his lyric phrasing, gentle in his imagery and gentle in his treatment of character. He finds excitement in all three of these but it is not the loud, spotlighted kind of excitement that Broadway often applauds. Harnick can be considered an optimist because of the very loving and forgiving subtext in all his work. But this is no pie-eyed optimism that reduces life to song and dance. Harnick's lyrics are rich with details that are painful and uncompromising. Like the finest lyricists, Harnick writes for the character above all else. His gentleness in this area is remarkable. We may laugh at the character's foolishness or indecision or self-deception but our laughter is one of recognition, not derision. The comedy is never at the expense of the character. Tevye's dreams in "If I Were a Rich Man" are sometimes ridiculous but we understand them. The imagined staircases—one for going up, another (even longer) for going down and a third "just for show"—reveal his naivete but secure our affection for him. The lyrics can be gentle because the characters Harnick chooses to lyricize are often gentle themselves. There are few villains in the Harnick musicals and when they do exist they are rarely abrasive. The corrupt officials in *Fiorello!*, the criminal element in *Tenderloin*, and the Russian Gentiles in *Fiddler on the Roof* are viewed with compassion, humor and tolerance. Like Hammerstein, Harnick sees the power to understand as the redeeming factor in people. Because he is writing for a Broadway more hardened than Hammerstein's postwar theatre, Harnick must avoid overt sentimentality. But at heart he is as guileless as the Master.

Also outstanding in Harnick's craftsmanship is the ability to blend opposing emotions in one song. In an almost Chekhovian manner, he sees tragedy and comedy coexisting in a lyric. The comedy may be self-deprecating or even bitter but it gives the character the strength to survive. Marie in *Fiorello!* is wounded in love so she vows to marry "The Very Next Man" who asks her. The silliness of her notion is offset by the frustration that is behind it. We laugh at her but her dignity is maintained. *Fiddler on the Roof* is filled with conflicting emotions in its songs, particularly in the already mentioned "Sunrise, Sunset" and "Far from the Home I Love." "Matchmaker, Matchmaker" is sometimes performed as a light frolic but it is also filled with dread and uncertainty. "Anatevka" fluctuates between pride and despair. In the hands of many songwriters these tender moments could become vulgar or self-indulgent; only a writer of Harnick's sensibility could make such fragile emotions real. One would be hard pressed to find a brassy, expansive song in Harnick's repertoire. Yet one would have more difficulty finding one that is dull or lifeless. That is the special talent of Sheldon Harnick. He finds excitement in the ordinary. In a theatre too often impressed with glorious noise, Harnick speaks in a whisper.

NOTE

1. Al Kasha and Joel Hirschorn, *Notes on Broadway: Conversations with the Great Songwriters* (Chicago: Contemporary Books, 1985), p. 169.

17

Also in the
1940s and 1950s

Lyricist Johnny Mercer spent most of his working days in Hollywood writing notable film scores and turning out a steady stream of song hits. But he returned to Broadway on occasion and the result was often noteworthy. Mercer's stage musicals suffered from weak librettos, bad timing and ill luck. Considering how successful he was in Hollywood, it is surprising he returned to the theatre as often as he did. In addition to his four Oscar-winning songs—"In the Cool, Cool, Cool of the Evening," "On the Atchison, Topeka and the Santa Fe," "Moon River" and "The Days of Wine and Roses"—Mercer provided lyrics for such film musicals as *You Were Never Lovelier*, *Blues in the Night*, *The Fleet's In*, *Star Spangled Rhythm*, *The Harvey Girls*, *Daddy Long Legs* and *Seven Brides for Seven Brothers*. Among his song hits are "That Old Black Magic," "Laura," "Jeepers Creepers," "Too Marvelous for Words," "I'm Old Fashioned," "Accentuate the Positive," "Satin Doll," "You Must Have Been a Beautiful Baby" and many others; but none of these was written for the theatre. Johnny Mercer represents the kind of popular songwriter who during the early decades of the century would have been on Broadway all the time. But the movies and the economics of Broadway saw to it that he went elsewhere.

John H. Mercer was born in Savannah, Georgia. As a child he loved the songs of Victor Herbert, Irving Berlin and Jerome Kern and he wanted to be a singer. He worked his way to New York, where his first jobs were as an actor and band vocalist. Some singing assignments led to lyricwriting and by 1930 his songs were heard in a number of Broadway revues. But Hollywood called and Mercer didn't return to Broadway until 1946 with *St. Louis Woman*. His collaborator was Harold Arlen and their score is one of the musical theatre's best. *St. Louis Woman* was a melodramatic tale of love and jealousy among a group of black characters in turn-of-the-century St. Louis, and much of the show sank under the weight of its ponderous book. But the score contains Mercer's finest lyric work for the theatre and reveals heartbreaking insight into character as well as poetic use of the vernacular. The duet "Come Rain or Come Shine" is joyously expansive. "Legalize My Name" is a comic plea for matrimony ("City Hall me!") that is sassy and forthright ("you've had all the samples that you gonna get"). "I Had Myself a True Love" is a powerful torch song with domestic imagery and straightforward phrasing. Other memorable songs from *St. Louis Woman* include "Sleep Peaceful, Mr. Used-to-Be," "Ridin' on the Moon," "A Woman's Prerogative (To Change Her Mind)" and "Any Place I Hang My Hat Is Home," a brilliant song of wandering loneliness with the haunting phrase "Howdy stranger, so long friend." This was definitely not a score written by a Hollywood hit peddler. Mercer was back on Broadway with *Texas, Li'l Darlin'* (1949), with music by Robert Emmett Dolan, and *Top Banana* (1951), in which Mercer composed his own melodies for his lyrics even though he could not read music. Mercer's only Broadway hit was *Li'l Abner* (1956), with music by Gene dePaul and a lively libretto based on the popular Al Capp comic strip characters. The whole musical is rather one dimensional but some of Mercer's lyrics are engaging. "The Country's in the Very Best of Hands" is a rousing celebration of nothing, a tribute to the razzle-dazzle of political doubletalk. "I'm Past My Prime" is an entertaining character song and "If I Had My Druthers" is a lazy, random number. "Jubilation T. Cornpone" is a snappy ensemble piece and "Namely You" an agreeable duet. *Li'l Abner* is not an exceptional musical by any means but it again illustrates Mercer's talent for regionalisms.

 Saratoga (1959) was Mercer's most ambitious theatre project. Edna Ferber's novel *Saratoga Trunk* told the epic story of a Creole in 1880s New Orleans and later Saratoga, New York. Putting such a series of events on the musical stage might have resulted in another *Show Boat*, but Morton DaCosta's libretto for *Saratoga* was melodrama without stature. The Arlen/Mercer score has two notable songs: the pragmatic "Game of

Poker," about the hit-or-miss qualities of love, and "Love Held Lightly," a tender ballad. Mercer's last Broadway effort, *Foxy* (1964), was also Bert Lahr's last stage appearance; it was not a fitting finale for either man. One of the surprising aspects of Johnny Mercer's remarkable career is the variety and versatility one finds in his work. Did the man who wrote "Jeepers Creepers" really write "Come Rain or Come Shine"? Hollywood demanded hit songs on a variety of subjects and he delivered. When Broadway asked for rich, evocative character songs he also delivered. His Broadway work often found pain and poetry in simple emotions. Mercer may have become one of the musical theatre's most influential lyricists.

Three lyricists who aptly represent the sheer vitality of the musicals of the 1950s are Richard Adler and Jerry Ross, who wrote together, and Carolyn Leigh, who wrote with composer Cy Coleman and others. These three songwriters rarely came up with words of great subtlety or inspired tenderness; but they did write some of the most energetic and rousing lyrics of the period. Their songs seem to shout "hey, there—look at us!" Whether it's a love song, a complaining lyric, an optimistic credo, or a character's self-revelation—they all seem to proclaim their emotions with brassy pride and confidence. The most unusual aspect of the team of Adler and Ross is that both wrote the music and the lyrics. This rather odd arrangement might create some awkwardness (how do two people compose one melody?) but these "two young Loessers," as Leonard Bernstein called them, flourished under the unusual arrangement.[1] Not only are the Adler-Ross songs vivacious and tuneful, they contain pleasant surprises along the way.

Richard Adler was born in New York in 1921 into a musical family and studied playwriting at the University of North Carolina. While working as a copywriter for an advertising firm, he started writing songs; but he did not seriously pursue a musical career until he met Jerry Ross in 1950. Ross was five years his junior but, in a way, a seasoned theatre veteran. Born into a poor Bronx family, Ross had been on the stage since childhood, acting in Yiddish theatre groups. He started writing songs while in his teens and later took a few music courses at New York University. Frank Loesser was impressed by Adler and Ross and published some of their early work. One song, "Rags to Riches," became fairly popular in 1953. That song, and others, caught the attention of producer John Murray Anderson, and he asked the young team to contribute to his new revue *John Murray Anderson's Almanac* (1953). When

Loesser decided not to do the score for the musical version of Richard Bissell's popular book *7 1/2 Cents*, he suggested Adler and Ross to the producers. With hardly any advance sales, *The Pajama Game* opened in 1954 and delighted audiences for two and a half years. The libretto by director George Abbott and Bissell was a fast-paced frolic about labor-management problems in a pajama factory. The musical steered clear of anything remotely controversial and concentrated on the love interests of the characters. The score was a dazzling display of youthful energy and abandon. The two hits of the show were the captivating tango "Hernando's Hideaway" and "Hey, There," a romantic solo that was really a duet with the hero singing along with his own voice on the dictaphone. "Think of the Time I Save" and "I'll Never Be Jealous Again" were the outstanding comedy numbers and "I'm Not at All in Love" was a playful waltz. "Steam Heat," remembered now for introducing Bob Fosse's distinct choreographic style, is a fascinating novelty number on its own. The whole score seems like a lively parade; what the songs lack in character or subtlety they make up for in irresistible fun.

Adler and Ross came back the next year with *Damn Yankees* (1955), a musical version of Douglas Wallop's book *The Year the Yankees Lost the Pennant*. The libretto, by Abbott and Wallop, was a clever mix of the baseball myth and the Faust legend. The songs for *Damn Yankees* are reminiscent of those for *The Pajama Game* but they still please. This time the tango is "Whatever Lola Wants" and Gwen Verdon, in her first starring role, made it seem new. The rousing hoedown number is "Shoeless Joe from Hannibal, Mo.," and the frantic "Who's Got the Pain?" recalls *The Pajama Game*'s "Racing with the Clock." "(You Gotta Have) Heart" is a barbershop quartet–like romp, the Devil (Ray Walston) gets a dandy softshoe in "Those Were the Good Old Days," and the team came up with a splendid duet in "Two Lost Souls." Most agreed that *Damn Yankees* wasn't quite as good as *The Pajama Game*; it was clear that Adler and Ross did not have the versatility of their mentor Frank Loesser. But audiences knew that future Adler-Ross shows would provide more delightful songs. Unfortunately, it was not to be. In 1955, shortly after *Damn Yankees* opened, Jerry Ross died of a lung ailment. He was twenty-nine years old.

Carolyn Leigh had only a handful of shows on Broadway but she had an extensive career writing popular songs in the early fifties. Her theatre lyrics have the same kind of bounce as those in Adler and Ross's shows, and Cy Coleman, her most frequent collaborator, writes music in a similar vein. Leigh's lyrics display moments of cleverness that are more sophisticated than Adler and Ross, but she shouts "hey!" in the same boisterous manner. She was born in the Bronx and attended Queens College and New York University. After graduation she wrote for radio programs and advertising companies. (The number of theatre lyricists who once wrote ad copy is quite high but it should not be surprising. Both occupations require a talent for brevity, succinctness and cleverness.) As the television field expanded, Leigh was hired to write scripts and lyrics for revamped operettas on NBC-TV. Cy Coleman and Leigh's first collaboration was the song "A Moment of Madness," which Sammy Davis, Jr., recorded. It met with some success and the team continued with several other songs, some of which became popular: "Witchcraft," "It Amazes Me," "Firefly" and "The Best Is Yet to Come." The most well known song by Leigh during this period was "Young at Heart", with music by Johnny Richards. Intended as a play with music, *Peter Pan* opened in California and toured the country prior to its New York opening. Leigh wrote a half dozen songs with composer Mark Charlap, including "I'm Flying," "I Won't Grow Up" and "I've Got to Crow." The producers then decided to turn the show into a full-scale musical and Jule Styne was hired to fill out the score. Styne brought his own lyricists with him (Comden and Green), so Leigh's Broadway debut with *Peter Pan* in 1954 was somewhat overshadowed by the more established songwriters. But her contribution (about half of the final score) is substantial, and her songs in the musical are as well remembered as those by Comden and Green. Leigh's first Broadway score with Coleman was *Wildcat* (1960). The show was a vehicle for television star Lucille Ball, and Coleman and Leigh wrote the score with her personality in mind. The score is occasionally fun. The roaring hoedown number, "What Takes My Fancy," was a high point of the evening, but the song that survived and became more popular later was "Hey, Look Me Over."

The best lyrics Leigh ever wrote were for *Little Me* (1962), another musical tailored to the talents of a television star: Sid Caesar. It was Neil Simon's idea to have his old TV boss play seven different roles of various ages and nationalities. Fictional heroine Belle Poitrine, from "the wrong side of the tracks," rises to fame and fortune and along the way encounters a succession of men, all played by Caesar. Simon recommended Coleman and Leigh, and their score complemented the libretto's daffy quality. Coleman's music is at its wittiest and Leigh's lyric work is superb. In all the Neil Simon–scripted musicals that followed, none would see book and lyrics match so succinctly as in this show. If Simon was a lyricist, the result would sound something like Leigh's work in *Little Me*. Two of the musical's breeziest songs, "I've Got Your Number" and "Real Live Girl," became popular outside of the show, though they lost much of their charm removed from the play's context. "The Truth" and "I Love You" have lyrics that are both smart and engaging. "Deep Down Inside" is another jubilant Coleman-Leigh number. "The Other Side of the Tracks" and the title song are incisive character numbers. There's even a Maurice Chevalier spoof, "Boom Boom," and a slap-happy "show biz" song called "Be a Performer."

After two Broadway scores and over twenty singles, Coleman and Leigh's collaboration ended. Coleman's career would continue with hit musicals written with lyricists such as Dorothy Fields, Michael Stewart, and Comden and Green. Leigh's subsequent career was not so successful. In 1967 she collaborated with movie composer Elmer Bernstein on the score for *How Now Dow Jones*, a foolish musical about big business and a couple who plan to wed once the Dow Jones average hits 1,000. "Step to the Rear" was a dazzling if empty crowd pleaser and proved to be an ideal song for political conventions. There is an effective duet, "They Don't Make 'Em Like That Anymore," and a flavorful song of self-revelation, "Just for the Moment." But most of the lyrics in *How Now Dow Jones* lack warmth or charm. What was once inspired fun was now loud and abrasive. What distinguishes the lyrics of Richard Adler, Jerry Ross and Carolyn Leigh is their stimulating celebration of optimism despite all odds. Wildcat Jackson sings that she's "fresh out of clover, mortgaged up to here." The image is filled with humor and resiliency. Comparisons with Cohan are not out of place. There is a cockiness in these lyrics that provokes joy. Instead of national or ethnic pride, there is a sense of self-preservation. No wonder these characters kept shouting "hey!" They were convinced that they were worth noticing; and they were noticed. But for too short a time.

In many ways composer/lyricist Bob Merrill has led a charmed life. Having been successful in so many different areas of show business, Merrill often struck gold with each new venture. He was born Henry Robert Merrill Lavan in Atlantic City and raised in Philadelphia. He first attempted an acting career but World War Two interrupted that, and Merrill found himself writing and producing radio shows for the armed forces. After the war he worked himself up from a CBS porter to the head of NBC's writers' department. When he was twenty-one Merrill went to

Hollywood to once again try acting but ended up as a dialogue coach at Columbia Pictures. While working on a western in Arizona he was asked to write some novelty songs. Unable to read music or play any instrument, Merrill wrote a few songs, plucking out the melodies on a toy xylophone. Writing tunes in this way he came up with a series of hit songs, including such memorable ditties as "Candy and Cake," "Belle, Belle, My Liberty Belle," "If I Knew You Were Comin' I'd've Baked a Cake" (with Al Hoffman and Clem Watts), "Honeycomb," "Mambo Italiano" and "How Much Is That Doggie in the Window?" Merrill returned to television in 1948, becoming a casting director at CBS, but what he really wanted to do was write for the musical theatre. He worked on a musical version of Eugene O'Neill's *Anna Christie* (1921), which interested George Abbott, who wrote a libretto. *New Girl in Town*, as it was titled, opened on Broadway in 1957 and ran for over a year. It is an uneven musical at best. Abbott's adaptation is intelligent and competent and Merrill's score is occasionally superb. But the uneasy mixture of buoyant musical comedy and O'Neill's unromantic point of view never quite worked. Gwen Verdon was outstanding as Anna, but audiences came to see the dancing Verdon of *Damn Yankees*, so what was intended as musical drama became a showcase for a musical comedy star. "It's Good to Be Alive" is an exceptional song of optimism that avoids sentimentality. "On the Farm" is almost Brechtian in its harsh, bitter humor. There are some robust dance numbers ("At the Check Apron Ball" and "Roll Yer Socks Up") and a wonderfully sarcastic song called "Flings" in which Thelma Ritter noted that "they got to be flung by the young." *New Girl in Town* is a flawed work and rarely revived but the score is ambitious and fertile; a surprisingly potent debut for the author of "How Much Is That Doggie in the Window?" Merrill's next Broadway effort was also based on an O'Neill play but a more likely source for a musical. *Take Me Along* (1959) was a breezy, joyous version of O'Neill's only comedy, *Ah! Wilderness* (1934). As with *New Girl in Town*, a star threw the musical off balance. Jackie Gleason's jubilant performance as Uncle Sid, a supporting character in the play, shifted much of the focus away from the central father-son relationship. It was to be expected, for the show's most exhilarating songs were sung by Sid: "Sid Ol' Kid," "I Get Embarrassed" and the title song. Merrill wrote an exemplary ballad, "Staying Young," for the father, and its revealing reprise later in the show was very affecting. There is clever lyric work about the wonders of sin in "Wint's Song," and "Little Green Snake" is an unusual serio-comic number about Sid's alcohol problem.

Carnival (1961) is perhaps Merrill's finest score. An imaginary world of make-believe, innocence and magic is deftly portrayed in music and lyrics that have a European feel about them. The libretto by Michael Stewart was based on the 1953 film musical *Lili* but Merrill wrote a new score for Broadway. The movie's "Hi Lili, Hi Lo" had been popular but Merrill countered with the equally simple and charming "Theme from *Carnival*," better known as "Love Makes the World Go Round." The tale of an orphan girl who joins a seedy traveling carnival and discovers love was hardly riveting material, but Gower Champion's inspired direction and Merrill's gently enticing score made *Carnival* appealing enough to run for 719 performances. The lyric work throughout is commendable. "Mira" is an effective character song that whispers rather than proclaims. "Sword, Rose and Cape" is a dashing number that playfully conjures up fairy tale images. "Humming" is a delightful comic song with expert lyric structure. "Always Always You" and "Her Face" are fine ballads, and the slowly building "Grand Imperial Cirque de Paris" is gripping. The score for *Carnival* is unusual in that it is subdued and yet turned into a big Broadway hit. By this time Merrill was thought of highly enough to be brought in to help others' shows so, when Jule Styne needed a lyricist for *Funny Girl* (1964), he called on Merrill. Writing lyrics for another man's music seemed to cause no difficulty for Merrill, for he wrote his most famous score and his most popular song, "People." That hit outshone the better ballads and various musical comedy songs in the show. "The Music That Makes Me Dance" is an exquisite torch song and a commendable substitute for the real Fanny Brice's "My Man." "His Love Makes Me Beautiful" is in the style of Berlin's Follies standard "A Pretty Girl Is Like A Melody," and "Rat Tat Tat" captures the Ziegfeld era. "Cornet Man" is a flavorful rag, and some of the comedy songs ("Sadie, Sadie" and "You Are Woman") are very ingenious. The big optimistic number, "Don't Rain on My Parade," is reminiscent of Styne and Sondheim's "Everything's Coming Up Roses" and pales in comparison. The character songs for the supporting players ("Find Yourself a Man" and "Who Taught Her Everything She Knows") are weak. It is a varied score and delivers when it must, but Merrill's lyric work is uneven.

The rest of Merrill's Broadway ventures were not successful. The legendary fiasco *Breakfast at Tiffany's* never opened in New York. *Henry, Sweet Henry* (1967), based on the book and movie *The World of Henry Orient*, was mildly charming. Alice Playton, in a minor role, stole the show with her two songs "Poor Little Person" and "Nobody Steps on

Kafritz." Throughout the score the rhymes are forced and awkward, the ballads are predictable, and the attempts at lyric humor fall flat. Merrill reteamed with Styne again in 1972 and supplied the lyrics for *Sugar*, the musical version of the film comedy *Some Like It Hot* (1959). The score was competent and tunefully pleasant but negligible; the highlights of the show were not the songs but the scenes taken from the film. The musical numbers gave *Sugar* a sassy Prohibition era feeling. "When You Meet a Man in Chicago" has a period flavor, and the spoof on Weill/Anderson's "September Song" called "November Song" ("even naughty old men need love") was a dandy vehicle for Cyril Ritchard. Merrill's career paralleled the declining trend in Broadway musicals in the 1970s. His *Prettybelle* (1971) and *The Prince of Grand Street* (1978) both closed out of town. It seemed the charm had worn out.

Bob Merrill may not rank as highly as other songwriters to come out of the 1950s but at times he has a grace and style that is extremely satisfying. His lyrics are sometimes sloppy, particularly in some of his rhyming and abrupt line endings, but they often paint vivid pictures. When a score is as magical as *Carnival*, for example, one doesn't notice or even mind the little imperfections along the way. Merrill may be a better magician than a lyric craftsman but sometimes Broadway desperately needs magicians.

Meredith Willson only wrote three Broadway scores, but his long and distinguished career in music quickly earned him veteran status. In many ways Willson was the personification of everything celebrated in his *The Music Man*. He was born in Mason City, Iowa, in 1902. His mother was the local piano teacher and Willson studied piano, piccolo and flute as a boy. Having played in various civic and school bands, Willson decided to pursue a musical career, so he went to New York City where he studied at Juilliard. He was only nineteen years old when John Philip Sousa chose him as first flutist for his famous band. By 1924 Willson was a member of the New York Philharmonic under Toscanini. He eventually became music director at ABC and then NBC, writing his own music as well. His first symphony ("San Francisco") was completed in 1937. After serving in the Army during World War Two, Willson became musical conductor for several popular radio shows.

It was Frank Loesser who first suggested to Willson that he write a musical about his early years in Iowa. Willson used to entertain friends with stories about small town life during the early years of the century. But putting these stories together into a play was a much more difficult matter. Writing his own libretto, Willson went through thirty-two drafts of the book and eventually got assistance from playwright Franklin Lacey. *The Music Man* opened in 1957 and immediately became a beloved classic. It was corny but funny, nostalgic yet innovative. In addition to the standard musical comedy songs, there were barbershop quartet pieces, stirring marches, rhythmic dialogue scenes and fast-talking monologues that were quite unlike anything heard before on Broadway. As old-fashioned and homespun as *The Music Man* may seem, it is also very adventurous and unconventional. The score is rich with variety and warmth. Only the popular "Till There Was You" has a typical Broadway sound to it; the rest of the songs seem to come from another genre. "Seventy-six Trombones" is a skillful Sousa replica. The same melody becomes the fragile "Goodnight, My Someone." The talk-songs, such as "Rock Island," which gets its rhythm from a train, and "Trouble," patterned after a salesman's hustling patter, are mesmerizingly effective. "The Piano Lesson" is a musical scene played against a piano student practicing the scales. And "Lida Rose" sounds so authentic that many think it is an old barbershop quartet number from the period. Almost every song in *The Music Man* is a bold departure from the expected. Willson's music sometimes recalls Cohan, but his lyrics are sharper and wittier. What makes the songs so appealing is their humor. Willson looked back on the past fondly but with a slyness that kept the ideas fresh. *The Music Man* does not age because it reveals little of the age in which it was written. Produced in 1957 or 1987, the musical always creates its own world.

Since Willson's own life was the inspiration for *The Music Man*, it should not be surprising that his subsequent shows were not as effective. His craftsmanship remains high but the writing seems more manufactured. *The Unsinkable Molly Brown* (1960) is set in the same time period as *The Music Man* and has another dynamic central character, but this musical rarely rings true despite the fact-based story. *The Unsinkable Molly Brown* does have some spirited songs that play well on stage. Molly's credo "I Ain't Down Yet" is a joyous march that helps unify the material. "I'll Never Say No" is an appealing ballad and "Belly Up to the Bar, Boys" sounds like a turn-of-the-century favorite. And the revival-like "Are You Sure?" has the sort of magnetism that propelled *The Music Man*. *Here's Love* (1963) has more heart but less to recommend. Based on the 1947 film *Miracle on 34th Street*, the musical has book, music and lyrics by Willson. Much of it is pleasant but just about all of it is forgettable. "It's Beginning to Look a Lot like Christmas" resurfaces each December though *Here's Love* rarely does. The musical has all the expected innocence and optimism that Willson treasures. Thematically it follows right in line with his other works: the miracle of Santa Claus, the happy-go-lucky fate of Molly Brown, the magical power of music in a small Iowa town. *Here's Love* is the poor descendant of a rich idea. Meredith Willson's career celebrated miracles. Although he started writing for the musical theatre at a much older age than most songwriters, he was eternally youthful in his writing. His convictions were not as lofty as, say, Oscar Hammerstein's were; but they were as deeply felt. Willson used comedy to say what meant so much to him. His lyrics, in particular, are warm affirmations of life without being preachy or moralistic. And few have woven homespun emotions with an energetic wit as well as Willson did in *The Music Man*. He truly believed in the possibility of miracles. In one show he gave Broadway its own little miracle.

John Latouche never had a hit musical during his sixteen-year Broadway career but his librettos and lyrics are superb examples of quality craftsmanship, versatility and humor. Because his musical theatre projects were more daring than commercial, Latouche was highly regarded in the profession; even the critics consistently praised his efforts. But, for one reason or another, none of Latouche's musicals was a box office success. *Cabin in the Sky* (1940), which Latouche wrote with composer Vernon Duke, was an imaginative fantasy that utilized Negro folklore, but it only lasted on Broadway for 156 performances. (A 1944 movie version was more successful.) The score for *Cabin in the Sky* mixes rustic charm with Broadway sophistication, resulting in a unique theatre piece. Heaven is simply a "Cabin in the Sky," the title song states; "Love Turned the Light Out," another lyric says. "Honey in the Honeycomb" has a wry tone while "Takin' a Chance on Love" has a worldly wise quality to it. Latouche worked with Duke again on two revues (*Banjo Eyes* in 1941 and *The Lady Comes Across* in 1942) and adapted Chopin's music for *Polonaise* in 1945. He provided the splendid lyrics for Duke Ellington's *Beggar's Holiday* (1946), an updated jazz version of John Gay's *The Beggar's Opera*. Once again the show was a critical success but audiences stayed away.

Latouche's finest work for the musical theatre was his libretto/lyrics for *The Golden Apple* (1954), with music by Jerome Moross. This satirical yet engaging musical retold the tale of Ulysses set in turn-of-the-century America. The musical is almost continuously sung although it retains a musical comedy feel rather than an operatic one. The lyricwriting throughout is impeccable: "Lazy Afternoon" is a languorous solo for Helen of Troy, "It's the Going Home Together" is both comic and romantic, "Doomed, Doomed, Doomed" is a riotous rag, "By Goona-Goona Lagoon" lampoons those mellow South Seas ballads, and "Scylla and Charybdis" is a delightful Gallagher and Sheen takeoff. *The Golden Apple* opened Off-Broadway to excellent reviews but the producers immediately moved it to a Broadway house where it only lasted 125 performances. Latouche teamed up with Moross again in 1955 for the short-lived *The Vamp* and provided some lyrics for Leonard Bernstein's *Candide* (1956). Latouche's untimely death in 1956 at the age of thirty-eight cut short the career of one of Broadway's finest and least recognized lyricists.

Sammy Cahn, on the other hand, was one of the most successful songwriters in America. He spent most of his career in Hollywood where he won the Oscar for best song four times ("All the Way," "High Hopes," "Three Coins in a Fountain" and "Call Me Irresponsible"), but at heart Cahn was a Broadway lyricist. *High Button Shoes* (1947), with music by Jule Styne, was a daffy but innocent piece of Americana that ran for 727 performances. The cheery "Papa, Won't You Dance with Me?" and the warm duet "I Still Get Jealous" are the standouts in the score, but there are also the rousing ensemble number "There's Nothing Like a Model T," the comic "Nobody Ever Died for Dear Old Rutgers" and the frolicsome "On a Sunday by the Sea." Cahn returned to Broadway in the 1960s but fared less well. *Skyscraper* (1965) was based on Elmer Rice's 1945 comedy *Dream Girl* but the James Van Huesen/Cahn score was disappointing. The same team musicalized Harold Brighouse's British favorite, *Hobson's Choice*, in 1966 and called it *Walking Happy*. The title song is a joyous romp but the rest of the score is strained; English character comedy is not within Cahn's range. Neither was the gentle book (and movie) *Lilies of the Field*, which Cahn and Jule Styne turned into the musical *Look to the Lilies* (1970). Cahn did return to Broadway triumphantly in 1974 with *Words and Music*, a revue of his past songs, in which he also appeared. Sammy Cahn is in many ways a lightweight songwriter but one capable of a memorable lyric.

Few songwriters have had such distinguished music to write lyrics for as Robert Wright and George Forrest have. These two lyricists had a series of musicals in the forties and fifties utilizing the music of classical composers. Their adaptations of world-renowned music into Broadway scores was always done with care and intelligence and their lyrics

were often exemplary. *Song of Norway* (1944) was an operetta about
the life of Edvard Grieg, using his own compositions for the songs.
The whole enterprise was rather rhapsodic and overromanticized but had
some pleasing musical moments, most notably when Grieg's "Wedding
Day in Troldhaugen" became the enticing "Strange Music." *Gypsy Lady*
(1946) resurrected old Victor Herbert melodies, and *Magdalena* (1948)
used music by Brazilian composer Heitor Villa-Lobos. Both scores have
some admirable qualities but are more curiosities than satisfying musical theatre experiences. *Kismet* (1953) was the most successful of the
Wright/Forrest projects. Alexander Borodin's compositions were used
this time and they blended beautifully with the exotic setting for this
"Musical Arabian Night." "Stranger in Paradise" (based on Borodin's
"Polovtsian Dances") and "Baubles, Bangles and Beads" (a reworking
of the "String Quartet in D") are the familiar favorites, but the score is
filled with lyrics that are clever ("Rhymes Have I" and "Gestitulate"),
enchanting ("Sands of Time") and sly ("Night of My Nights"). The most
effective mixture of Borodin with Wright and Forrest is the intoxicating
"And This Is My Beloved," a vocal quartet that uses another section
of the "String Quartet in D." In 1978 an all-black version of *Kismet*
called *Timbuktu* opened on Broadway for a modest run. Wright and
Forrest wrote their own music as well as lyrics for *Kean* (1961), a musical biography of actor Edmund Kean that failed to run. *Anya* (1965)
returned to their old formula, this time with Rachmaninoff providing
the music, but the legendary Anastasia story did not translate well to
the musical stage. Wright and Forrest resurfaced on Broadway twenty-
five years later with their music and lyrics for *Grand Hotel* (1989),
which is discussed in Chapter 22 with composer/lyricist Maury Yeston.

The musical theatre during the 1940s and 1950s was enhanced by the
contributions of four poet/writers: Ogden Nash, Truman Capote, Richard
Wilbur and Langston Hughes. Nash provided the cunning lyrics for the
musical fantasy *One Touch of Venus* (1943). Although the plot was a
worn-out tale about a statue that comes to life, Kurt Weill's music, S. J.
Perelman and Nash's libretto, and the presence of Mary Martin in her
first starring role were enough to turn *One Touch of Venus* into something
extraordinary. Nash's lyrics throughout are adroit. "Very, Very, Very,"
"The Trouble with Women" (the trouble with women is men, the lyric
concludes), and the title song are all notable, but the hauntingly romantic
"Speak Low (When You Speak Love)" and the straightforward "That's
Him" are highpoints in an exceptional score. Unfortunately Nash never

wrote a full theatre score again, but some of his lyrics were used in a number of revues, notably *Two's Company* (1952) and *The Littlest Revue* (1956), both with Vernon Duke. In 1973 there was a musical revue, *Nash at Nine*, that set Ogden Nash poems to music by Milton Rosenstock, but it pleased neither critics nor audiences.

Truman Capote's stories have often been dramatized on stage and on film, but he wrote an original libretto and the lyrics for the musical *House of Flowers* in 1954. The story, about two feuding brothels on a West Indies island, had its problems but the Harold Arlen/Capote score was admirable. The tender "A Sleepin' Bee," the calypso number "Two Ladies in de Shade of de Banana Tree," the touching "I Never Has Seen Snow" and the title song all show fine lyric craftsmanship. Despite its short run, *House of Flowers* became something of a cult favorite. But when a revised version opened Off-Broadway in 1968, it did not fare any better at the box office than the original. Capote did not return to the musical theatre although a musicalization of his book *The Grass Harp* by Kenward Elmslie and Claibe Richardson played briefly in 1971.

The poet Richard Wilbur's predominant association with the theatre has been his translations of Moliere's plays. But in 1956 Leonard Bernstein convinced Wilbur to write the lyrics for his comic operetta version of Voltaire's *Candide*. John Latouche, Dorothy Parker and Bernstein himself provided additional lyrics, but Wilbur's work shone most brilliantly. The mock aria "Glitter and Be Gay," the expansively romantic duets "Oh, Happy We," "My Love" and "You Were Dead, You Know," and the exhilarating "Make Our Garden Grow" are masterworks of lyricwriting. Despite Bernstein's finest Broadway score and a stunning production, *Candide* could not survive Lillian Hellman's heavy-handed libretto and closed after seventy-three performances. But the musical became Broadway's most beloved flop and the original cast recording became a best seller. The 1974 revival substituted a new libretto by Hugh Wheeler, a few new lyrics by Stephen Sondheim, and crafty direction by Harold Prince; *Candide* was finally a hit.

Black poet/novelist/dramatist Langston Hughes also wrote lyrics for Broadway and Off Broadway during this period. But unlike the other poets mentioned, who took occasional and brief excursions into the musical theatre, Hughes worked on one production after another for over twenty years. He saw theatre, particularly musical theatre, as a potent medium for revitalizing interest in black culture. His plays and musicals were written for black audiences but on Broadway they were seen mostly by white audiences and judged by critics who knew little of the culture these works celebrated. Hughes resented how white artists had stolen the black idiom and translated it into clichés. "You've taken my blues away," he once wrote in a poem; "they don't sound like me."[2] He sought to restore this deep-rooted culture in a series of dramas and musicals starting in the 1940s. Because of his reputation as a poet, Hughes was asked by Kurt Weill to write the lyrics for *Street Scene* (1947), an operatic version of Elmer Rice's 1929 urban slice-of-life drama of the same title. Here finally was a chance for Hughes' ideas to come to life on the Broadway stage. But Rice was asked to do the libretto and, wishing to retain the characters of his original play, he only allowed Hughes one black character in the piece: a janitor. Despite his disappointment and frustration, Hughes provided a remarkable set of lyrics for *Street Scene*. The duet "Moon-Faced, Starry-Eyed" became somewhat popular, but most of the songs were too closely tied to specific characters to travel well. "What Good Would the Moon Be?" is a moving ballad sung by a woman who laments the futility of moonlight without love; she has been offered a loveless life of luxury by a racketeer. "Somehow I Never Could Believe" is a piece of bitter frustration while "Remember That I Care" and "We'll Go Away Together" are optimistic duets. For the lone black character, Hughes wrote the stirring "I Got a Marble and a Star." But the most striking lyric in *Street Scene* is "Lonely House," the cry of a soul alone in a crowded world. "Funny—you can be so lonely with all these folks around," he sings. "The night for me is not romantic"; not in a lonely house . . . in a lonely town.

The rest of Hughes' career was one attempt after another to create a true black musical. *Troubled Island* (1949) took the form of an opera, *Simply Heavenly* (1957) had a Harlem setting, and *Black Nativity* (1961) and *Tambourines to Glory* (1963) both used a good deal of gospel singing in the score. *Jerico-Jim Crow* (1964) was an ambitious attempt to tell the history of black Americans from slavery to the 1960s. In each case the production was not understood by the ordinary theatre community and failed to reach the appropriate audience. But the lyric work was usually of the highest standard. Hughes died in 1967, only a few years before the renaissance of the black musical theatre of the 1970s and 1980s. Those musicals, appealing to both black and white audiences, would not have been possible without the years of groundwork laid by Langston Hughes.

NOTES

1. Stanley Green, *The World of Musical Comedy* (New York: A. S. Barnes & Co., Inc., 1980), p. 270.

2. Langston Hughes, "Note on Commercial Theatre," in *Selected Poems of Langston Hughes* (New York: Alfred A. Knopf, 1968), p. 190.

18

Sunday Clothes: Jerry Herman

Among the many challenges facing anyone who attempts to look critically at the American musical theatre of the past three decades is the question of what to do with Jerry Herman. Unabashedly old-fashioned, often predictable, occasionally very successful and unquestionably talented, Herman can neither be easily dismissed nor roundly praised. To some, his work represents all that has gone wrong with the Broadway musical: big, empty shows with vulgar caricatures passing themselves off as personalities. To others, Herman is one of the few reminders of what made Broadway great: bright, optimistic musical comedies filled with singable songs and high-flying entertainment value. *Hello, Dolly!* may be the superlative example of American musical comedy or the low point of slick Broadway desperation, depending on your viewpoint. Herman is the predominate force in each of his musicals not just because he writes both the music and lyrics but because each show breathes his philosophy of high-powered optimism and glamour. Take him or leave him, Jerry Herman is an important part of the Broadway mentality. Deny him and you ignore a sizable portion of the musical theatre; glorify him and you sell Broadway short.

Herman was born in 1932 in New York but grew up in Jersey City, New Jersey, where his family moved when he was young. He received no formal musical training but before long Herman was playing the piano by ear. He studied drama at the University of Miami, where he first wrote music and lyrics for college revues, one of them, *I Feel Wonderful*, transferring to Off Broadway in 1954. Herman moved to New York after graduation and worked as a cocktail lounge pianist while he continued his songwriting. He scored a handful of Off-Broadway shows and one of his songs appeared in Hermione Gingold's Broadway revue *From A to Z* (1960). Herman's first Broadway score was *Milk and Honey* (1961), a musical about the middle-aged romance of two American tourists vacationing in Israel. Don Appell's libretto was sensitive, if a bit awkward, but Herman's score attracted attention. The music, utilizing an ethnic strain mixed with a traditional Broadway sound, is spirited, especially in the ensemble numbers "Independence Day Hora" and "The Wedding," The title song is an interesting intermingling of a rousing anthem with a sarcastic counterpoint. Lyrically, the score is primitive. "Shalom" is somewhat engaging and enjoyed some popularity. Molly Picon's comic songs, "Chin Up, Ladies" and "Hymn to Hymie," are predictably clichéd. The ballads "There's No Reason in the World" and "I Will Follow You" are adequate but vague. As would often happen in his subsequent scores, the song title tells all and the lyrics rarely develop the idea. But *Milk and Honey* firmly placed Herman on Broadway and the young songwriter's career was off and running.

When he heard that David Merrick was planning a musical version of Thornton Wilder's *The Matchmaker* (1955), Herman auditioned for the producer by writing four songs for the proposed show. Merrick hired him but, concerned about using an unknown composer, the producer backed his investment with Michael Stewart and Gower Champion, the librettist and director from his successful production of *Carnival* (1961). *Hello, Dolly!*, as it was eventually titled, had difficulties out of town and Bob Merrill, Charles Strouse and Lee Adams were brought in to help fix things. Widespread rumors aside, they did not write parts of the score. But under the pressure from Merrick, Herman wrote the musical's best number, "Before the Parade Passes By." By the time *Hello, Dolly!* opened on Broadway in 1964 it was a highly polished, unpretentious musical comedy that delighted audiences for 2,844 performances.

The timing of *Hello, Dolly!*'s appearance was ideal. Broadway hadn't had a major comic musical for some time. The traumatic side effects from the assassination of John Kennedy two months before were gradually wearing off and the audiences were ripe for a jubilant, escapist entertainment set in a colorful past. But the success of *Hello, Dolly!* was more than a matter of favorable circumstances. Champion's snappy staging, Carol Channing's quirky but winning performance and Herman's tuneful score must also be credited. *Hello, Dolly!* has become a staple in the musical theatre repertoire and no small part of the credit goes to Herman. The score for *Milk and Honey* departed from the Broadway norm because of its ethnic character, but the score for *Hello, Dolly!* was pure show business. Ostensibly the play's setting is the New York and Yonkers of the 1890s but everyone knows that we are nowhere but on the stage of a big Broadway hit. The songs do nothing to capture the period but instead act as a tribute to the Broadway musical. Herman's score ignores two decades of innovation and experiment. It is stubbornly old-fashioned and it defies us not to embrace it. For the most part we do. "Put On Your Sunday Clothes" is contagious. It celebrates simplicity in such an unaffected way that the stage overflows with joy. "Ribbons Down My Back" and "It Only Takes a Moment," the only two songs in *Hello, Dolly!* that are not belted, are pleasing and actually develop character. "So Long, Dearie" is a brassy, sexy lament that is inappropriate for the plot and the character but is appealing on a "show biz" level. As for the title number, the most popular song to come from Broadway for years before and after, it is one of the musical theatre's great acts of hocus-pocus. Excitement is generated out of thin air as we celebrate the illusion that there is something to celebrate. Without connecting to the rest of the musical, the song "Hello, Dolly!" is a grand parade searching for a holiday. The number represents everything wonderful and shallow about Herman's work.

Mame (1966) resembles *Hello, Dolly!* in many ways, most obviously for being another "Big Lady Show," as Ethan Mordden labels it.[1] Mame Dennis is as oversized as Dolly Levi, although Angela Lansbury did display a bit more subtlety. With the familiar Patrick Dennis story that was previously a book, a play and a film, *Mame* seemed more like a revival than a new musical. But once again the production values were expert and Herman's songs showed no signs of weariness. The score starts out quietly with "St. Bridget," moves into forced enthusiasm with "It's Today!," "Open a New Window" and the title song, and then embraces pretentiousness with "If He Walked Into My Life." Once again the songs tell us nothing of the period, in this case the Roaring Twenties and the Depression years. Any of Dolly Levi's songs would suffice for Mame Dennis (and vice versa) but Herman tries for pathos in *Mame* and it doesn't sit well. The title song is again a tribute to a star masquerading as a character. The comic songs, "Bosom Buddies" and "Gooch's Song," are obvious and crude. Two bright spots in the score are the unmotivated but cheery "We Need a Little Christmas" and the fun dance number "That's How Young I Feel." *Mame* was less accomplished than *Hello, Dolly!* but it was nearly as popular and remains so. As long as there are Big Lady stars, these two musicals will survive.

Herman's next three musicals moved into more demanding territory that challenged the songwriter's formula. Unhappily, all three were box office failures. *Dear World* (1969) attempted to musicalize Jean Giraudoux's whimsical fantasy, *The Madwoman of Chaillot*. To transfer this gentle comedy to the big musical stage is a problematic task at best; the clumsy Jerome Lawrence/Robert E. Lee libretto and Herman's blaring score were surely not the solution. Some of the score has a French flavor to it but lyrically much of it is Shubert Alley. Ballads such as "I've Never Said I Love You" seem more nightclub lounge than Paris cafe and do not mix well with the sections of the Giraudoux dialogue that are retained in the musical. But there are some lovely moments in *Dear World*. "Each Tomorrow Morning" and "Kiss Her Now" come close to the original's charm. "Garbage" is an interesting list song and the Countess's "And I Was Beautiful" is effective. But the subdued quality found occasionally in the score is destroyed by two loud and incongruent numbers: "One Person," a Cohan-like rouser, and the catchy title song that recalls a TV commercial jingle for some unnecessary product. *Dear World* often sounds like a battle between Herman's desire to make hits and to create theatre. In one admirable number, "The Tea Party," he attempts an extended musical scene that follows the divergent trains of thought of the eccentric lady friends of the Countess. It was the most ambitious piece of lyricwriting Herman had yet assayed. *Dear World* closed after 123 performances despite the presence of Angela Lansbury as the Countess. The musical that pointed to new directions for Herman was dismissed and the audiences waited for another Big Lady Show.

They didn't get it in *Mack and Mabel* (1974). Mabel Norman, the silent screen comedienne, is the most fully realized character in the Herman repertoire. As Bernadette Peters played her, Mabel was part waif, part star. Herman found a voice for her in "Look What Happened to Mabel," "Wherever He Ain't" and "Time Heals Everything." The character of Mack Sennett was more vague and Robert Preston's competent but distanced performance kept it that way. But even his songs have flesh and blood, in particular the duet "I Won't Send Roses." *Mack and Mabel* is Herman's favorite score and without question his best. Instead of the plastic emotions of "If He Walked into My Life," Herman gave *Mack and Mabel* the tender torch song "Time Heals Everything." "Tap Your Troubles Away" is actually satiric, an unusual quality for Herman. "Hundreds of Girls" is playful but tongue in cheek. The score makes another loud attempt at enthusiasm ("The Big Time") and another "here she is" tribute ("When Mabel Comes in the Room") but all in all it is an exceptional score.

Herman didn't think Franz Werfel's *Jacobowsky and the Colonel* (1944) would make a suitable vehicle for a musical but he wanted to work with Joel Grey, so he did the score for *The Grand Tour* (1979). Michael Stewart got libretto help from Mark Bramble, but this odd comedy about anti-Semitism didn't lend itself to the traditional musical form. In 1980 Herman contributed some songs to the transplanted British revue *A Day in Hollywood—A Night in the Ukraine*. Having started his career writing for similar kinds of revues, Herman was in his milieu. But the book musical was still his ideal and his last three had flopped. So when the musicalization of the French play and film *La Cage Aux Folles* came along he grabbed it.

Harvey Fierstein's libretto turned the sensitive yet hilarious Jean Poiret story of two middle-aged homosexuals into a labored, obvious farce. Herman's score is just as crass and the result is another Big Lady Show; instead of Dolly or Mame it is Albin, the neurotic drag queen of a French nightclub. "A Little More Mascara" wouldn't be out of place for Dolly Levi, and one could almost hear the unconventional Mame Dennis singing "I Am What I Am" without losing much impact. The sweet romantic songs "With You on My Arm" and "Song on the Sand" are easily hummable but lyrically impotent. "The Best of Times" is another empty testimonial to nothing in particular and the title song manages to be crude and old hat at the same time. Despite its seemingly controversial subject matter, *La Cage Aux Folles* (1983) was a hit. By looking backward, Herman came up with the most popular musical of the season. His worst instincts had been proven valid and the audience left the theatre humming the oft-reprised songs.

Jerry's Girls, a revue comprised of Herman favorites and near-favorites, toured the country and then opened on Broadway in 1985. Since then Herman has made occasional nightclub appearances performing songs from his past shows. Should circumstances be favorable, we will again hear a new Herman score on Broadway. One hopes that the Big Lady

will be left behind. Broadway can always use a hit but it could use a
score with the quality of *Mack and Mabel* even more.

How does Jerry Herman fit into the development of the musical theatre? He has been very successful when he has given audiences what
they thought they wanted. "Commercial is what my middle name is,"
he once noted.[2] Some compare him to Irving Berlin in regard to this
commercialism. But Berlin's work is always about simple emotions:
Herman's is too often a celebration of commercialism. Few can write
melodies as easily digested as Herman's. This, according to some, also
recalls Berlin. But when it comes to lyrics Herman too often disappoints.
His words do more than serve the music; they sacrifice themselves for
the catchy tune. Herman believes in lyrics that are uncomplicated and
can be appreciated on first hearing. But uncomplicated to whom? How
little can an audience grasp on one hearing? Perhaps he underestimates
his audience.

Many of Herman's songs have become popular by avoiding the uncommercial pitfalls of theatre music: distinct characters, appropriate situations
and thematic unity. He insists that there is a big difference between pop
music and show music; the title of an early song of his assures us "There's
No Tune Like a Show Tune." Yet few songwriters have blurred the
distinction between pop and theatre music as Herman has. He emulates
the style of the pre–World War Two musicals when theatre songs were
the popular music of the era. But by the sixties that was no longer the
case, so Herman's theatre music patterned itself after pop. Musically this
is suspect; lyrically it is dangerous. Since most pop music has little regard
for lyrics it is understandable that Herman's scores suffered. But the true
frustration comes from the fact that Herman has the talent and sensitivity
to write theatre lyrics. By ignoring these instincts he has given us some
major hit shows. But is he doing the musical theatre a favor?

There is something else that Herman has given to Broadway and it
should not be underestimated. From time to time a touch of glamour is
needed. In the rough- and-tumble sixties Herman showed that the musical
theatre could still dazzle. The glamour may have been artificial but it was
needed all the same. Everyone puts on their Sunday clothes in a Jerry
Herman musical. It shows in the pride and optimism of the score as much
as in the visual aspects of the production: Broadway in its Sunday best.
"Glamour plays a very important part in my conception of Broadway,"
he has stated.[3] It's an undeniable part of the musical theatre and few
provide it as well as he does. So Herman's most important long range

contribution might be twofold: he made the Broadway musical accessible and he made it glamourous. On occasion he made it beautiful underneath as well. That's when the Sunday clothes become more than dressing for store window mannequins. That's when Broadway breathes. That's real glamour.

NOTES

1. Ethan Mordden, *Broadway Babies: The People Who Made the American Musical* (New York: Oxford University Press, 1983), pp. 158–59.

2. Al Kasha and Joel Hirschorn, *Notes on Broadway: Conversations with the Great Songwriters* (Chicago: Contemporary Books, 1985), p. 181.

3. Otis L. Guernsey (ed.), *Broadway Song and Story: Playwrights, Lyricists, Composers Discuss Their Hits* (New York: Dodd, Mead and Co., 1985), p. 199.

19

Trying to Remember:
Tom Jones and Lee Adams

In 1960 two lyricists, one from Texas and the other from Ohio, made their first significant New York contributions in musicals about the joys and pains of youth. Lee Adams captured the faddish, silly aspects of adolescence in *Bye Bye Birdie*, while Tom Jones explored the more whimsical and bittersweet side in *The Fantasticks*. Throughout their careers, their most potent moments would always be those dealing with youthful ambition and a feeling for beginnings. To appreciate the lyrics of Jones and Adams, one must put them in the context of this sense of beginning. Both lyricists were most successful when enticing audiences into remembering the past; not the historical past but the personal past. "See it with your ears," Jones urges us in *The Fantasticks*. "Hear it with the inside of your hand." One must respond to the work of these two men in a sensual rather than analytical manner. We must think as the young, not as older subjects of the "tyranny of time."

Tom Jones was born in Littlefield, Texas, in 1928, the son of a turkey hatcheryman. His ambition was to be a stage director, so he studied drama at the University of Texas. In 1951 he met a fellow student, Harvey Schmidt, who was majoring in art and shared his enthusiasm for the musical theatre. Although Schmidt could only play the piano by ear, he provided the music for Jones' lyrics. Their efforts were produced on campus and, later in New York, they contributed songs to several of Julius Monk's revues at the Upstairs-at-the-Downstairs. Although the collaborators had been working on a musical adaptation of Edmond Rostand's *Les Romanesques* for several years, the project did not come to light until director Word Baker asked them to turn the work into a one-act musical for a summer season at Barnard College. This short version, called *The Fantasticks*, ran its scheduled week at Barnard in 1959 where producer Lore Noto saw it. He offered to produce a full-length version Off Broadway and raised the necessary $16,500 to open at the small Sullivan Street Playhouse. When *The Fantasticks* opened there in 1960 it received less than enthusiastic reviews, but word of mouth kept the show alive and the popularity of the song "Try to Remember" helped it along. Once *The Fantasticks* did catch on it never let go; it is still running as of this writing, thirty years later.

Jones wrote the libretto for *The Fantasticks* as well as the lyrics. It is often difficult to determine where the songs start because Jones' lead-in dialogue is usually written in verse. Both book and lyrics are fragile, poignant and charming. The words are highly poetic but rarely cloying. They have a naiveté that charms rather than irritates. We can forgive their emotional excesses just as we forgive the young characters' shortsighted ambitions. "Try to Remember," the signature song for the show, sets the musical's premise: these things can only come alive if the audience remembers. The imagery in the song is simple but expansive ("love was an ember about to billow") and the poetic techniques are fanciful ("when life was slow and oh so mellow"). Jones uses alliteration unabashedly ("When grass was green and grain was yellow") and pushes internal rhymes to their bearable limit ("Although you know the snow will follow") but it all works. The youthful enthusiasm of the characters dictates much of the score. Luisa's "Much More" is a touching and giddy character song, and her duet with Matt, blatantly entitled "Metaphor," is a mock-operatic lampoon of the very imagery that the play thrives on. While the comic songs for the two fathers are rather routine, most of the score for *The Fantasticks* is exceptional. There is a consistency of tone and vocabulary throughout. Vegetation, sunlight, moonlight, illusions, reality and theatrical posturing itself all recur with effective frequency. "Soon It's Gonna Rain" uses natural elements to accent a highly romantic duet. "I Can See It" presents optimism and pessimism side by side as the worldly wise El Gallo and the eager Matt view the future differently. "Round and Round" is a dream sequence that hints at a nightmare. By the end, Jones' lyrics simplify into the elegant but unembellished "They Were You."

The Fantasticks is one of the most produced of American musicals, both in this country and in over fifty foreign nations. Its universality stems from its defiance of any specificity. The musical does not age because it has no time reference. Young audiences today respond to it much as similar audiences did in 1960. As for older patrons, they must accept it on its own terms and "try to remember." Jones continued to work solely with Schmidt and together they had a productive career throughout the sixties. But none of their later projects can match *The Fantasticks* for consistent high quality.

David Merrick brought the team to Broadway in 1963 with their musical version of N. Richard Nash's *The Rainmaker* (1954), retitled *110 in the Shade*. The tale of a spinster who falls for a con man had some similarities to *The Fantasticks*, especially regarding illusions being created and destroyed, but the libretto (by Nash) lacked a delicate touch. The Jones/Schmidt score, on the other hand, is filled with tenderness, especially in the ballads "Love, Don't Turn Away" and "Is It Really Me?," both sung by the insecure Lizzie (Inga Swenson). "Everything Beautiful Happens at Night" and "Another Hot Day" show some of the naturalistic sensuality of the team's earlier work, and "Simple Little Things" has its charm. The rainmaker's "Melisande" is a fanciful conjuring trick, and "Little Red Hat" is one of Jones' best comic lyrics. But *110 in the Shade* was too gentle for the Broadway of its day (*Hello, Dolly!* and *Funny Girl* were the big hits that season) and only managed to run for 250 performances.

With *I Do! I Do!* (1966) Jones and Schmidt entered the mainstream of commercial musical theatre. Jones adapted Jan de Hartog's *The Fourposter*, a sentimental play about fifty years of a marriage. The adaptation was pretty straightforward and Jones even kept the cast size to two, a bold move for a musical. But the show turned into a star vehicle for Mary Martin and Robert Preston, whose personal charm and fine-tuned interaction with each other outshone the material. Much of the score for *I Do! I Do!* is obvious and simpleminded. In their efforts to musicalize everyday domestic emotions, Jones and Schmidt expanded the sentimentality to a size appropriate for superstars. "My Cup Runneth Over" is pretentious, "Where Are the Snows?" is hollow, and the title song is irritatingly wholesome. Most embarrassing of all is "Flaming Agnes," a showstopper that says nothing. The team did provide a likeable, if inappropriate, softshoe number, "A Well Known Fact," which Preston danced in his bare feet. There are some believable moments in "Goodnight," and "What Is a Woman?" is touching. But this sort of show was not what Jones and Schmidt were all about and they never returned to its like again.

Celebration (1969) was a return to Jones' belief in primitive, bare-bones theatre. It was his first libretto not based on an existing work and it was highly allegorical. Set on a wooden platform on a dateless New Year's Eve, *Celebration* broke most conventions by going back to theatre's first convention: simple storytelling around a fire. The project was meant to be somewhat off-putting and it was, even for brow-beaten 1969 audiences. The plot, a fable of sorts, is about the battle between youth and age, between winter and summer, between idealism and reality. There is a Greek choruslike ensemble of Revelers led by Potemkin, an even more cynical version of El Gallo. The whole show was actually more engrossing than it sounds, if a bit cold at times. Jones directed so there was an uncompromising consistency in book, staging and lyrics.As for the score, it is rich with imagination but keeps affections at a distance. Luisa's naive "Much More" now becomes "Somebody," an ambitious character song sung by the worldly heroine who is ironically called Angel. Potemkin's brutal "Survive" and "Not My Problem" are coldhearted but interesting. The wealthy Mr. Rich has some dandy vaudeville-type numbers ("Where Did It Go?" and "It's You Who Makes Me Young") and a wry song called "Bored." An innocent but determined orphan has the musical's tenderest songs, particularly "My Garden" and "Love Song." Too offbeat for general audiences, *Celebration*, not too surprisingly, lasted only fourteen weeks on Broadway but it contains some of Jones and Schmidt's finest work.

Burnt by the compromises of *I Do! I Do!*, disillusioned by the failure of *Celebration*, and stung by the closing out of town of their next show, *Colette* (1970), the partners returned to Off Broadway where they opened the Portfolio Studio, an experimental workshop theatre, to try out small, intimate musicals. The studio presented a series of showcase productions of their own work, the most notable being *Philemon* (1975). This dark tale about a clown in ancient Rome had the coldness of *Celebration* but little of the vitality. The songs seemed strained and the overall effect was one of indifference. Although the team has not had a major New York production since, they are still active. Their musical version of *Our Town*, called *Grover's Corners*, was produced in various cities in the 1980s and may yet be seen on or Off Broadway.

Most of the musicals that Lee Adams worked on did not approach the serious nature of Jones' work but both men explored the same ground: youthful ambition and the destruction of illusions. The Adams musicals are particularly American in their subject matter and point of view. He is closer to the Broadway musical comedy vein than Jones but Adams sometimes reveals moments of painful honesty. He is a fine craftsman and, with his composer/collaborator Charles Strouse, provided some excellent scores for Broadway in the 1960s.

Lee Adams was born in Mansfield, Ohio, in 1924. Although he loved the theatre he felt that journalism was his calling. He attended Ohio State University with that in mind but wrote lyrics for original college musicals as well. After graduation Adams went to New York where he enrolled at Columbia University's School of Journalism. Throughout his subsequent jobs on various newspapers and magazines he continued to write lyrics but did not take it seriously until he met Charles Strouse in 1949. Strouse, a struggling composer who worked as a rehearsal pianist, and Adams teamed up to write original scores for the weekly revues at the Green Mansions summer resort. They then scored a series of Off-Broadway revues, most notably Ben Bagley's *Shoestring Revue* (1955) and its 1957 sequel.

Their first Broadway effort, *Bye Bye Birdie*, went through several drafts, dozens of songs and numerous backers' auditions before it opened in 1960 with only a small box office advance. Newcomer Michael Stewart, an old friend from Green Mansions, wrote the witty libretto that celebrated the vivacious and harmlessly chaotic lifestyle of American youth. In attitude and style it was a sort of flipside to *West Side Story*. The Elvis Presley–like Conrad Birdie character gave the show its premise, but the musical was really about the parallel romances of two different generations. Business for *Bye Bye Birdie* was slow at first but, like *The Fantasticks* Off Broadway, it became that season's sleeper on Broadway. The musical is continually revived by amateur groups, so many have dismissed it as a high school vehicle. But time has proven *Bye Bye Birdie* to be something more. The faddishness has worn off (it was, after all, a satire on faddishness) and it is clear how well structured and durable a piece it is. The score has also survived nicely. Strouse and Adams display the jubilant spirit of the young generation in "The Telephone Hour" and "A Lot of Livin' To Do." But they also find the sweet pathos of adolescence in "One Boy" and "How Lovely to Be a Woman." The adults also get their share of comedy ("Kids"), romance ("Baby, Talk To Me") and bounce ("Put on a Happy Face"). There's a lively female duet called "What Did I Ever See In Him?" and even a mock tribute to Ed Sullivan, "Hymn For a Sunday Evening." It is a vibrant musical comedy score and Adams' lyric work throughout is fresh, precise and engaging. The team graduated from high school to college with their next musical, *All American* (1962), but the result was less than joyous. Ray Bolger played a Hungarian immigrant professor at a small Southern college. Mel Brooks' original libretto was disappointing, Joshua Logan's direction was heavy handed, and much of the Strouse/Adams score failed to sparkle. The lovely ballad "Once Upon a Time" became popular and there was a pleasant softshoe, "If I Were You," but the rest is forgettable.

Strouse and Adams wrote their most powerful score for *Golden Boy* (1964), an updated musical of Clifford Odets' 1937 drama of the same name. The Italian-American boxer Joe Bonaparte became the black boxer Joe Wellington from Harlem (Sammy Davis, Jr.) in the new version scripted by Odets himself. But Odets died in 1963, leaving an incomplete libretto that Adams and playwright William Gibson finished. *Golden Boy* opened to respectable reviews but a less than profitable run. Nevertheless, the score for *Golden Boy* is very potent and reveals traits that are not to be found in the team's other works. "Night Song," which sets the mood for the musical and establishes Joe's character, is a masterful lyric that paints vivid pictures and evokes subtle emotions. There are two very effective ballads, "Lorna's Here" and "I Want To Be With You," and a chilling ensemble number, "No More," about the various levels of rejection in the world. "Don't Forget 127th Street" is a contagious group number that is filled with irony and self-knowledge. "This Is the Life," though a familiar type of persuasive song, avoids the expected clichés and continually surprises, especially in its clever rap song section that forshadows the black musicals of the 1970s.

The team returned to musical comedy with *It's a Bird, It's a Plane, It's Superman* (1966). The popular comic strip was not treated as camp in David Newman and Robert Benton's tight, resourceful libretto. Superman and the ideals he stood for were portrayed with the earnest fun found in the original. Harold Prince directed smashingly and the critics gave their approval, but audiences stayed away. They have continued to stay away, for the show is rarely revived. When *Superman* was in preparation, the pop art craze was at its peak. Andy Warhol gave the craze the look and *Batman* on TV gave it a voice. But the fad soon passed and by the time *Superman* opened it was already waning. One popular song came from the score, "You've Got Possibilities," but there were others that had the same sassy, urban spirit: "So Long, Big Guy," "The Woman for the Man (Who Has Everything)," and "Ooh, Do You Love You!" Superman has a revealing solo called "The Strongest Man in the World" (he has the "heaviest heart in the world") and Lois Lane's "What I've Always Wanted" is agreeable. It is not a superior score but it is playful and intelligent.

Applause (1970) was the biggest hit of that season and it provided Adams with his most commercially successful show. Betty Comden and Adolph Green adapted the 1950 film *All About Eve* into a musical theatre setting, and Lauren Bacall scored a triumph in the Bette Davis role. The story is a good one and Ron Fields' direction and choreography made it seem new but the score is second rate and Adams' lyrics disappoint. The sincere enthusiasm of *Bye Bye Birdie* becomes forced and empty in *Applause*. "But Alive," "Something Greater" and even the noisy title song ring false; the words are not convincing and the imagery is flat. The humor in "One of a Kind" and "Good Friends" is artificial as is the logic in "Fasten Your Seat Belts," a song inspired by·the film's most famous line. There is real tenderness in "Think How It's Gonna Be," but the pathos in "Hurry Back" and "The Best Night of My Life" is plastic. "Who's That Girl?" is the score's brightest spot, a delightful spoof of a freewheeling 1940s kind of song.

Although Strouse and Adams continued to work on some television specials and on a musical in London (*I and Albert* in 1972), *Applause* was their last Broadway success together. Their *A Broadway Musical* (1978) attempted to capture the backstage dealings in producing a musical. It was showcased Off Broadway first, but on Broadway it closed on opening night. It is a vicious, bitter piece, but there is one memorable song: "Yenta Power," a savage number about the group sales promoters on Broadway. In 1981 the team resurrected some of the characters, authors and cast of *Bye Bye Birdie* and brought them up to date in the musical sequel *Bring Back Birdie*. But the magic was clearly gone and the show closed after four performances. In 1977 Strouse teamed up with lyricist Martin Charnin and they came up with one of the decade's biggest hits, *Annie*. As for Adams, he continues to work on various projects but none, as of this writing, has come to successful fruition.

The best lyrics by Tom Jones and Lee Adams survive because their words manage to remain forever young. Their lyrics are the sounds of youth and they remain new and exciting if one is willing to take a youthful approach. El Gallo asks his audience to picture a scene; see it "not with your eyes, for they are wise," he tells them. Sometimes the work of Jones and Adams should not be viewed with wisdom but with the senses only. That may seem like an apology for immature writing but it is not. These men, at their finest, wrote with the profound blindness of youth.

20

A Quiet Thing: Fred Ebb

The most promising and intriguing songwriting team to come out of the sixties is John Kander and Fred Ebb. The lyricist of the team is Ebb, a consistently dedicated and intelligent lyric writer who usually works with material that is challenging and bold. Big-time success has eluded Kander and Ebb because their musicals are rarely mainstream products appealing to a wide audience. And when they write the score for a hit, credit is often given to other forces. Has a team ever been more overshadowed by dominant directors (such as George Abbott and Harold Prince), over-powering superstars (Lauren Bacall, Liza Minnelli) and all-encompassing director/choreographers (Bob Fosse, Gower Champion) than this one? No wonder, after more than twenty years of quality work, they are still so little known. Kander and Ebb are too often the men who write the score for somebody else's hit or flop musical.

Fred Ebb was born in New York City in 1932 and attended New York University and Columbia. His first collaborator was composer Paul Klein, with whom he wrote individual songs and contributed to a hand-ful of Off-Broadway revues in the late 1950s. He worked with other composers and also wrote sketches for the television show "That Was the Week That Was." But the turning point in his career came in 1962 when music publisher Tommy Valando introduced Ebb to John Kander. The new team's first efforts were some individual songs, two of which ("My Coloring Book" and "I Don't Care Much") became hits. Producer

Harold Prince knew Kander from his 1962 musical *A Family Affair* and hired the team to write the score for *Flora, the Red Menace* (1965), their first Broadway show together. The musical was intended as a vehicle for Barbra Streisand, who had gained stardom with *Funny Girl* the year before. When Prince couldn't get Streisand, he cast nineteen-year-old Liza Minnelli and she filled the bill smashingly. But *Flora, the Red Menace* was less than a success, running only for eighty-seven performances. Based on Lester Atwell's novel *Love Is Just Around the Corner* about American communists during the Depression, the libretto was by Robert Russell and George Abbott, the show's director. The apolitical Abbott saw to it that the subject matter was softened and romanticized until the communists were merely silly, and there was no point to the story. Yet Kander and Ebb's score for *Flora, the Red Menace* is bright and thrilling, a dazzling debut for the team. Some of the comic songs ("The Flame," "Knock, Knock," "Palomino Pal") are a bit obvious and dated but when the show called for knowing character songs ("All I Need," "Sign Here"), a charming duet ("Not Every Day of the Week") or high energy star solos ("Sing Happy," "Dear Love"), Kander and Ebb came through with superior material. The finest song in the score is the ballad "A Quiet Thing," an engaging solo about life's rewards sometimes coming in subtle ways: "happiness comes in on tip toe." It is a tender, inspired song, the kind to come from seasoned professionals, not beginners. It is still one of Ebb's best lyrics. *Flora, the Red Menace* has been revived with book changes, and the musical may yet gain wider popularity. But in 1965 it was merely the vehicle that gave Liza Minnelli her big start rather than the show that introduced Kander and Ebb.

The team got involved in *Cabaret* (1966) only after producer/director Prince couldn't get Dorothy Fields as lyricist. Although based on John Van Druten's 1951 play, *I Am a Camera*, Joseph Masteroff's libretto for *Cabaret* went back to Christopher Isherwood's stories about Berlin in the 1920s. It was Masteroff's idea to use a cabaret as a metaphor for the rise of Nazi Germany. The idea opened up exciting song possibilities and Kander and Ebb provided their most famous score. *Cabaret* was a remarkable achievement for its time and one of the great transitional musicals. In many ways it is daring, cynical and uncompromising; in other ways it is traditional. The scenes in the Kit Kat Club take on a Brechtian quality, while the main story of two parallel relationships is patterned after the *Oklahoma!* model. Surprisingly, this mixture of two very different styles works effectively. Kander and Ebb's score can also be divided into the cabaret numbers ("Wilkomen," "Don't Tell Mama," "If You Could See Her"), which have a sting to them, and the book songs ("It Couldn't Please Me More," "Married," "Why Should I Wake Up?"), which provide traditional musical comedy satisfaction. While the Kit Kat Club songs are the more challenging, there is excellent lyric work in both categories. The duet "Perfectly Marvelous" disappoints, but most of the other book songs are quite resourceful even when they deal with the sentimental aspects of the plot. Two of the lyrics, "So What?" and "What Would You Do?," are powerful solos in the Weill/Brecht style. (Both were sung by Weill's widow Lotte Lenya in the original production.) At the cabaret, where the songs are more thematic, Ebb's lyrics soar. "Two Ladies" has a Cole Porterish sense of the risqué but with a dark undercurrent. The chilling "Tomorrow Belongs To Me" is deceptively engaging. Even the title song, which has become a popular upbeat party number over the years, is lyrically very pessimistic in the context of the show. Because *Cabaret* successfully combined traditional musical comedy and the darker conceptual musical, it was popular—the team's only mainstream hit.

Producer David Merrick was impressed with Kander and Ebb's work and hired the team for *The Happy Time* (1968), the sentimental story of a family in French Canada based on Samuel Taylor's popular 1950 comedy of the same name. The scope of the story, the subject matter and the characters were all on a modest scale and the team provided a charming, intimate score. But under Gower Champion's direction and choreography the project was inflated to *Hello, Dolly!* proportions. Champion turned the simple tale into a multimedia show with photographic projections that dwarfed the action and upstaged the characters. Also lost in all the spectacle was a beautiful score. *The Happy Time* gave Kander and Ebb the opportunity to write on a more personal level, and the score is warm and truthful. It was, for the most part, a quiet thing. There are two enchanting ballads ("I Don't Remember You" and "Among My Yesterdays"), a lovely duet ("Seeing Things") and a title song that immediately captivates. Even the lively numbers ("A Certain Girl" and "The Life of the Party") are joyous without being overpowering. In his lyrics for *The Happy Time*, Ebb shows a mastery of romanticism comparable to Lerner and a tenderness worthy of Harnick. But very few noticed.

Working with Hal Prince once again, Kander and Ebb wrote the score for *Zorbá* (1968), the unsatisfying musical version of the popular book and the film *Zorbá the Greek*. Part of the problem with *Zorbá* was the production teaming. With the producer (Prince), cast members (Herschel Bernardi, Maria Karnilova), librettist (Joseph Stein) and designers (Boris Aronson, Patricia Zipprodt) all from *Fiddler on the Roof*, audiences and critics anticipated a similar show. *Zorbá* was no *Fiddler on the Roof* and, more pointedly, it was quite the opposite in temperament and theme. *Zorbá* was about a fatalistic zest for life, an irresponsible approach to living without family, community and shared love. The closer the score got to this theme ("Life is what you do while you're waiting to die"), the less audiences liked it. Kander and Ebb's contribution to *Zorbá* was of mixed quality. Kander attempted Greek-sounding music and Ebb tried a sort of broken English for the natives of Crete; neither worked very well. This European folklore was not within their talents. There are still some songs from *Zorbá* that deserve notice: a pathetically joyous "Happy Birthday to Me" for the aging courtesan, the ballad "The Butterfly," and a charming duet "Goodbye, Canavaro."

70, Girls, 70 (1971), the next Broadway musical the team worked on, was the victim of a series of unfortunate circumstances that resulted in the shortest run of any of their shows (thirty-five performances). Ebb and Norman L. Martin coauthored the libretto based on Peter Coke's geriatric comedy *A Breath of Spring*. The story of a group of senior citizens who turn to robbery in order to finance their crumbling old folks' home was unconventional and required a certain amount of silliness and fantasy on the part of the audience. Instead people didn't know how to react and sat dumbfounded as the veteran performers sang and danced like spry chorus kids. People confused the ads for *70, Girls, 70* with those for the concurrent musical *Follies*, a serious approach to aged performers trying to relive the past, and the show was lost in the confusion. There was also a dark shadow cast over the whole production when David Burns died of a heart attack during a preview performance in Philadelphia. The whole misadventure quickly disappeared, but the score for *70, Girls, 70* is as alive and kicking as few Broadway scores are. It was Kander and Ebb's most vivacious (too vivacious, many felt) set of songs yet. Since the whole point of the musical was to show old people not acting like old people, the songs are fast, lively and raucous. High-spirited numbers like "Coffee (in a Cardboard Cup)," "Broadway, My Street" and "See the Light" are showstoppers in the old vaudeville style. The sweet songs ("Do We?" and "Go Visit Your Grandmother") are very sly with tongue-in-cheek lyrics, and the optimistic numbers ("Believe," "Yes" and the title song) are too much fun to get preachy. And "The Elephant Song" added another delightful lyric to Ebb's growing list of outstanding comic songs. *70, Girls, 70* is a cult favorite of many who never saw it, but the musical is probably beyond a major revival; audiences still wouldn't get it. In terms of the creative growth of Kander and Ebb the show was a cheerful step forward.

Chicago (1975) was the team's most successful musical after *Cabaret*, but its box office appeal must be credited to the stars, Gwen Verdon and Chita Rivera, and the signature production by director/choreographer Bob Fosse rather than the score or script. Ebb coauthored the libretto with Fosse, basing their "musical vaudeville" on the 1926 play of the same name. The story of murderess Roxie Hart and her publicity-hungry lawyer became very dark and cynical in Fosse's concept of a tawdry and gaudy vaudeville show. All the characters were liars and cheats, and the issues raised were drowned in cynicism. *Chicago* was dazzling and fascinating but, ultimately, empty and tiresome. Unlike the understated, chilling Kit Kat Club songs, the score for *Chicago* is overtly sinister. *Cabaret* suggests; *Chicago* shouts. Ebb's lyrics are finely crafted throughout but they have no subtlety and the songs do not build because, with everything blankly stated at the top, there is nowhere to go. The opening "All That Jazz" was sensational; unfortunately nothing following could top it. By the second act everything became predictable as Fosse ran out of ideas. The concluding duet "Nowadays," a gentle softshoe, was anticlimatic after two hours of razzle dazzle. But there is superb lyric work in *Chicago*. Ebb found many playful ways to express the show's single theme. The debonair "All I Care About (Is Love)" makes cynicism fun. "The Cell Block Tango" and "When Velma Takes the Stand" use narrative wryly, and optimism is wickedly lampooned in "A Little Bit of Good." Ebb captures the twenties' lyric style in several of the songs but none better than the droll "Mr. Cellophane," a parody of Bert Williams' famous "Nobody." *Chicago* was a unique theatrical experiment that did not satisfy in conventional musical theatre terms. The song "Razzle Dazzle" claims that audiences will buy anything if it is glossy and flashy enough; *Chicago*, despite its adventurous ambitions, too often was just that.

With *The Act* (1977), the team was reunited with Liza Minnelli once again. The show was another triumph for the star but the book by George Furth, the direction by Martin Scorcese (later replaced by Gower Champion), and Kander and Ebb's score fared less well. *The Act* was about a film star who loses her husband and watches her career falter, all told in the format of a Las Vegas nightclub act. Aside from Minnelli's performance, the whole venture was rather uninvolving and the score did not help matters. There is little variety from song to song because the limited premise only allowed for Las Vegas–style numbers. Even the ballads are too high-powered. No quiet thing here. Ebb's lyrics disappoint because they try to develop a show business persona instead of a character. "Shine It On," the signature song for the show, is all empty bluster. The ballads "There When I Need Him" and "It's the Strangest Thing" are predictable. Only the comic songs temporarily come to life: a sexy romp called "Arthur in the Afternoon" and "Little Do They Know," a satirical number sung by the disgruntled dancers who have to support the star.

Their next project, *Woman of the Year* (1981), was also a vehicle, this time for Lauren Bacall. If the team was limited by the script's premise in *The Act*, they seemed to be limited by the questionable musical talents of their star in *Woman of the Year*. Bacall's songs were musically simpleminded and lyrically embarrassing. She was not helped much by Peter Stone's script, which reduced the clever screenplay it was based on to a one dimensional tale about a cartoonist and an intellectual. The various directors who worked on the production (Robert Moore, Joe Layton, Tommy Tune) couldn't solve its many problems. Ebb's lyrics come across as manufactured rather than inspired. Again it is in two comic songs that Ebb shows some of his usual flair: the delightful duet "When You're Right, You're Right" and the nasty but enjoyable "It Isn't Working," sung about the characters' marriage but applicable to the whole production.

After two disappointments, Kander and Ebb revealed in *The Rink* (1984) that their superior talents had not evaporated. The libretto by Terrence McNally wasn't much better than the team's last two musicals but it did have solid characters, some issues worth dramatizing, and intriguing song possibilities. The story was a dreary affair about a mother, her estranged daughter, and their reunion at their home situated over an amusement park rollerskating rink. Chita Rivera and Liza Minnelli played mother and daughter but *The Rink* was no star vehicle. Both characters were far from glamorous and the songs were character pieces instead of talent showcases. Here was a musical with integrity, as bold as *Chicago* but without the "razzle dazzle." Kander and Ebb's score for *The Rink* is outstanding. The opening ballad, "Colored Lights," immediately sets the mood for the show: intimate, reflective, painful. Several of the musical numbers ("Blue Crystal," "Not Enough Magic," "All the Children in a Row") are extended dramatic scenes, and the lyricwriting is exceptional. The script often strays into calculated melodrama but Ebb's words are honest and moving. The simple ballad "Marry Me," for example, is more potent than the long dramatic confrontations that surround it. The show's lighter moments are musical, most notably with the comic duet "The Apple Doesn't Fall (Very Far From the Tree)." And there is a frolicsome title song that delights, even though it seems awkwardly tacked onto the plot. Audiences, understandably, disliked *The Rink* and even the two stars couldn't keep it running any longer than 204 performances. But the score is exciting enough to revive interest in Kander and Ebb and promises for the future. With work this good, it is always worth the wait.

Arriving on the Broadway scene during a time of great transition, Fred Ebb's work has qualities of both the well-structured 1950s musicals and the more conceptual projects of the seventies. This fluctuating between the old and the new can be seen from show to show and sometimes from song to song within the same show (as in *Cabaret*). But regardless of approach, the lyrics are usually succinct, clear, and true to the nature of the production.

The traditional side of Ebb's lyrics makes him accessible; the innovative side gives him distinction. The lyricist he most admired was Dorothy Fields and her crisp, decisive way with words can be seen in Ebb's work. Like Fields, he is very adaptable, moving from the plain and straightforward to the cynical and slightly cockeyed. By the time Ebb did *Chicago*, he was applying the Fields clarity to allegorical song subjects. Ebb is one of the few theatre lyricists who can experiment, develop a lyric thematically and still retain a traditional foundation. Performers like to sing Ebb's lyrics because of this quality. The words come out easily and clearly because they are so solid. Every lyric has a story-like element and each song progresses with a sense of narrative. There are several Ebb lyrics that are distinctive because they are musical narratives: "Meeskite," "Arthur in the Afternoon," "The Elephant Song," "Don't Tell Mama," "The Cell Block Tango," "Cabaret," "All the Children in a Row," "See the Light" and others. Ebb retains another element of the traditional in his use of the verse. Once a required part of every song, the verse was dropped by most lyricists when it became the prevailing style in popular music. But Ebb often uses the verse, even in his nontraditional efforts. The best Ebb verses are terse introductions to the song subject and add suspense to the narrative.

The less traditional side of Ebb's lyrics can be seen in his approach to character and setting. Many of the people in the Kander and Ebb musicals are unromantic: tawdry cabaret performers, fading stars, estranged family members, greedy lawyers, damaged wives, the unloved and the forgotten. They are often self-mocking, usually lack dignity, but are still fighting to survive. The settings for the musicals, from Depression New York to fascist Berlin to a crumbling amusement park, are also unromantic. Ebb's lyrics are vivid recreations of these places and people and, not surprisingly, the songs do not travel well outside of their milieu. There have been few Kander and Ebb song hits because they echo this anti-romanticism.

Kander and Ebb's musicals always deserve attention. Aside from *Cabaret*, big success has eluded them. But their little successes and even some of their failures are energetic reminders of the best musical theatre can offer. Fred Ebb's lyrics give one assurance that talented, challenging and satisfying qualities are still to be found in lyricwriting today, and that musicals will not become mute spectacles filled with noise instead of ideas.

21

Also in the
1960s and 1970s

Few composer/lyricists have had success come to them as easily as it came
to Stephen Schwartz. The first three musicals he wrote all ran over one
thousand performances each, and by the age of twenty-seven he had three
hits running simultaneously on Broadway—a feat few veteran theatre
writers can claim. Schwartz's good fortune has often been attributed
to others (such as Bob Fosse or Doug Henning) but there is no denying
the exciting and tuneful songs his scores often provide. Time has shown
that Schwartz is not always so lucky; but it has also shown that the high
quality of much of his work is a valuable contribution to the musical
theatre of the 1970s.

Schwartz was born in New York City and raised on Long Island, where
he started piano lessons at the age of six. He studied drama at the Carnegie
Institute of Technology and musical composition at Juilliard. In the sixties
he directed summer theatre productions and spent two years at RCA as
a record producer. His first score to be heard in New York was for
the Off-Broadway *Godspell*, (1971) which ran five years. This childlike
retelling of St. Matthew's gospel had a rock score typical in temperament
and sound but there was a level of craftsmanship, particularly in the
lyrics, that distinguished it. The score still holds up surprisingly well.
"Day by Day" became the show's recognized hit song but there is much
to be said for "We Beseech Thee," "All Good Gifts" and "Learn Your

Lessons Well." "Turn Back, O Man" is a comic vamp number that works well, and "All for the Best" is an inventive vaudeville softshoe. *Godspell* moved to Broadway in 1976 and was successfully revived again Off Broadway in 1988.

The success of *Godspell* convinced Leonard Bernstein to hire Schwartz to write lyrics for the modern sections of his *Mass* (1971), which opened the Kennedy Center in Washington. Schwartz's next musical, *Pippin* (1972), suffered from a negligible libretto—a *Candide*-like saga penned by Roger O. Hirson—but director/choreographer Bob Fosse scored a tour de force with his clever staging that disguised the lack of substance throughout. Too little credit has been given to Schwartz, and his score for *Pippin* has exemplary moments. The tantalizing opening, "Magic to Do," has delightful lyric work, as do the lively "On the Right Track" and "Simple Joys." The hymnlike "Morning Glow" is also pleasing, and the joyous "No Time At All," another vaudeville turn, has its own charm. Lack of substance notwithstanding, *Pippin* ran for 1,944 performances. *The Magic Show* (1974) didn't have a Fosse to hide its ineffectual story about a failing New Jersey nightclub that takes on a magic act. But it did have illusionist Doug Henning and, despite poor reviews, audiences searching for family entertainment kept it running for 1,920 performances. But Schwartz's score is mostly forgettable, with the weakest lyric work of any of his shows.

Schwartz's next project, *The Baker's Wife*, was based on the 1938 Marcel Pagnol film and would prove to be his greatest challenge. While much of Schwartz's previous work had a Motown sound, *The Baker's Wife* was a traditional musical play in the Rodgers and Hammerstein mold. The production toured across the country in preparation for its New York premiere, but with each city changes were made and gradually an intimate and engaging little musical became a big artificial dud. The show closed in Washington, D.C., in 1976 and Broadway never heard Schwartz's finest score. Many of the songs in *The Baker's Wife* have a stinging, personal quality not previously found in Schwartz's work. "Gifts of Love," "The Meadowlark," "Serenade" and "Where Is the Warmth?" are exceptionally beautiful and have a sensitivity found in too few musicals of the 1970s. The score also has its share of stale, routine numbers and predictable musical comedy turns, many of which were added in the attempt to make the gentle material more commercial. But the riches of *The Baker's Wife* far outweigh its faults, and the musical has been revived and revised over the years in various places in efforts to save this wonderful piece.

Schwartz wrote the book, four songs and directed *Working* (1978), a musical adaptation of Studs Terkel's best seller about different occupations. Six writers contributed to the score; Schwartz's portion contained the evocative "Fathers and Sons." But the unusual musical lasted only twenty-five performances. Schwartz was not represented on Broadway again until 1986, when the ill-fated *Rags* opened and closed after only four performances. This time Schwartz provided lyrics for Charles Strouse's music and the score was admirable. But Joseph Stein's libretto about immigrants in turn-of-the-century New York had too many problems and, despite a fine performance by opera singer Teresa Stratas, the musical failed. It is unreasonable to expect Stephen Schwartz's career to maintain the high success rate with which it started. But he is much more than a flash in the pan, and to expect quality work from him in the future is more than reasonable.

Lyricist Peter Udell is not so widely known but he is a writer of considerable talent and one of the few with a consistent vision. "I think the theme that runs through all my plays is hope," he has said.[1] It's a very Hammerstein-like sentiment; Udell is very close to the Master in his approach if not in his craftsmanship. Unfortunately, to be like Hammerstein in the sixties and seventies was courting disaster. Udell is interested in simple emotions expressed clearly. He shuns cleverness and sophistication and clings to the rural and homespun qualities of life; he is old-fashioned. But Udell and Gary Geld, his composer/collaborator, have consistently provided superior scores for productions that they strongly believed in.

Purlie (1970) was their first Broadway venture and it was a success; it ran for 687 performances, went on a profitable tour, and then returned to Broadway for another run in 1972. Based on Ossie Davis' racial comedy *Purlie Victorious* (1961), the musical accurately expressed the black idiom (Davis assisted with the libretto) and explored prejudice under the guise of musical comedy. Udell's lyrics are appropriately light-hearted for the farcical portions of the story ("New Fangled Preacher Man," "The Harder They Fall," "Big Fish, Little Fish"), while a deeper subtext can be found in the musical's more substantial moments ("Down Home," "First Thing Monday Morning"). Udell's most expansive lyrics are found in the songs of rejoicing: the boastful title song, the exultant gospel number "Walk Him up the Stairs" and the joyous showstopper "I Got Love." This last song is perhaps the closest anyone has come to a black equivalent for Hammerstein's "A Wonderful Guy"; both are unclever, repetitive and irresistible.

Shenandoah (1975) was a homespun tale of family, honor and war with clumsy plotting along the way. Despite mediocre reviews, *Shenandoah* ran even longer than *Purlie*. The melodrama got a bit thick at times, but there was a sincerity evident in the book, music and lyrics. The duet "We Make a Beautiful Pair," the straightforward "The Pickers Are Comin'" and the hymnlike "Pass the Cross to Me" are winning, and "Violets and Silverbells" is an agreeable wedding song. "Over the Hill" is an entertaining character song in the vein of *Oklahoma!*, and "Next to Lovin' (I Like Fightin')" has the kind of lyric energy that distinguishes much of *Purlie*. But other songs tend to annoy, such as the inane "Why Am I Me?" and the belabored soliliquies called "Meditations."

The three unsuccessful musicals by Udell and Geld that followed suffered from book and production problems. *Angel* (1978), based on Thomas Wolfe's *Look Homeward, Angel*, has some notable lyric work, including the inspiring "Like the Eagles Fly," the satirical "Make a Little Sunshine" and the lovely ballad "Railbird." *Comin' Uptown* (1979) was a musical *A Christmas Carol* set in Harlem. The urban setting was not conducive to the team's talents, perhaps, for very little of the score is noteworthy. *The Amen Corner* (1983), based on James Baldwin's play of the same name, returned to the gospel singing of *Purlie*, but the musical was dreary and uneventful. But even in those later musicals Udell retained his clear-headed, compassionate philosophy. Perhaps future theatregoers will look at the work of Peter Udell less skeptically.

For many years certain creative areas of the American musical theatre were closed to women artists. Female composers and directors, for example, were almost unheard of. But theatre lyricwriting, for some reason, was not denied them, and the history of Broadway recognizes several women who wrote lyrics. Since the turn of the century some of these writers have contributed to major Broadway successes. Rida Johnson Young penned the book and lyrics for Victor Herbert's *Naughty Marietta* (1910) and Sigmund Romberg's *Maytime* (1917). Dorothy Donnelly wrote the books and lyrics for Romberg's *Blossom Time* (1921) and *The Student Prince of Heidelberg* (1924). Anne Caldwell was another busy Broadway writer from 1912 until her retirement in 1928. Caldwell collaborated with Jerome Kern on eight musicals in which she provided lyrics and often the librettos. All three of these women were fully professional, well-respected writers who held their own in a business dominated by men. One can find nothing remotely feminist in their work, but they were able to bring a woman's touch to the songs, if not a woman's point of view. Few musicals or operettas of the 1910s and 1920s had much thematic substance in any case. In the thirties, forties and fifties the musical changed enough to allow a varying point of view. We have seen how the careers of Dorothy Fields, Betty Comden and Carolyn Leigh played a part in the developing musical theatre, but none of these writers could be labeled feminist. Their lyrics often convey a woman's insight into some issues (usually regarding male-female relationships), but there is no overt feminist outlook in their work. It would not be until the 1960s, when so many sacred cows perished, that a timely feminist musical was possible. Many were written, some were produced, few were notable. But there are three women lyricists whose work does bear closer study. Gretchen Cryer, Micki Grant and Carol Hall each contributed to the mainstream of musical theatre by bringing forward very individual sociopolitical and feminist ideas.

Gretchen Cryer and Nancy Ford are unique for being the first and most successful female songwriting team in the American musical theatre. Ford provided the music and Cryer the lyrics and librettos for a series of musicals off and on Broadway starting in the late 1960s. Their musicals have always tackled controversial topics and contemporary problems. But it is their high level of craftsmanship and their sense of humor that distinguish their musicals from the many others of similar intent that arose during a turbulent era. Born in rural Indiana, Cryer studied English literature at DePauw University, where she met and began writing with Nancy Ford. Her first Broadway job was as a chorus member in *Little Me* and later in *110 in the Shade*. While performing she continued to collaborate with Ford. Their first professionally produced musical, *Now Is the Time for All Good Men*, opened Off Broadway in 1967. A melodramatic tale about a conscientious objector, the musical boasted a strong if conventional score and an honest attempt to deal with a difficult subject. *The Last Sweet Days of Isaac* (1970) also opened Off Broadway but became a well-known hit, running for 485 performances. Cryer's libretto, two stories about the lack of communication in society, was breezy, satirical and intelligent. The score this time was rock but, in the lyrics particularly, was firmly rooted in the musical theatre tradition. Rock scores on and off Broadway were numerous by 1970 but *The Last Sweet Days of Isaac* was the first to illustrate that rock music and musical theatre could coexist in a show with pleasant results. In the first playlet, set in a stalled elevator, there is an intriguing song, "My Most Important Moments Go By," a delightful character song, "A Transparent Crystal Moment," and a revealing comic number, "Love, You Came to Me." The second half of the musical grows more somber and contains a protest song, "Herein Lie the Seeds of Revolution," a gospel number called "Yes, I Know That I'm Alive," and a chilling antiwar song, "Somebody Died Today." *The Last Sweet Days of Isaac* is dated now and revivals are difficult, but it is an important score not only for Cryer and Ford but for the development of the musical form.

The team's one Broadway musical was the short-lived *Shelter* (1973), a piece about technology and its effect on personal communication. Less vibrant than *The Last Sweet Days of Isaac* and too narrow for popular Broadway tastes, *Shelter* lasted only a month. Returning to Off Broadway, Cryer and Ford presented *I'm Getting My Act Together and Taking It On the Road* in 1978. Cryer's libretto, about a divorced singer/soap opera actress trying for a comeback, was somewhat autobiographical and featured Cryer herself in the central role. Some dismissed the show as feminist propaganda; others found it disturbingly accurate without being preachy. But there was little doubt about its potency and its popularity; it ran for 1,165 performances, one of the longest-running Off-Broadway musicals on record. *I'm Getting My Act Together* is the team's finest score. It combines the forthright, aggressive quality of their early work with a more polished, more personal viewpoint. "Smile" and "Dear Tom" are powerful songs that avoid bitterness and simplified solutions. "Put in a Package and Sold" is a wry commentary on the artificiality of show business, "Miss America" is a sardonic song about the illusions we have about womanhood, and "Old Friend" is a moving tribute about friendships that outlast love affairs. Cryer and Ford even include a vapid, pretty pop ballad, "In a Simple Way I Love You," to contrast the main character's past and future directions. The most characteristic song in the musical is "Strong Woman Number," a seriocomic piece about the frustrations of being a self-sufficient woman in the 1970s—the kind of woman that men find "so easy to leave." Cryer and Ford continue to write together and can often be found performing their work in nightclubs and workshops. It can only be hoped that one of the most topical and personal of all songwriting teams will once again be represented on or Off Broadway with a new musical.

Micki Grant, the black composer/lyricist, also began her career performing and, like Gretchen Cryer, often appeared in her own works.

Grant's lyrics also deal with the role of individuals, women in particular, within society at large. But Grant brings the perspective of a black woman and her songs are potent and unique. Grant was born in Chicago and was educated at the University of Illinois, Roosevelt University and de Paul University. She made her acting debut in New York in 1962 and continued to appear in several plays and musical revues Off-Broadway, most notably *Brecht on Brecht* (1963), *Tambourines to Glory* (1964) and *To Be Young, Gifted and Black* (1969). In 1970 Grant formed a partnership with producer Vinnette Carroll and they presented a series of musical revues for the Urban Arts Corps in New York. Grant wrote the music and lyrics for the Corps' most popular musical, *Don't Bother Me, I Can't Cope* (1971), which moved to Broadway in 1972 where it ran for 1,065 performances. Grant also appeared in this all-black musical revue, which explored various aspects of contemporary life. The score ranges from calypso to gospel to folk and the lyrics are sharp and funny. The title song is a playful comic number about the pressures of modern times, but there is a genuine desperation present as well. "Fighting for Pharoh" is a simple but eloquent anti-war song ("turn our children's history books around," it pleads), and there is a lovely, evocative song called "Questions" that has powerful, specific imagery ("which hand do I shake?"). The score for *Don't Bother Me, I Can't Cope* is one of the brightest to come from a modern musical revue; it enthralled black and white audiences for many months.

Grant scored nine other musicals in the 1970s even as she continued performing on stage and on television. *Your Arms Too Short to Box With God* was created for the 1975 Spoleto Festival in Italy and then moved to Broadway in 1976. It is a retelling of St. Matthew's gospel as presented at a black revival meeting. Grant provided half of the songs (Alex Bradford contributed the other half, including the wonderful title song) and again her sense of humor shone through the gospel music format. The lively "We're Gonna Have a Good Time," the driving "We Are the Priests and Elders," and the dramatic "It's Too Late for Judas" are highlights in an exciting score. The musical was revived on Broadway in 1981.

Other memorable musicals that Grant contributed songs to include Stephen Schwartz's *Working* (1978), new lyrics for some Eubie Blake tunes in the Broadway revue *Eubie* (1979), and the AMAS Repertory Theatre's *It's So Nice to Be Civilized* (1979), which moved to Broadway in 1980. Micki Grant may not enjoy the popularity of other contemporary composer/lyricists, but her work is important in the development of black musicals into mainstream Broadway products. Her lyric work is strongly focused, of high craftsmanship and cannot be ignored.

On the basis of one musical, *The Best Little Whorehouse in Texas*, composer/lyricist Carol Hall should be included with these influential women writers of the 1970s. A veteran of the music business, Hall made her Broadway debut in 1978. But that debut was not so much a beginning as a culmination of decades of training and experience. Hall was born in Abilene, Texas, in 1936. Her family owned a music store and Hall received classical piano training by her mother, a piano and violin teacher. By the age of twelve Hall was a piano soloist for the Dallas Symphony Orchestra. She was educated at Sweet Briar College in Virginia and at Sarah Lawrence College, where she studied music with avant-garde composer Meyer Kupferman. Always having loved the theatre and popular music, Hall spent her summers writing and producing small musical shows at a summer theatre in Virginia. After graduation in 1960 she went to New York hoping to write songs for the theatre. She met with little success so she started composing popular songs; before long her work was recorded by Mabel Mercer, Barbra Streisand, Harry Belafonte, Barbara Cook, Neil Diamond and others. Hall also composed songs for children's records, the television program *Sesame Street*, and for the acclaimed TV special *Free to Be You and Me*.

Still trying to break into Broadway musicals, Hall wrote a show called *Wonderful Beast* that was produced briefly at Cafe LaMama in 1977. But she really wanted to write a musical set in her native Texas. Writer and fellow Texan Peter Masterson suggested they musicalize the story of the Chicken Ranch, a Texas whorehouse made famous through a magazine article by Larry L. King. With King and Masterson providing the libretto and Hall the songs, *The Best Little Whorehouse in Texas* opened Off Off Broadway, then moved to Off Broadway, and finally to Broadway in 1978, where it ran for 1,584 performances. While much of the praise for the muscial went to director/choreographer Tommy Tune (another Texan), *The Best Little Whorehouse in Texas* has many merits. The libretto has trouble blending the caricatures with the more serious aspects of the story but it is a tight, entertaining book. Hall's score is an invigorating mixture of rousing comic numbers and tender, fragile songs. It is sometimes mock country-western, other times pure Broadway. Hall herself described the songs as "written by someone with a classical background who absorbed the Nashville sound and who always wanted a career on Broadway."[2] The musical's opening number, "20

Fans," sets the tone: folksy, irreverent and sly. But before long songs like "Girl, You're a Woman" and "Bus From Amarillo" reveal lyric work that goes much deeper than the cheerful tale of politics, preachers and prostitutes. "The Sidestep" and "The Aggie Song" are inventive comic numbers, and "Good Old Girl" is a tender ballad. The bittersweet "Hard Candy Christmas" is filled with jaded optimism, "No Lies" and "Doatsey Mae" are knowing character songs and "Twenty Four Hours of Lovin'" is a jubilant gospel number. Few Broadway scores of the 1970s have as much variety, energy and richness as Hall's for *The Best Little Whorehouse in Texas*. In 1985 Hall wrote the book, music and lyrics for the Off-Broadway musical *To Whom It May Concern*, an inventive piece that explored the thoughts of a church congregation. She has also performed, taking over the central role in Cryer's *I'm Getting My Act Together* during part of its long run.

The contributions of Gretchen Cryer, Micki Grant and Carol Hall are important not only for the individual musicals that they wrote but also for the pattern they have created allowing women to write about women for the musical theatre. Unlike the women lyricists who preceded them, these writers bring a personal vision that is possible because of their being women, not in spite of it. Cryer, Grant and Hall are more than products of their time; they are voices whose exact temperament had never been heard in the musical theatre before.

Martin Charnin is a man with many hats: lyricist, director, television producer, and actor (he played one of the Jets in the original *West Side Story*). His lyricwriting is perhaps the least of his many talents, but he has written several shows and he was most responsible for *Annie*, one of the major hits of the 1970s. Charnin began his writing career by contributing lyrics to a handful of revues on and Off Broadway in the late fifties and sixties. He collaborated with Richard Rodgers and provided lyrics for two of his later musicals: the less-than-admirable *Two by Two* (1970) and the embarrassing *I Remember Mama* (1979), which was Rodgers' last show. Charnin's lyrics were heard in other forgotten musicals (although many feel that *The First* in 1981 deserves a second chance), but with *Annie* (1977) he had an unqualified hit. Among the many elements that made *Annie* work—Thomas Meehan's crisp, nonsensical libretto, Charles Strouse's bouncy music, and a polished production directed by Charnin—the lyrics are the least impressive. But all those years in the profession did amount to something and Charnin provided some enjoyable lyrics for *Annie*. "Easy Street," "Little Girls" and "It's a Hard-Knock Life" are sassy and buoyant. "Maybe" is an agreeable little song of yearning and "A New Deal for Christmas" has a definite thirties quality to it. Other parts of the score are cloying: "I Think I'm Going to Like It Here," "NYC" and, unbearable even at first hearing, "Tomorrow." How much more effective Charnin is when he parodies such optimism, as in the droll "You're Never Fully Dressed without a Smile."

A disturbing trend found among Broadway songwriters during the 1960s and 1970s is the number of writers who scored one major hit musical and then never again produced any work of note. This was a pattern not found often in earlier decades. Sherman Edwards, for example, conceived the idea and wrote the music and lyrics for the 1969 musical *1776*. Edwards was a former high school history teacher and a pop songwriter of some success so it was more than sheer luck that produced a musical that ran for 1,297 performances. The score for *1776* is an odd but pleasing mixture of styles: period minuets, Broadway character songs, Gilbert and Sullivan–like choral numbers, folk ballads and even the musical patter of the auctioneer. The lyric work is often impressive, especially in the quiet "Momma, Look Sharp," the stirring "Molasses to Rum" and the elegant "Cool, Cool Considerate Men." But the musical theatre never heard from Sherman Edwards again. Much the same thing happened to Charlie Smalls, the composer/lyricist for *The Wiz* (1975). Smalls had a solid musical background—education at Juilliard, professional experience with bands and nightclubs, scores for films—and his work for *The Wiz* promised an exciting career on Broadway for this black songwriter. Smalls' score remains faithful to all the musical influences that went into *The Wiz*: gospel, rap songs, blues and pop. The lyrics are carefree and repetitive when appropriate ("Ease on Down the Road" and "Don't Nobody Bring Me No Bad News") or emotional and dramatic when necessary ("Home" and "Be a Lion"). *The Wiz* was perhaps the first musical that appealed equally to black and white audiences.

Joe Darion, on the other hand, has had a longer Broadway career but he also is known for only one musical. Darion has written for theatre, television, film, radio and the concert hall. He received some attention for his lyrics for *Shinbone Alley* (1957), a musical adaptation of Don Marquis' *archy & mehitabel* stories with music by George Kleinsinger. But recognition would not come until 1965 with *Man of La Mancha*. There is no question that some of Darion's lyrics for this popular musical have aged poorly; the whole show has as much a sixties mentality as a Spanish Renaissance feel. But if one considers how awful a Broadway musical version of Cervantes' massive *Don Quixote* could be, one realizes how considerable an achievement *Man of La Mancha* really is. Dale Wasserman's libretto makes the intricate tale stageworthy and Mitch Leigh's music wisely suggests rather than authenticates the sound of the period. Darion's lyrics usually retain an earthbound naturalism even when the story wishes to push them to grand opera proportions. "Dulcinea," "What Do You Want with Me?" and "To Each His Dulcinea" are rhapsodic but carefully restrained. On the other hand, "The Quest" (better known as "The Impossible Dream") is lofty and, perhaps appropriately, pretentious. Darion is less successful with his comic songs. "A Little Gossip," "I'm Only Thinking of Him" and "I Really Like Him" try for a folk charm but are predictable and unsatisfactory. But whatever its shortcomings, the score for *Man of La Mancha* is an expert accomplishment. Joe Darion did not disappear after *Man of La Mancha* but his succeeding works—*Illya Darling* in 1967 and *The Megilla of Itzik Manager* in 1968—were of little consequence.

Although Michael Stewart had started out as a lyricist, his fame in the 1960s was due to his librettos for such musicals as *Bye Bye Birdie*, *Hello, Dolly!* and *Carnival*. In 1977 Stewart wrote both the book and lyrics for *I Love My Wife*, a lame little musical about the sexual revolution in suburbia, which boasted an interesting score with music by Cy Coleman. "Hey There, Good Times" is a lively number that recalls Coleman and Carolyn Leigh's work a decade earlier. "Lovers on Christmas Eve" and "Someone Wonderful I Missed" are pleasing ballads and the title song is affecting. But much of the rest of the lyrics succumb to the juvenile humor of the libretto. *Barnum* (1980), again with music by Coleman, is more accomplished. Mark Bramble's libretto about the famous showman was negligible, but Joe Layton's inventive staging and the Coleman/Stewart score created the illusion that something sensational was going on. "The Colors of My Life" is an original ballad, "Bigger Isn't Better" and "Black and White" are highly entertaining and there is clever lyric work in "The Museum Song." Michael Stewart was a lightweight songwriter but some of his lyrics had a vitality that was sorely needed in the 1970s.

Another pattern that began in the 1960s and continues strong to this day is the transferring of promising Off-Broadway musicals to Broadway. When *Hair* moved from Joseph Papp's Public Theatre to Broadway in 1968 it brought more than an Off-Broadway sentiment with it. *Hair* turned what many considered a subculture into mainstream entertainment.

The score by Galt MacDermot (music), Gerome Ragni and James Rado (lyrics and libretto as well) was uncompromisingly rock and made no concessions to any of the Broadway traditions. The non-book story did not require character songs, for example; this was a score that existed on its own. But there was no question as to the theatricality of the songs, especially in numbers like "Ain't Got No," "Frank Mills" and the title song. The three hits from the score—"Let the Sunshine In," "Good Morning, Starshine" and "Aquarius"—were already popular by the time the revised version of *Hair* opened on Broadway. Others became well known because of the production: "Where Do I Go?" and "Easy to Be Hard," a ballad even conservative audiences could appreciate. Ragni and Rado knew how to write pop hits even if they never cared about writing a theatre score. (Their efforts for Broadway after *Hair* were disastrous.) But the recording of *Hair* became a best seller on a level that few musicals of the sixties or seventies enjoyed.

Grease (1972) also moved from Off Broadway to Broadway, where it stayed for seven and a half years. (For a while it was the longest-running musical on record.) There is not much to recommend in the songs for *Grease* but one cannot totally dismiss a show that was so popular. Jim Jacobs and Warren Casey wrote the book, music and lyrics, and it was readily agreed that their sense of parody was proficient. In a few of the musical numbers the songs moved beyond the fifites-milieu surface and hinted at real characters and emotions. "Alone at a Drive-In Movie" and "There are Worse Things I Could Do" seem more accomplished than mere camp; but they are atypical of the rest of the score.

Of all the Off-Broadway transfers, *A Chorus Line* (1975) has the grandest success story of them all. Starting as a discussion, then a workshop and then a full production at the Public Theatre, *A Chorus Line* moved to Broadway two months later and stayed there for over fourteen years, holding the new record for the longest run. For a musical that originated with performers talking about themselves, *A Chorus Line* is not about words at all. In fact, it's not even about characters or plot. This musical speaks fluently only when it moves and originator-director-choreographer Michael Bennett makes the movement seem like high art. The dreary book by James Kirkwood and Nicholas Dante is saved by the musical numbers which usually rise above the banal clichés that substitute for drama. Marvin Hamlisch's music and Edward Kleban's lyrics are at their best when they explore ideas with a montage approach: "At the Ballet," "I Hope I Get It" and "Hello Twelve, Hello

Thirteen, Hello Fourteen." "Sing!" is a comic solo that skillfully sustains a thin idea, "I Can Do That" is a breezy lyric and there is an enchanted quality to "The Music and the Mirror." Where Kleban falls short is in the forced comedy ("Dance: Ten; Looks: Three"), the non-dramatic narrative ("Nothing") and in the manufactured kind of pathos ("What I Did For Love"). *A Chorus Line* may be the quintessential Broadway musical of the post-fifties; it is high quality and high style but it is practically mute when it comes to the words.

There were also plenty of Off-Broadway musicals during this period that were more than content to stay there. *You're a Good Man, Charlie Brown* (1967) played for 1,597 performances without moving to Broadway. It was a modest musical in scope and talent that gained strength and charm through its simplicity. Clark Gesner wrote the book, music and lyrics and was faithful to the Charles M. Schulz comic strip that inspired the show. *You're a Good Man, Charlie Brown* is unique in that all the musical numbers are character songs. Even the multicharacter "The Book Report" concentrates on individuals, and the group numbers, such as "Baseball Game" and the title song, are focused on one character. "Happiness Is" was the heart-warming finale and did travel a bit; but, like all the songs, taken out of context it was less effective. *Your Own Thing* (1968), another Off-Broadway mainstay that ran for 933 performances, lampooned the sixties as *Grease* had the fifties. But *Your Own Thing* held together better (it was based on Shakespeare's *Twelfth Night*) and had some delightful moments of musical comedy. The music and lyrics are by Hal Hester and Danny Apolinar and, while some songs are unbearable even as parody, others ("The Middle Years," "Be Gentle" and "What Do I Know?") deserve more attention than a silly musical like *Your Own Thing* affords them.

The Robber Bridegroom and *Man With a Load of Mischief* only had modest runs Off Broadway but boasted superior scores. *The Robber Bridegroom* began as part of the repertory of the touring Acting Company. After a brief stay in New York it reopened on Broadway in 1976. Based on a tall tale by Eudora Welty, *The Robber Bridegroom* relied on farce, folklore and a mystical feeling for the fanciful. The score (music by Robert Waldman, lyrics by Alfred Uhry) uses a lot of bluegrass but adheres to the musical comedy format. "Steal With Style" and "Pickle Pear and Lilybud" are top-notch character songs. "Ain't Nothin' Up" is a dreamy piece that captivates, and "Love Stolen" is a dashing solo about love triumphant. *The Robber Bridegroom* gave the appearance of a comic free-for-all but all the shenanigans were held together by an exemplary score.

Man With a Load of Mischief (1966) was a much classier affair, telling a romantic tale about six inhabitants of a nineteenth-century wayside inn. John Clifton wrote the music and, with Ben Tarver, the lyrics for this unique Off-Broadway musical. The score is sumptuous and, once heard, not easily forgotten. The lyrics stay within the romanticized decorum of the period with the sextet of characters and voices drifting in and out as in a chamber piece. The imagery in the songs is sweeping but the lyrics never fall into excess. Clifton and Tarver use metaphor as well as verse narrative effectively. "Masquerade," "Little Rag Doll" and "Hulla-Baloo-Balay" are standouts in a score that never disappoints. *Man With a Load of Mischief* was perhaps the antithesis of the rock musicals that would dominate Broadway and Off Broadway for a time, so the little musical was rarely produced during the years following its run in 1966–1967. But *Man With a Load of Mischief* is being rediscovered along with many other works of the sixties and seventies that did not conform to the current fashion. Perhaps we are still learning to appreciate what we lost when rock came in.

NOTES

1. Al Kasha and Joel Hirschorn, *Notes on Broadway: Conversations with the Great Songwriters* (Chicago: Contemporary Books, 1985), p. 303.

2. Stanley Green, *The World of Musical Comedy* (New York: A. S. Barnes & Co., Inc., 1980), p. 377.

22

The Writing on the Wall: The 1980s

Composer/lyricist William Finn can possibly serve as a metaphor for the 1980s. Finn was represented Off Broadway near the beginning and again at the end of the decade. Both Finn and the 1980s appeared to be very promising at first; by 1990 the promises seemed unfulfilled and disappointment set in. There were many lyricists who made their debut during the decade and several of them are still very promising. But too often these new talents were defeated by flawed librettos, unpopular productions or the poor economic climate. There were more encouraging lyricists in the 1980s than in the previous decade, but the musical theatre of the 1980s did less to nurture them. None should be dismissed yet. The process takes longer these days, and only the 1990s will be able to tell which of these songwriters will make the greatest impact.

William Finn must still be watched. He was educated at Williams College as an English major and he wrote three original musicals there with such unlikely subject matter as the Rosenbergs' case, prostitution and Aubrey Beardsley. After graduation Finn made his living writing history plays for the junior high school level. Playwrights Horizons first gave a workshop production of one of his scripts, and in 1981 Second Stage produced his *In Trousers*, a small musical about a bisexual named Marvin. The unusual piece drew some attention but it was its sequel, *March of the Falsettos* (1981), that prompted raves from critics and audiences alike. As would become more popular during the 1980s,

March of the Falsettos was completely sung and lyrics and libretto were indistinguishable from each other. The plot revolves around Marvin, his ex-wife, his male lover, his adolescent son and the psychiatrist who treats them all. The music was pleasing and the small production was inventive but it was the lyrics that were most impressive. The opening number, "Four Jews in a Room Bitching," makes it clear that this is not an ordinary approach to musical theatre. What follows are musical arguments ("The Thrill of First Love," "The Chess Game"), fantasy (the title song), a mini-opera ("Marvin at the Psychiatrist") and five-way bewilderment ("Love Is Blind," "This Had Better Come To a Stop"). There is not a campy or cheap moment in the score; everything is honest and knowing. Yet the musical has a highly stylized, almost surreal quality to it. The songs are too specific to become popular outside of the show's context but "The Games I Play" and "I Never Wanted to Love You" are among the most effective ballads to come out of the 1980s.

After *March of the Falsettos* Finn contributed lyrics here and there but not until 1989 was a full score of his heard Off Broadway again. *Romance in Hard Times* was a confusing muddle and what quality there was in the songs was sabotaged by Finn's libretto. Critics quickly took back all the praise they had heaped on *March of the Falsettos*. William Finn is probably a sporadic talent and the promise of his early work cannot yet be dismissed.

Lyricist/librettist Howard Ashman and his composer/collaborator Alan Menken first gained some notice with their Off-Broadway musical *God Bless You, Mr. Rosewater* (1979), based on the Kurt Vonnegut novel. It only ran for forty-nine performances but the odd little musical foreshadowed the offbeat approach that Ashman and Menken would take with the popular *Little Shop of Horrors* (1982). Again Ashman wrote the libretto and lyrics, building on Roger Corman's low-budget movie of the same name, but the musical version far surpassed the campy quality of the cult film. *Little Shop of Horrors*, like *March of the Falsettos*, creates its own reality, utilizing the freedom of the musical comedy genre. Ashman and Menken had a lot of fun spoofing the early 1960s in *Little Shop of Horrors* but the musical went beyond parody. The nerdy Seymour is a caricature, yet when he sings about "Skid Row" or pleads with the plant to "Grow For Me," a true character is revealed. The scatterbrained Audrey lampoons the popular culture of the sixties in "Somewhere That's Green" but the song has more than a touch of heartbreak to it. Perhaps the most mesmerizing song in the score is "Suddenly Seymour," a duet for two of life's losers that turns into a full-blown romantic number filled with "sweet understanding."

Ashman teamed up with composer Marvin Hamlisch for *Smile* (1986), a tale about a junior beauty contest based on the 1975 film. Ashman directed as well as provided the libretto and lyrics, but *Smile* suffered from inconsistency of tone, pointless satire and poorly developed characters. But the score has its moments of honesty and affection and Ashman displays a sense of subtlety at times. One hopes that Ashman will not be lost to the movies (he and Menken wrote the admirable score for Disney's *The Little Mermaid* in 1989) and will return to the musical theatre before long.

The career of lyricist Richard Maltby, Jr., stretches back to the 1960s but only in the 1980s did he emerge as a major talent. Maltby is the son of an orchestra leader and was educated at Yale, where he met fellow student David Shire, who would become his most frequent composer/collaborator. Their 1961 Off-Broadway musical *The Sap of Life* was short lived but showed promise. Their revue *Starting Here, Starting Now* (1977) was the team's first success, modest as it was. This Off-Broadway revue's score is a refreshing, romantic celebration of life and love and has received hundreds of productions regionally over the years. The next year Maltby's intimate little revue of the works of Thomas "Fats" Waller opened for a limited run at the Manhattan Theatre Club. Maltby conceived and directed the revue and wrote lyrics for a half dozen Waller songs. *Ain't Misbehavin'* (1978), as the show was titled, was so popular it moved to Broadway, where it ran for 1,604 performances; many still consider it the finest revue of the eighties.

In 1983 Maltby's first and, to date, only Broadway musical with Shire opened: *Baby*. Sybille Pearson's libretto, about three very different couples expecting or hoping for a baby, was ambitious and witty, if a bit too clinical for some tastes. But it was the Maltby/Shire score that triumphed. The songs subtly shift in style from one couple to another but the whole is consistent and harmonious. Maltby's lyrics are filled with insightful humor, conversational clarity and contagious joy. From the eager trio "I Want It All" to the reflective "Patterns," the character development in the songs recalls the dexterity of Stephen Sondheim. The comic frolic "Fatherhood Blues" and the discerning "Easier to Love" are also highlights in this exceptional score. But *Baby* was too small, too personal for a Broadway musical (it clearly belonged Off Broadway) and lasted only seven months. But the musical has often been effectively revived in smaller theatres across the country. Maltby next adapted the English lyrics for and directed Andrew Lloyd Webber's *Song and Dance* when the American version opened on Broadway in 1985. The "song" section of the musical was an extended solo turn by Bernadette Peters, and Maltby's lyric work is honest and engaging. Maltby and Shire wrote some small musical revues in the eighties that were revised and polished into the Off-Broadway revue *Closer Than Ever* (1989). Like *Starting Here, Starting Now*, this revue was a sparkling look at life, but this time the viewpoint was more mature and explored various decisions and compromises. The full story of Richard Maltby's career can only be partially examined at this writing. His biggest hit, *Miss Saigon*, is yet to open on Broadway, but it is the most popular musical in London, where it premiered in 1989. Maltby adapted Alain Boublil's French libretto/lyrics for *Miss Saigon*, set to music by Claude-Michel Shonberg. It looks as though Maltby, after more than thirty years of lyricwriting, will finally score a megahit.

Maury Yeston, a composer as well as a lyricist, has a more formal musical background than most songwriters. Yeston was educated at Yale and Clare College/Cambridge University. While he was still a student his first orchestral pieces were performed by notable groups. Yeston has written several concert works (his *Goya: A Life in Song* was recorded in 1989), two books on music theory and currently teaches at Yale. He made his Broadway debut with his music and lyrics for *Nine* (1982). Yeston's songs were somewhat overshadowed by director/choreographer Tommy Tune's dazzling staging, but the score is an exceptional one. Arthur Kopit and Mario Fratti's libretto reduced Federico Fellini's film *8 1/2* to tired clichés, but the lyrics often lifted the production up to an adult level of originality. "Guido's Song," the main character's confession of his paradoxical nature, is entertaining and revealing. "Be On Your Own" is highly dramatic and "Only With You" is a sad love tribute sung to too many women. Yeston's lyric work ranges from the complex ("Germans at the Spa," "Not Since Chaplin") to the simply moving ("Growing Tall" and the title song) but the most intriguing lyric in the score is "My Husband Makes Movies," a painfully absorbing portrait of the private and public personas of the two major characters.

Yeston was not represented on Broadway again until the end of the decade, when he did revisions for *Grand Hotel* (1989). Composer/lyricists Robert Wright and George Forrest had previously attempted musical versions of Vicki Baum's novel, but this production, with a libretto by

Luther Davis, was dominated by Tommy Tune's highly theatrical vision of a dark Berlin of 1928. When *Grand Hotel* was in trouble out of town, Tune called in Yeston, who revised the lyrics of nine of the Wright/Forrest songs and wrote seven new numbers for the show. When the musical opened in New York, Tune once again garnered most of the praise for his ingenious staging but Yeston, Wright and Forrest provided some excellent support. "Maybe My Baby Loves Me" and "Who Couldn't Dance With You?" (both by Wright/Forrest) are infectiously joyous. Yeston's "I Want To Go To Hollywood" and "Bonjour Amour" are very touching in their subtext. Yeston also has an expansive love duet called "Love Can't Happen", and his revised lyrics make "Fire and Ice" and "Roses at the Station" very poignant.

Rupert Holmes' Broadway debut with *The Mystery of Edwin Drood* (1985)—during its Broadway run the title was shortened to *Drood*—was impressive for several reasons, not the least being that Holmes wrote the libretto, music, lyrics and even the orchestrations for the "musical mystery." Holmes has both a classical and popular musical background. He was born in England to an American father, who later taught music at Juilliard, and a British mother, who instilled in him a devotion for English composers. Holmes was educated at the Manhattan School of Music, then went into the pop music business, where he produced, arranged and/or composed several albums. His songs often had a narrative ("Escape" or "The Piña Colada Song" was his biggest hit) and, with his fascination with British mystery/thrillers, it was understandable that his first theatre piece would be a musical version of Charles Dickens' unfinished novel. Holmes wrote several different endings for *The Mystery of Edwin Drood* and let the audience at each performance decide who had "done it." The gimmick made the musical unique but it also kept the events and characters at such an analytical distance that the whole venture was often uninvolving. The score is rich and varied, employing operetta, British music hall, melodrama and traditional musical comedy. The action involves suspects rather than fully realized characters, but sometimes the lyrics are quite emotional. The duets "Perfect Strangers" and "Moonfall" are effective in very different ways. The rousing opener "There You Are," the vaudevillelike "Off To the Races" and the exhilarating chorus number "Don't Quit While You're Ahead" are all highly entertaining. "The Wages of Sin" is a melodramatic solo that is neatly stylized; the inspiring finale, "The Writing on the Wall," is also memorable. *The Mystery of Edwin Drood* proved to be a disappointment to those expecting a full-bodied musical, but there was no question of a formidable talent at work.

One of the most sensational productions of the decade was *Dreamgirls* (1981), Michael Bennett's high-powered vision of the entertainment world as seen through a sixties pop group. Tom Eyen wrote the libretto and lyrics for the musical and Henry Krieger composed the music. Much of the score echoes the Motown sound of that era but some songs rely on the traditional musical comedy format. Sometimes the musical numbers are designed to show off the vocal gymnastics of the performer ("And I'm Telling You I'm Not Going," for example), rather than pursuing character or plot. But "One Night Only" is a driving lyric that pushes the action forward and "When I First Saw You" is a complex and moving ballad. Eyen's most ambitious lyric is "Cadillac Car," an extended musical sequence that parallels social changes with the growth of the characters. While *Dreamgirls* without Michael Bennett's staging is a less-than-flawless vehicle, the work of Tom Eyen is very encouraging.

Krieger worked with lyricist Robert Lorick on *The Tap Dance Kid* (1983) and, while the production was not as slick as *Dreamgirls*, there was much in the musical to recommend. Charles Blackwell's libretto, about the dance world's influence on a black family that is striving for social acceptance, was often powerful and the Krieger/Lorick score was consistently expert. "Another Day," "Four Strikes Against Me" and "Someday" are winning character songs. The dreamy "Man in the Moon" and the warm "I Could Get Used to Him" are also effective. Lorick uses some tricky word play in "Like Him," an interesting mother/daughter duet, and "William's Song" is a highly explosive musical monologue. *The Tap Dance Kid* had a modest Broadway run but the score deserved better.

Edging into the limelight as the decade ended was David Zippel with his lyrics for *City of Angels* (1989). Zippel's work had been heard around New York throughout the 1980s but usually in disjointed pieces. He contributed to the Off-Broadway revue *A . . . My Name is Alice* (1984), wrote the lyrics for the short-lived Kipling musical *Just So* (1985) and provided songs for Radio City shows and for such recording artists as Barbara Cook, Michael Feinstein, Debbie Shapiro and Ann Reinking. But *City of Angels* made him a full-fledged Broadway lyricist. Larry Gelbart's libretto and Cy Coleman's music got all the notice but Zippel's contribution must be acknowledged. While the double film-noir plot depended on jokes and gimmicks to sustain itself, the lyrics were often substantial, honest and well crafted. "What You Don't Know About Women" and "You're Nothing Without Me" are pleasing duets that artfully mix real and fictional characters. "It Needs Work" displays a depth of character not found in the libretto. Zippel also found an accurate voice for the 1940s-era songs coming from the radio studio with "Ev'rybody's Gotta Be Somewhere" and "Ya Gotta Look Out For Yourself."

Judging by one Broadway and one Off-Broadway musical, perhaps the most promising lyricist to debut during the 1980s was Barry Harman. *Olympus On My Mind* (1986) had a modest run at two Off-Broadway theatres, and *Romance, Romance* (1988) had a less-than-profitable run of 297 performances on Broadway. Harman wrote the librettos and lyrics for both, and his work in each deserves considerable attention. While not as innovative as William Finn and some others, Harman's more traditional musicals are skillfully written and consistently satisfying. *Olympus On My Mind* was a musical farce much along the lines of *The Boys from Syracuse* and *A Funny Thing Happened On the Way to the Forum*. The basis for this musical is the Amphitryon legend with a cast of gods and humans who are light footed, expressive and larger than life. The music by Grant Sturiale is appropriately daffy and anachronistic, and Harman's lyrics move from the witty to the tenderhearted. The musical opens with the zany "Welcome to Greece," a collegiate-like spoof in which the jokes pay off nicely. "Heaven On Earth" is a rhapsodic duet with the god Jupiter trying to seduce the mortal Alcmene. "The Gods on Tap" is a merry chorus number championing the power of divine intervention; it cleverly takes the form of a tap dance. "Love—What a Concept" is a comic-sad song about discovering human emotion, and "At Liberty in Thebes" is a mirthful number celebrating feminine sexual freedom. Harman also reveals a deft talent for the ballad form as well; "Something of Yourself" and "Wait til It Dawns" are original and attractive.

Romance, Romance was really two intimate little musicals about two sets of lovers. Harman moves from the silliness of *Olympus On My Mind* to a more mature and deeply felt temperament in *Romance, Romance*, and Keith Hermann's gentle music helps set the mood. The first playlet tells of a love affair in nineteenth-century Vienna. Music and lyrics are elegant and poetic but quite truthful. If *Olympus On My Mind* reminded one of Stephen Sondheim's *Forum*, this mini-musical recalled his *A Little Night Music*. "Oh, What a Performance" is an intriguing look at role-playing within the period's mores. "Yes, It's Love" is a fresh and engaging solo about a familiar theme. "I'll Always Remember That Song" is a lively polka, and "The Night It Had To End" mixes whimsy and intellect. The second playlet is set in the Hamptons today. Harman shifts gears subtly and the parallels between the two stories unfold easelessly. "It's Not Too Late (For Love)" is used in both acts with slightly altered lyrics and tempos. "Think of the Odds" is a cynical song about platonic love, and "So Glad I Married" has a dangerous subtext. Few musicals explore the intricacies of marriage as successfully as the lyrics in this section of *Romance, Romance*. But the four-character musical looked puny in a Broadway house and its charm was not high powered enough to attract an audience. *Romance, Romance* was only mildly entertaining, but Harman's lyric power was full bodied and exciting.

Final mention must be made of some other lyricists who debuted during the 1980s. Craig Carnelia's music and lyrics for *Three Postcards* (1987) are noteworthy. Carnelia had contributed songs to *Notes: Songs* (1978), *Working* (1978), *Is There Life After High School?* (1982) and other shows but his sensitive and revealing lyrics for Craig Lucas' *Three Postcards* point to a writer worth watching. Douglas J. Cohen's *No Way To Treat A Lady* (1987) did not please all, but one could not help but credit the talents of the man who wrote the book, music and lyrics for this odd little musical. The same can be said for Peter Tolan's satirical Off-Broadway revue *Laughing Matters* (1989) and Michael Colby's music hall melodrama *Charlotte Sweet* (1982). Tolan provided both music and lyrics for his revue, while Colby wrote the all-lyrics libretto for *Charlotte Sweet* with music by Gerald Jay Markoe. Many dismissed Roger Miller's songs for *Big River* (1985) as too country western for Broadway, but Miller's score has some fine lyric work with exemplary character development. Broadway could do much worse than have Roger Miller score another musical in the future. And there is no question that it should welcome back William Dumaresq, who wrote the lyrics for Galt MacDermot's *The Human Comedy* (1983). This sentimental and near-operatic version of William Saroyan's novel moved from the Public Theatre to Broadway in 1984; despite favorable reviews it only lasted ten weeks. Both the MacDermot/Dumaresq score and Broadway deserved better.

"I have read the writing on the wall," Rupert Holmes' lyric boasts. "What a bloody marvel we survive!" The new generation of America lyricists left several images on the wall for us to interpret. Some of the writers move ahead with innovation, others embrace tradition, still others are influenced by the invasion of British musicals and the pop opera trend. Economics has reduced the number of musicals produced (at least on Broadway), so it is inaccurate to read too much into any one product. Even the most influential musicals of the past—such as *Show Boat*, *West Side Story*, *Company*—could not immediately change the direction of the musical theatre; much of Broadway continued on in its various forms. Only in the long run did these shows eventually influence the way the musical spoke. So no one musical or songwriter from the 1980s can hope to correctly tell us what that writing on the wall says.

The art of lyricwriting has survived the rock invasion, the shift from words to dance, the predominance of spectacle over substance, and all the other trends that doomsayers declare as the death blow for the musical theatre. But lyrics are still as important as they've ever been. In fact, the recent tendency toward all-sung musicals and all-lyric librettos can point to a newfound appreciation for lyricwriting. Unfortunately these pseudo-operas sometimes reduce lyrics to sung prose. A musical like *Aspects of Love*, for example, is devoid of true lyricism even though the singing never stops. Such an approach to writing musicals is unlikely to be the predominant writing on the wall; there are too many other images up there as well.

If one insists that lyrics are the voice of the musical theatre, then lyrics will be necessary as long as musicals have anything to say. At times it does seem "a bloody marvel we survive." But most of the time it should be evident that the musical theatre cannot help but express itself and it is the lyricist who will be there to put it into words.

Bibliography

Abbott, George. *Mister Abbott*. New York: Random House, 1963.

Altman, Richard, with Mervyn Kaufman. *The Making of a Musical* (Fiddler on the Roof). New York: Crown Publishers, 1971.

Atkinson, Brooks. *Broadway*. New York: Macmillan Publishing Co., Inc., 1974.

Bernstein, Leonard. *Findings*. New York: Simon and Schuster, 1982.

Bordman, Gerald. *American Musical Comedy: From Adonis to Dreamgirls*. New York: Oxford University Press, 1982.

———. *The American Musical Revue: From the Passing Show to Sugar Babies*. New York: Oxford University Press, 1985.

———. *American Musical Theatre: A Chronicle*. New York: Oxford University Press, 1978.

Carter, Randolf. *The World of Flo Ziegfeld*. New York: Praeger Publishers, 1974.

Cohan, George M. *Twenty Years on Broadway*. New York: Harper and Brothers, 1924.

Dietz, Howard. *Dancing in the Dark*. New York: Quadrangle/The New York Times Book Co., 1974.

Donaldson, Frances. *P. G. Wodehouse: A Biography*. New York: Alfred A. Knopf, 1982.

Engel, Lehrman. *The American Musical Theatre: A Consideration*. CBS Legacy Collection Books, 1967.

———. *Their Words Are Music: The Great Theatre Lyricists and Their Lyrics*.

New York: Crown Publishers, 1975.

Ewen, David. *The Complete Book of the American Musical Theatre*. New York: Henry Holt & Co., 1958.

Fordin, Hugh. *Getting To Know Him: A Biography of Oscar Hammerstein II*. New York: Random House, 1977.

Freeland, Michael. *Irving Berlin*. New York: Stein and Day, 1974.

Gershwin, Ira. *Lyrics on Several Occasions*. New York: Viking Press, 1959.

Goldman, William. *The Season*. New York: Harcourt, Brace and World, Inc., 1969.

Gottfried, Martin. *Broadway Musicals*. New York: Harry N. Abrams, Inc., 1980.

————. *A Theatre Divided*. Boston: Little, Brown & Co., 1967.

Green, Benny. *P. G. Wodehouse: A Literary Biography*. New York: The Rutledge Press, 1981.

Green, Stanley. *Encyclopedia of the Musical Theatre*. New York: Dodd, Mead and Co., 1976.

————. *The World of Musical Comedy*. New York: A. S. Barnes & Co., Inc., 1980.

Guernsey, Otis L. (ed). *Broadway Song and Story: Playwrights, Lyricists, Composers Discuss Their Hits*. New York: Dodd, Mead and Co., 1985.

————. *Curtain Times: The New York Theatre 1965–1987*. New York: Applause Theatre Book Publishers, 1987.

————. *Playwrights, Lyricists, Composers on Theatre*. New York: Dodd, Mead and Co., 1974.

Hammerstein, Oscar, II. *Lyrics*. Milwaukee: Hal Leonard Books, 1985.

Hart, Dorothy, and Robert Kimball (eds.). *The Complete Lyrics of Lorenz Hart*. New York: Alfred A. Knopf, 1986.

————. *Thou Swell, Thou Witty: The Life and Lyrics of Lorenz Hart*. New York: Harper & Row, 1976.

Hemming, Roy. *The Melody Lingers On: The Great Songwriters and Their Movie Musicals*. New York: Newmarket Press, 1986.

Henderson, Mary C. *Theatre in America*. New York: Harry N. Abrams, Inc., 1986.

Herbert, Ian (ed.). *Who's Who in the Theatre, Vol. I*. Detroit: Gale Research Co., 1981.

Hughes, Langston. *Selected Poems of Langston Hughes*. New York: Alfred A. Knopf, 1968.

Jablonski, Edward. *Gershwin*. New York: Doubleday & Co., 1987.

Jablonski, Edward, and Lawrence D. Stewart. *The Gershwin Years*. Garden City, N.Y.: Doubleday & Co., Inc., 1958/1973.

Kasha, Al, and Joel Hirschorn. *Notes on Broadway: Conversations with the Great Songwriters*. Chicago: Contemporary Books, 1985.

Kimball, Robert (ed.). *The Complete Lyrics of Cole Porter*. New York: Alfred A. Knopf, 1983.

Kimball, Robert, and William Bolcom. *Reminiscing with Sissle and Blake*. New York: Viking Press, 1973.

Kimball, Robert, and Alfred Simon. *The Gershwins*. New York: Atheneum, 1973.

Lerner, Alan Jay. *The Musical Theatre: A Celebration*. New York: McGraw Hill Book Co., 1986.

———. *The Street Where I Live*. New York: W. W. Norton & Co., 1978.

Lerner, Alan Jay, and Benny Green (ed.). *A Hymn to Him: The Lyrics of Alan Jay Lerner*. New York: Limelight Editions, 1987.

Lynes, Russell. *The Lively Audience: A Social History of the Visual and Performing Arts in America, 1890-1950*. New York: Harper & Row, 1985.

McCabe, John. *George M. Cohan: The Man Who Owned Broadway*. Garden City, N.Y.: Doubleday & Co., Inc., 1973.

Mordden, Ethan. *Better Foot Forward: A History of American Musical Theatre*. New York: Viking Press, 1976.

———. *Broadway Babies: The People Who Made the American Musical*. New York: Oxford University Press, 1983.

Morehouse, Ward. *George M. Cohan: Prince of the American Theatre*. New York: J. B. Lippincott, 1943.

———. *Matinee Tomorrow: Fifty Years of Our Theatre*. New York: McGraw Hill, Inc., 1949.

Nolan, Frederick. *The Sound of Their Music: The Story of Rodgers and Hammerstein*. New York: Walker & Co., 1978.

Prince, Harold. *Contradictions: Notes on 26 Years in the Theatre*. New York: Dodd, Mead and Co., 1974.

Rodgers, Richard. *Musical Stages*. New York: Random House, 1975.

Schwartz, Charles. *Cole Porter: A Biography*. New York: Dial Press, 1977.

Smith, Cecil, and Glenn Litton. *Musical Comedy in America*. New York: Theatre Arts Books, 1981.

Suskin, Steven. *Show Tunes: 1905-1985*. New York: Dodd, Mead and Co., 1986.

Taylor, Deems. *Some Enchanted Evenings: The Story of Rodgers and Hammerstein*. New York: Harper & Brothers, 1953.

Taylor, Theodore. *Jule: The Story of Composer Jule Styne*. New York: Random House, 1979.

Wilk, Max. *They're Playing Our Song*. New York: Atheneum, 1973.

Willson, Meredith. *But He Doesn't Know the Territory*. New York: G. P. Putnam's Sons, 1959.

Wodehouse, P. G. and Guy Bolton. *Bring On the Girls! The Improbable Story of Our Life in Musical Comedy*. New York: Simon and Schuster, 1953.

Woll, Allen. *Black Musical Theatre: From Coontown to Dreamgirls*. Baton
    Rouge: Louisiana State University Press, 1989.
Zadan, Craig. *Sondheim and Co*. New York: Harper and Row, 1986.

Index

"Monkey Doodle-Doo," 14

"Monkey in the Mango Tree," 84

"Moon-Faced, Starry-Eyed," 159

"Moonfall," 203

"Moon River," 145

"Moonshine Lullaby," 13

Moore, Robert, 182

Mordden, Ethan, 42, 163

Morehouse, Ward, 2

"Morning Glow," 186

Moross, Jerome, 155–56

"Most Beautiful Girl in the World, The," 65

Most Happy Fella, The, 115–16, 118

"Mountain Greenery," 67

"Mr. Cellophane," 181

"Mr. Goldstone, I Love You," 121

"Mr. Monotony," 13

Mr. President, 13–14

Mr. Wonderful, 138

"Much More," 169, 172

"Museum Song, The," 195

"Musical Moon," 4, 6

"Music and the Mirror, The," 197

Music Box Revue, 11

Music in the Air, 34

Music Man, The, 7, 117, 153–55

"Music That Makes Me Dance, The," 152

"My Buddy," 90

"My City," 77

"My Coloring Book," 177

"My Cup Runneth Over," 171

"My Darling, My Darling," 114

My Fair Lady, 98–101, 104–5

"My Flag," 4

"My Funny Valentine," 63, 65, 69

"My Garden," 171

"My Gentle Young Johnny," 139

"My Heart Belongs to Daddy," 61

"My Heart Stood Still," 65, 67

"My Husband Makes Movies," 202

"My Love," 158

"My Love is a Married Man," 97

"My Lucky Star," 89

"My Man," 152

My Man Godfrey, 104

"My Most Important Moments Go By," 190

"My Mother's Wedding Day," 98

My One and Only, 50

"My Own Morning," 111

"My Romance," 65, 67

"My Ship," 49

My Sister Eileen, 109

Mystery of Edwin Drood, The, 203

"My Time of Day," 115

"Namely You," 146

Nash at Nine, 158

Nash, Ogden, 157–58

Nash, N. Richard, 171

Naughty Marietta, 188

"Necessity," 82

"Nesting Time in Flatbush," 26–27

"Never," 111

"Never, Neverland," 110

"Never Will I Marry," 116

"New Ashmolean Marching Society . . . ," 114

"New Deal for Christmas, A," 194

New Faces of 1952, 137

"New Fangled Preacher Man," 187

New Girl in Town, 151

Newman, David, 174

New Moon, The, 33–34

"New Sun in the Sky," 73

New Yorkers, The, 61

"New York, New York," 108

"Next to Lovin'," 188

"Nice Work If You Can Get It," 49, 51–52

"Nickel Under the Foot," 92

Nickolson, Nick, 10

"Night and Day," 59, 61

"Night It Had To End, The," 206

About the Author

THOMAS S. HISCHAK is Associate Professor of theatre history and criticism at State University of New York-Cortland. He has published numerous plays.